BEYOND THE STUDIO

Broadcasting House,
Ormeau Avenue, 2000

BBC NI

BEYOND THE STUDIO

A History of
BBC Northern Ireland

JONATHAN BARDON

THE
BLACKSTAFF
PRESS

BELFAST

First published in 2000 by
The Blackstaff Press Limited
Blackstaff House, Wildflower Way, Apollo Road
Belfast BT12 6TA, Northern Ireland

Jonathan Bardon has asserted his right under the
Copyright, Designs and Patents Act 1988
to be identified as the author of this work.

Typeset by Techniset Typesetters, Newton-le-Willows, Merseyside

Printed in Northern Ireland by by W. & G. Baird Limited

A CIP catalogue record for this book
is available from the British Library

ISBN 0-8650-685-6

www.blackstaffpress.com

ACKNOWLEDGEMENTS

Pat Loughrey, the former Controller Northern Ireland, must have my heartfelt thanks. His love of history and passion for broadcasting ensured that this project always had support at the very top.

Austin Hunter helped in so many ways. His deep knowledge of the photographic archive was invaluable, and his tireless efforts to identify everyone in the photographs uncovered many stories and considerably enriched this book.

Gráinne Loughran and Clare McVeigh at the BBC Archives at the Ulster Folk and Transport Museum were enthusiastic and supportive, always willing and keen to help out with the research. Tim and Jeremy Shields in the Information Archive of BBC Northern Ireland were also very helpful during the research.

Nan Magee, characteristically, lent superb practical support within my office in the early days of the project and was followed later by Claire Archibald and Laura Spence. Wendy Dunbar, Carina Rourke and Patsy Horton of Blackstaff Press have shown a dedication to this publication well beyond the call of duty.

My thanks must go also to many BBC colleagues past and present who gave freely of their memories. This is their story.

Last, but most importantly, my greatest debt is to Jonathan Bardon whose close association with the BBC over many years as distinguished writer, broadcaster and more latterly a member of the Broadcasting Council for Northern Ireland, perfectly equipped him to undertake the arduous research task. He has, I believe, written a fascinating book which is a fine chronicle of the BBC in Northern Ireland, rich in historical anecdote, and which will endure as a reference book in times to come.

PICTURE ACKNOWLEDGEMENTS

My thanks must go also to all the photographers who have captured images on behalf of the BBC over many years – in particular Wilfred Green, Chris Hill, Pacemaker and John Harrison.

ROSEMARY KELLY
HEAD OF PUBLIC AFFAIRS
BBC NORTHERN IRELAND

CONTENTS

FOREWORD

IN OCTOBER 2000 HUNDREDS OF PEOPLE squeezed into the normally spacious Studio 1 in Broadcasting House, Belfast, to share memories and memorabilia of a radio programme which was broadcast to the children of Northern Ireland from 1946 until 1964. For many it had become required childhood listening and for some of us an inspiration for life. *Children's Hour Remembered* was a celebration of the work of Cicely Matthews, presenter and organiser of *Children's Hour*, and the occasion was a reminder of how often this small and remote part of the greater BBC has produced programmes and presenters that inspired the loyalty and affection of the audience.

During this golden age of wireless, broadcasts were generally scripted down to the very last word, but Cicely, as a pioneer of unscripted spontaneity, introduced a form of interactivity and listener participation which was at that time extremely rare in broadcasting. In short the BBC in Northern Ireland, for all its stiffness in those years, could often be innovative, unselfconsciously inclusive and mould-breaking.

Ever since the first broadcast from 2BE, the Belfast station, in 1924, the BBC in Northern Ireland has been broadcasting to a divided society. However, it is worth recalling that during the early period David Curry's *Irish Rhythms* (though offensive alike to traditional musicians and those hostile to 'Irish' culture in general) became the most popular network and overseas radio series ever produced in Belfast – a sort of *Riverdance* of its day; and that Joseph Tomelty's *The McCooeys* brought almost all Northern Ireland to a halt each week.

The Troubles of the last thirty years led to the expansion and development of news output. As community divisions grew more stark the BBC in Northern Ireland frequently found itself buffeted by one side or another and was seen by some only in this one dimension of its activities. Whilst news programming was and remains the cornerstone of the schedules, the reality is that a rich variety of programmes which sought to give context and definition to our entangled cultures were created and flourished on radio and television during that time. Former Governor of the BBC in Northern Ireland, Sir Kenneth Bloomfield, summed up memorably our role as 'both a mirror and a window – a mirror in which we can see ourselves and each other, and a window through which we can look at the world and it can look back at us'.

This book was inspired by the recognition of the BBC as the chronicler of life in Northern Ireland. Throughout its seventy-year history it has expanded audience horizons through its drama, documentaries, education, music and arts and entertainment programming as well as identifying and nurturing talent which has had impact far beyond these shores.

The convergence of telecommunications, development in information technology, the internet and broadcast media is creating a communications revolution, transforming our economy, society and culture. The BBC is at the heart of this in Northern Ireland. Whilst we continue to nurture our audience on analogue we are also already serving the interests and needs of those who have converted to digital – on television, radio (more and more of BBC RADIO ULSTER is streamed online across the world), and online itself.

The challenge for us now is to take the values from an earlier era with us into our digital future.

ROSEMARY KELLY
HEAD OF PUBLIC AFFAIRS
BBC NORTHERN IRELAND

1

BEGINNINGS
'PIONEERS IN SO GREAT A VENTURE'

ON 14 NOVEMBER 1923 JOHN REITH, Managing Director of the British Broadcasting Company, reported to his board that 'a scheme was being prepared for broadcasting from a station in Northern Ireland'. On 14 February 1924 the region learned that it was to have its own radio station in Belfast with the call sign of 2BE, which would not only relay programmes from stations on the other side of the Irish Sea but also would make its own programmes with its own staff.

E. Godfrey Brown, head of music at Methodist College, Belfast, was the first member of staff to be appointed. Though he would have to take a cut in salary, he accepted the post of Director of Music. As he recalled: 'the thought of being one of the pioneers in so great a venture, coupled with the promise of an Orchestra which I felt would benefit the City and the Philharmonic Society was sufficient to make me give up my duties at the College'. Soon after, to his surprise, he saw a man struggling up the hill to his home in Holywood, County Down, with a typewriter on his shoulder, and a day or two later the railway carrier delivered a large parcel of headed writing paper.

The station's first studio was on the first floor of a disused linen warehouse at 31 Linenhall Street. Brown found the rooms almost bare, with 'a small portion of the main building partitioned off as the Engineers Quarter and in which some apparatus was already installed. Two engineers, Ingram and Goodyear, had arrived . . . Both had been working all night and one had gone to his lodgings to sleep and the other was enjoying a snooze alongside his electrical apparatus.' Next, Major Edmund Thomson MC, a Scot with experience in amateur drama, arrived as senior assistant to the Station Director and announcer. Tyrone Guthrie, the junior assistant, had just graduated from Oxford, where he had distinguished himself in undergraduate drama productions. Then the new Station Director, Major Walter Montagu Douglas Scott, joined his colleagues. According to Brown, Scott's previous career

had largely been given over to irregular soldiering in Africa and elsewhere, and to big game shooting. His knowledge of music was negligible and the other artistic outlooks were about ditto, but he had a charming personality. His business training apparently had been acquired in the orderly room as adjutant to a Regiment. The major's first request to me was 'will you please go and get two nice and well educated girls as typists and private secretaries, one for yourself and Mr. Thomson and one for me'. He added: 'I don't want to advertise, it's such a nuisance sorting them out.'

The main burden of the first broadcasts would fall on Brown's shoulders and he set about recruiting seventeen members for the station's orchestra 'drawn from the best orchestras in England', including Pauline Barker, a harpist from the Carl Rosa Opera Company.

While a special submarine cable was being laid from Scotland there were serious doubts about the reliability of the normal commercial cable: the Belfast station at the outset would have to devise its own schedule of programmes. Arthur Burrows, the BBC's Director of Programmes, warned Belfast that

> a wireless audience includes women and children and others unaccustomed to broad humour. Nothing must be transmitted by wireless that will offend sensitive folk, and in the event of particularly tragic material being broadcast it may be advisable to warn invalids and others to put down their 'phones for a specified period.

The opening date for the station was set for 15 September 1924. That morning Brown brought his Wireless Orchestra into the studio for rehearsal and to his alarm 'the transmission was hopeless – far too much resonance'. The Chief Engineer, Peter Eckersley, over from London for the occasion, decreed that the whole studio would have to be draped. Staff rushed out to Cornmarket and bought a large consignment of white cotton sheets for the ceiling, pillars and walls, and a thick drugget to be laid on the floor. Members of the orchestra helped to swathe the room until the engineers were satisfied that the echo had been eradicated. 'The studios, all draped in white, had an extraordinary effect', Brown remembered, 'and one lady of the Orchestra said, "I simply cannot play in there, it's just like a sepulchre" and so it was.'

'Hello, hello, this is 2BE, the Belfast station of the British Broadcasting Company, calling.' With these words Tyrone Guthrie, the announcer for the evening, began broadcasting in Northern Ireland. The orchestra played the national anthem and then there was a technical hitch and the station went off the air for around fifteen minutes. When broadcasting resumed there was a short local news bulletin followed by about an hour and a half of music, starting with Sullivan's overture *Di Ballo*, punctuated by a couple more unscheduled breaks in transmission. The evening ended with a short address from the Director of the station.

Next morning, the most enthusiastic verdict came from the *Irish News*:

> In countless numbers of houses within the magic circle of the Belfast Broadcasting Station, amateur 'listeners-in' waited with baited breath for the first message from the Director last evening. To say that their vigil was rewarded is to put it mildly, for, according to reports from every district of the city, and from distant parts of the north-east, users of even the cheapest crystal sets were able to enjoy the delightful programme

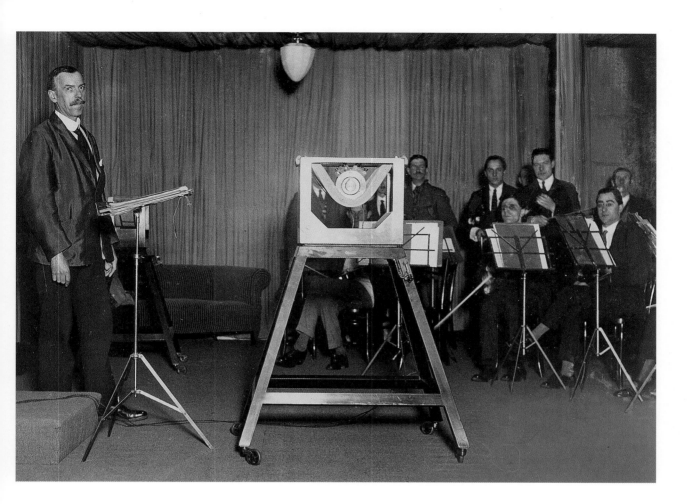

submitted. The clearness with which the various items were heard was commented upon by wireless enthusiasts, who were loud in their praise of the efforts of the officials of the station to provide such interesting programmes as they have arranged for the week.

The *Northern Whig* critic listened only to the final twenty minutes; having failed to hear the national anthem played at the start, he was indignant that the programme did not conclude – as it did in London – with 'God Save the King': 'I would suggest that if the Belfast Broadcasting Station cannot be closed down in the same manner as all British stations, then close it up altogether. Anyone in Ulster who cannot listen to our National Anthem has no right to be catered for by a British company.' The *Evening Telegraph*, a Dublin newspaper with unionist sympathies, was surprised that the only accents heard were English, but nevertheless provided a detailed and appreciative critique:

> It is an evidence of the standard of musical taste in Belfast that the appeal to popularity embodied so much really good music . . . the male voice choir of the Queen's Island is an admirable combination. We are so accustomed to associate the name of Queen's Island with the 'savage breast' that it is a delightful experience to learn that it is so fully conscious of the charms of music to soothe.

Godfrey Brown, previously Head of Music at Methodist College in Belfast, was the first employee of 2BE and all but ran the Belfast station in its early years. The uncertainty of the cable connection across the Irish Sea meant that the station's musicians were under relentless pressure to provide continuous entertainment when 2BE was on the air.

BBC NI

2BE's Control Room in 1924. This was housed in an attic above the electricity power station on Albertbridge Road in Belfast, the transmitter aerials being slung between the tall twin chimneys of the power station.

BBC NI

However, one disgusted listener wrote: 'I see from the papers that there is a large increase in the sales of radio sets. I am not surprised. After last night's programme I am selling mine too.'

The formal opening of the station followed on the night of Friday 25 October at the Ulster Hall. By that time over five thousand licences had been issued in Belfast, and though a wireless set could be bought for 7s. 6d., most citizens were listening in on crystal sets. The hall was packed and at nine o'clock all BBC stations were connected to Belfast, so that the formal proceedings were broadcast throughout the United Kingdom. Many heard a weather forecast for the first time. Then, the news from London was relayed into the hall and there were bursts of cheers and laughter when it was announced that Eamon de Valera had been arrested by the Royal Ulster Constabulary in Newry, County Down. At the Belfast City YMCA in Wellington Place a loudspeaker was placed above the main entrance and crowds of people gathered round to hear speeches by the Chairman of the BBC, Lord Gainford; the Lord Mayor of Belfast, Alderman Sir W. G. Turner J.P., the Duke of Abercorn, Governor of Northern Ireland; Dr Richard Livingstone, Vice-Chancellor of Queen's University; and Sir James Craig, the Prime Minister. Craig amused his audience by suggesting that 2BE stood for Belfast, 'the second city of the British Empire'. The centrepiece of the broadcast was a specially commissioned composition by Norman Hay, a fantasy on Irish folk tunes.

Despite evident audience appreciation, John Reith noted in his diary: 'there was actually a disgraceful series of muddles, beginning with our not knowing if Gainford's address was to be simultaneously broadcast or not. Also there was a row about precedence in the procession, the Lord Mayor insisting on walking with Gainford and the Governor into the Ulster Hall. Further, the programme ran 25 minutes short.' Brown remembered that last minute changes were 'rather a trying business' and in a postmortem next day 'poor Major Scott came in for some of the blame' – Reith noted that he 'made a real row about the previous night'. Regular broadcasting had begun in the region, however, keeping Brown and his station orchestra at more than full stretch for the remainder of the year, while the engineers toiled to eradicate the numerous technical hitches which prevented the regular relay of programmes from London and other regions.

The Belfast station of the BBC opened just two and a half years after the creation of Northern Ireland. Uncertainty about the island's political future had brought opposing passions to the surface in Ulster, making civil war seem imminent in 1914. Then in 1920, as Westminster was formulating elaborate constitutional remedies, a sectarian conflict more vicious and lethal than all the northern riots of the previous century put together swept across the province. The Government of Ireland Act brought Northern Ireland into being in the spring of 1921 at a time of intense intercommunal warfare and this violence reached a fearful crescendo during the first six months of 1922.

Considering what had gone before, it is remarkable how swiftly peace returned and there was not a single sectarian murder between 1923 and 1932. Northern Ireland's society remained bitterly divided, however; nearly all the Belfast station staff were either English or Scots, anxious not to offend local sensibilities. Brown was English but he was constantly consulted by his colleagues because he had lived in Ulster for some years. Indeed, Brown was regarded as the real head of the regional service in the early years. The commercial cable was only suitable for speech and, until the submarine radio cable had been laid and connected, the responsibility of providing programmes fell mostly on his shoulders. Members of his Wireless Orchestra were hard-worked and the burden was only slightly eased when their numbers were augmented by drafting in recruits from the Belfast Philharmonic Society orchestra one evening a week. On one occasion, after a sextet had played itself to a standstill, an appeal went out to listeners – 'Would anybody with talent please go round to Broadcasting House?' In almost no time there was a queue of fiddlers, pianists, mouth organists, mandolin players and comics in Linenhall Street. Auditions were quickly held and within an hour a variety show went on the air. Talks, sketches, plays and features were the responsibility of Tyrone Guthrie. He recalled the problems of broadcasting from the heavily draped studio in Linenhall Street:

The light fell from great chamber-pots suspended by muffled chains from the muffled girders in the muffled ceiling — a cold, hard glaring light.

Three minutes in this chamber of horrors would have meant asphyxiation; so there was a 'plant' which filled it — and us — with ozone. One minute of deep breathing of this ozone was, we were assured, the equivalent of a fortnight at Blackpool; the funny little smell of rotten eggs was merely proof of its invigorating, tonic, bracing excellence. You can imagine the effect upon the spirit of those who had to perform here — the smell, the gross, crass ugliness of it all, the neuralgic glare from the chamber-pots, and, above all, the acoustic deadness. A cheery 'Good day' or a ringing roundelay fell with a dull thud into a sterilized blank; the backchat of two comedians sounded like one mute telling dirty stories to another mute in the undertaker's parlour.

None the less, we crusaders of the ether were constantly cheered and uplifted by the thought that nobody was listening. Sometimes now I wake at night and blush in the dark to think that, occasionally and by a few, our prentice efforts were heard.

The sound effects team at the Belfast station during the early years.

BBC NI

Growing numbers in Belfast and its environs were listening, however, and the station was soon to learn about local sensitivities. When the *Radio Times* published details of the St Patrick's Day programme for 17 March 1926, 'Crystal user' in the *Irish News* pointed out that, even though Prime Minister Sir James Craig had announced the day to be a bank holiday, he 'and every

other good Irishman living within the 2BE wavelength will find that these sentimentalities are regarded as out of date by the Olympians who guard the microphone in Linenhall Street'. Belfast's sole contribution was to be an evening of ballroom music. Major Scott hastily replaced the dance music with an hour of Irish music. The Station Director's headaches had only just begun: the programme from Dublin – a half-hour programme of the Irish army's No.1 Band, conducted by Colonel Fritz Brase – was not relayed as scheduled at 9.15 p.m. The *Irish News* correspondent strongly hinted that the BBC in London had been lobbied successfully by the Northern Ireland premier. For the remainder of the interwar period controversies were to rage – often for weeks – with almost every St Patrick's Day broadcast.

The shortcomings of Major Scott had already been observed at first hand by Reith and the dilatory fashion in which he passed on instructions from London and responded to mail became ever more evident. In July 1926 Scott was relieved of his post and replaced eventually by Gerald Beadle, an Englishman who had spent a year with the BBC setting up a station for Durban in South Africa. Beadle, when he had become Director of BBC Television Broadcasting, recalled his reception in Belfast:

> When I arrived in Northern Ireland I was made to feel for the first time in my life that I was a person of some public importance . . . I was invited to become a member of the Ulster Club, where almost daily I met members of the Government; the Governor, the Duke of Abercorn, was immensely helpful and friendly, and Lord Craigavon, the Prime Minister, was a keen supporter of our work. In effect I was made a member of the Establishment of a province which had most of the paraphernalia of a sovereign state and a population no bigger than a moderate sized English county.

Beadle made up his mind to create 'a closer liaison between the Government and the BBC'. He wrote to Reith for advice and concluded: 'I am sure that our position here will be strengthened immensely if we can persuade the Northern Government to look upon us as their mouthpiece.' With the events of the 1926 General Strike to the fore in his mind, and in particular how close then the BBC came to being taken over by the British government, Reith made it plain to Beadle that the Belfast station could not be put at the disposal of Sir James Craig and his government. Nevertheless, in the BBC's Year Book of 1928, Beadle wrote: 'The broadcasting Station, though in no sense under the control of the Northern government, does to a considerable degree co-operate with it.'

This cosy relationship with the Unionist government was to some extent offset by Beadle's enthusiasm for collaboration with 2RN, the Dublin station which began broadcasting on 1 January 1926. From April 1926 there was a wide range of joint programmes of classical music, light entertainment and folksongs, and the Abbey Theatre Company travelled north on several occasions to broadcast their productions. On St Patrick's Day 1930, two plays, one from the South and one from the North, together with a story in dialect from County Tyrone and traditional music, were broadcast throughout the United Kingdom without attracting adverse comment.

The special St Patrick's Day programme for the following year, broadcast entirely from Belfast for the national programme, prompted a storm of protest, however. Many condemned the items for their banality, and while the *Manchester Guardian* felt that the Dublin station should have been asked to contribute to give 'a more composite picture of Ireland', Northern Ireland newspapers and those who wrote to them for weeks afterwards were appalled that so little of what could be regarded as distinctive Ulster culture had been included.

That the letter columns of the newspapers were often filled with passionate observations on the merits or otherwise of programmes, and on whether there was enough 'high-brow' or 'low-brow' entertainment, demonstrates the growing number of listeners in the region. The pressure on the Belfast station, and on the orchestra in particular, to churn out programmes with very limited resources was eased considerably when a powerful transmitter at Daventry came on air in August 1927. Daytime national programmes could more easily be relayed, though interference was still too great at night. Beadle, indeed, had to resist pressure from London to abandon drama productions and to curtail still further live music broadcasts. Improving technology and the greater freedom provided by the BBC Charter did, however, extend the range of programmes to include outside broadcasts, covering such events as the laying of the foundation stone of Parliament Buildings at Stormont in 1928, the launch of ships from Harland and Wolff at Queen's Island, and sporting events, including motorcycle races on the Ards Circuit and the Irish Derby from the Curragh. Beadle had persuaded his superiors in London to scrap the heavily draped studio in Linenhall Street and replace it with three new studios: No. 1 studio was spacious enough for orchestral concerts and operatic productions; No. 2 was used for talks, children's programmes and chamber music; and No. 3, with a purpose-built control room, was where most plays were broadcast. The Belfast Station Director spent much of his time travelling to London where he lobbied, often persuasively, to protect regional broadcasting from excessive centralisation.

Beadle moved on in 1932 and was replaced by George Marshall, a Scot who had been Director at Edinburgh and then Newcastle upon Tyne. Marshall, like his predecessor, ran into fierce controversy: the St Patrick's Day programme in 1933 was condemned widely for its uneven quality, but it was the Belfast station's 'ballyhoo' performance − characterised by execrable 'Irish' accents − on Christmas Day which aroused most ire.

These were years of heightened tension in Northern Ireland. In the 1920s the economy of the whole region had languished in profoundly altered world trading conditions and it was thrown into crisis when the shockwaves of the 1929 Wall Street Crash crossed the Atlantic. Not a single ship was launched at Queen's Island between 10 December 1931 and 1 May 1934. For a brief moment the unemployed of both religions acted together in the Outdoor Relief riots in Belfast during October 1932. Sectarian tensions were once again aggravated, however, by the election of a Fianna Fáil government in Dublin and the subsequent confrontational approach of de Valera to Anglo-Irish relations, and by inflammatory speeches made by Unionist politicians. Following George V's jubilee celebrations, fifteen people were killed in Belfast during sectarian riots over the summer of 1935. In such an atmosphere the broadcasters in Linenhall Street operated with extreme caution; even then it proved impossible to avoid giving offence. In April 1934, for example, it was decided to include sports results in Sunday news bulletins. The *Northern Whig* correspondent was incensed and observed that 'the majority of the citizens of our province do not want this class of news in the Sunday programmes'.

On 9 May 1934 the Belfast station became the Northern Ireland Region: henceforth 'a *Regional* programme would be radiated from the Belfast transmitter — that was, a programme of local items, music, plays, talks, etc., reflecting the life of the province, together with certain items selected from other regional programmes'. It was an arrangement which caused widespread dissatisfaction. In future, those who wanted to hear the national programme had to tune in to Droitwich, far beyond the reach of crystal set owners. Meanwhile, local broadcasting was far short of being regional, still accessible only to those in the greater Belfast area. For many people in Northern Ireland the opening of the Lisnagarvey transmitter at Blaris, on 20 March 1936, was a highly significant occasion and owners of wireless sets in Derry, Omagh and Enniskillen could hear BBC broadcasts for the first time. In the Lisnagarvey machine room motor generators converted the mains electricity to the type required by the transmitter and a six cylinder, 600-horsepower diesel engine stood ready should there be a cut in mains power. The cigar-shaped, lattice steel mast, 475 feet high, was supported by two sets of stays. Two lines permanently rented from the Post Office connected the Belfast studios to the Lisnagarvey control room. It was now possible for Linenhall Street to provide a genuinely regional service and in the three and a half years before the Second World War some attempt was made to broadcast programmes of interest to all listeners in Northern Ireland.

Beadle had been primarily responsible for persuading Reith that a Director of Regional Relations should be appointed. That Director, Charles Siepmann, following an intensive investigation, wrote a confidential report in September 1936 on the Northern Ireland Region. He provided head office with a penetrating analysis of Northern Ireland and of the characteristics that made the region so different from any other in the BBC:

> The bitterness of religious antagonism between Protestants and Catholics invades the life of the community at every point and for our purposes conditions almost everything we do . . . in the official life of Northern Ireland the Roman Catholic by virtue of his religious faith is virtually at a discount. Roman Catholicism for purposes of party politics means fusion with the Free State and the political existence of

Ulster is of course based on the determination to oppose such fusion at any price . . . The government is in effect that of a loyalist dictatorship. Constituencies have been so devised as where possible to split the Roman Catholic vote. There is virtually no opposition . . .

Such then are the circumstances in Northern Ireland, a small area, a small population, awkwardly divided between town and country, slender cultural resources, cross-currents of bitter religious antagonism and a lamentable dearth of talent both among authors and artistes . . .

Siepmann was excoriating about a great deal of the region's output. He recommended that all drama production and studio-based variety should end and that emphasis should instead be given to talks and features. The final decision on the drama department was left to the Regional Director and Marshall refused to wield the axe there because he believed that the broadcasting of local plays was essential for the support of regional culture. Immediate action was taken, however, to attract new scriptwriting talent. Denis Johnston was engaged to research and write features, and because he was already a playwright of some distinction, he was to extend his work to bring about a striking improvement in the quality of broadcast plays. The quality and range of regional broadcasts were also enhanced by a more adventurous use of outside broadcasts. A BBC recording van arrived in 1937 to gather material for *Summer Over the British Isles*, a feature for the national programme: listeners all over the United Kingdom were able to enjoy impressions of the Ould Lammas Fair at Ballycastle in County Antrim. The van was borrowed by the regional station to make, for example, a programme of a ceilidh in a County Tyrone cottage, but Belfast did not get its own vehicle until after the war.

The war, when it came in September 1939, brought an end to regional broadcasting. The plan to disperse the production centres was implemented: all transmitters were synchronised on two wavelengths to prevent enemy aircraft from using regional frequencies to assist them in finding their targets. Nearly all members of the orchestra joined the British armed forces and most other staff were transferred to England. The Assistant Director of Programmes, Henry McMullan, remembered the last night of broadcasting, 3 September 1939:

There was nobody in the building except me, the commissionaire and the engineers. The last broadcast consisted of a series of announcements. I remember the last of all being a request for anyone with nursing experience in Northern Ireland to register. This was, of course, because of what was thought to be the imminent threat of bombing. 'Good night! Good bye! Regional broadcasting is coming to an end until the end of the war.' I remember going down the stairs and getting into my car and that was the first time I had ever driven at night with the headlights almost completely blacked out. It was most eerie. I drove back home in a state of utter depression.

During the war, McMullan operated as a BBC war correspondent.

Only George Marshall and two programme staff, Ursula Eason (who had

produced *Children's Hour* since 1932 and was now acting Programme Director) and drama assistant James Mageean remained at the Linenhall studios. By the end of 1939 the Post Office could make a line to Glasgow available on occasion and this made possible a limited contribution of programmes for the Home and Forces Services from Belfast. Lord Craigavon gave a talk, *Ulster's Part in the War*; variety programmes, sports commentaries and the immensely popular *Irish Rhythms* were transmitted to the forces; and music recitals, talks, St Patrick's Day programmes and thirty-minute contributions to *Children's Hour* were produced for the Home Service. Head office was keen to use artistes and material from Éire – at first, when it was hoped that de Valera could be persuaded to bring his state into the war, and then for the benefit of the thousands of southern Irishmen serving in the British armed forces – but

For a brief period in the late 1930s BBC Northern Ireland was able to borrow the mobile recording unit from London. The photograph shows the duplicate recording positions and associated switch gear. Local programme makers – Denis Johnston and Raymond Glendinning in particular – took full advantage of the van to make some notable recordings in the Ulster countryside.

BBC NI

Marshall implacably opposed such co-operation whenever he could. John Andrews became Prime Minister after the death of Craigavon in 1940 and he energetically weighed in to support the Regional Director. When Andrews heard that a regular Irish magazine programme was in preparation, he wrote to the Director-General, observing that

the object of the broadcasts will be to interest 'Ireland', both North and South, and Irishmen everywhere, in the war effort, by telling them and the world how Irishmen are helping in the present struggle.

This, in my view, would be an insidious form of propaganda which would entirely misrepresent the position of Northern Ireland in the United Kingdom and would slur over the neutral and most unhelpful attitude which Eire has taken up during the war . . . and I feel strongly that steps should be taken to put a stop to propaganda of this character in whatever quarter it may originate. Why not leave Eire to plough her lonely furrow?

F.W. Ogilvie, the former Vice-Chancellor of Queen's University who had succeeded Reith as Director-General in 1938, refused to be moved, and the programmes, entitled *Irish Half Hour*, were made in the BBC's wartime production centre at Bangor in north Wales.

Ursula Eason was the first woman to be appointed to a senior position in BBC Northern Ireland. During the Second World War she was acting Head of Programmes, with the unenviable task of being second in command under the lugubrious Director, George Marshall.

BBC NI

Later Marshall persuaded head office to allow Belfast to produce its own *Ulster Half Hour*; these programmes, made on a shoe string, attracted a great deal of criticism for their poor quality, the radio critic of the *Northern Whig* speaking for many by describing them as 'uneven and badly blended'. Marshall did, however, win an important victory in these years, which was to have major implications for the future: material for programmes referring to Northern Ireland made elsewhere by the BBC first would have to be submitted to the Regional Director for approval.

Work on the foundations of the new Broadcasting House began in the autumn of 1938 and by the spring of 1939 the steel framework was complete. Construction was so well advanced by September 1939 it was agreed to finish the building in spite of the war. Broadcasting House was designed to contain a large concert hall, a drama suite comprising three studios and a disc reproducing room, two talks studios and a general purposes studio. Then in April 1941 the Luftwaffe struck Belfast and on the night of 14–15 April almost a thousand citizens died. The Germans returned on the night of 4–5 May and, aided by a cloudless moonlit sky, their bombers inflicted devastating blows on the shipyard, the docks and the city centre. Astonishingly, while great conflagrations still raged, the ceremony – low key though it was – to open the unscathed Broadcasting House went ahead on Monday 5 May 1941.

Broadcasting House, the city's finest Art Deco building, was still largely a shell but the few remaining staff moved into it straight away on the grounds that its walls, eighteen inches thick, would afford good protection from blast in the event of another raid. No programmes were made in Belfast until early in 1940 and thereafter output was limited to the requirements of the Home and Forces services. Journalists referred to the 'white elephant of Ormeau Avenue' but the presence of a new Broadcasting House was a clear indication that the BBC intended to restore original broadcasting after the war.

In fact, it did on 29 July 1945, but Northern Ireland was denied a wavelength of its own. International agreements limited the number of wavelengths available to the BBC and because Northern Ireland was by far the smallest region, it was decided that it would have to share the wavelength of 285.7 m with the North East England Region. Originally intended as a temporary arrangement, listeners would have to listen half the time to programmes targeted at audiences in places such as Newcastle upon Tyne and Durham, while those in the north-east of England would be forced to accustom themselves to the concerns of what was then considered the backwater of the United Kingdom.

Marshall addressed listeners on what was being prepared for the postwar schedules. There would be a five-minute news bulletin each evening, except on Sundays; a fortnightly news commentary; a Saturday sports bulletin; a *Children's Hour* programme every week; a monthly religious service and a programme of hymns every week; talks for farmers; regular plays, starting with Patricia O'Connor's *Highly Efficient*; and some special features.

A Northern Ireland Advisory Council of the BBC, 'broadly representative of the general public of the region', was appointed. 'I have consulted numerous people,' Marshall informed the Director-General, 'including the Prime Minister . . . You will note that I have included three Nationalists, which, I would say, is about the right proportion . . .' Sir Henry Mulholland, brother-in-law of Prime Minister Sir Basil Brooke, was the first chairman. Mulholland had his work cut out, for there could be sharp exchanges between members, particularly when the colourful Harry Midgely, a former Labour MP who had now become a true-blue Unionist, was present at meetings. When members suggested that discussion of partition should be permitted in local broadcasts, the chairman had no hesitation in ruling such a subject out of order.

Henry McMullan had been appointed Programme Director on his return from the war and he now strove to enhance the regional service. In this he was greatly assisted by Sam Hanna Bell, a writer with a secure reputation, as features producer, and by John Boyd as talks producer. Both men had contributed to the distinguished literary journal *Lagan* and Boyd had been editor. Bell was eager to make full use of the recording van bought at the time American troops were stationed in Northern Ireland.

McMullan extended the region's news gathering with the help of C.L. Frankland, an English journalist who had been information officer at Stormont. The continuing ban on items referring to events and developments south of the border proved a growing irritant not only to those who compiled bulletins but also to John E. Sayers of the *Belfast Telegraph,* who presented the news talk programme *Ulster Commentary* every fortnight. The Director-General himself authorised the reporting of results of Gaelic games on Sundays in 1946 but the reaction of unionist listeners was so fierce that he felt obliged to reverse his decision soon afterwards. Head office's reluctance to cause offence to the Protestant majority was vehemently reinforced by Marshall's frequent representations. His staff were not sorry to see him go. In *The Middle of My Journey* Boyd recalled that Marshall was

> a Scot with an unsmiling, granite-like face, who was reputed to spend a good deal of time in the Ulster Reform Club in Castle Place. Marshall retired soon after my arrival and never took any opportunity to speak to me, being content to pass me by in the corridor with a slight nod ...When Marshall retired I was told he spent more and more of his time in his club and that his fellow members took to avoiding him once he had relinquished the reins of office . . . I cannot recall anyone saying a complimentary word on his behalf until many years later I met Joyce Cary in Oxford . . . in his brisk, inconsequential manner, he suddenly asked me if I knew Marshall. 'I heard he went to seed. Is that true?'
>
> 'Yes, I believe so.'
>
> 'What a pity! He was a splendid-looking chap when I knew him at Oxford. Very good company and very talented . . . You know, he could very well have become a concert pianist. He was a first-class player – or at least he had that potentiality. Poor George! So that's what happened to him.'

Andrew Stewart, the Scot who took over from Marshall in 1948, brought fresh air into Broadcasting House and lifted the ban on reference to the border – indeed, Sayers was able to devote whole programmes of *Ulster Commentary* to the question of partition. Stewart was only a few months in his new job when he was visited by the Director of the Spoken Word, George Barnes, who was over to make a report to the Director-General. Barnes began his analysis with these observations:

> The feeling that first struck me about the country is the intensity of political feeling, resentment is quickly taken and bitterly expressed. ('Would you be liberal if rats were gnawing at your constitution day and night?') Neither party, for instance, will trust even its own members to broadcast an objective talk on 'This Week in Stormont'. I was told that this feeling is indigenous and no longer religious, though the line of religious difference follows the political line. It is deepened by parochialism . . .
>
> The position of the BBC needs examination against this background.

He deplored the sharing of the 285.7 m wavelength and its poor reception in 'the west, the Catholic fringe, which is both a fruitful source of programmes and the place most cut off from British influence'. 'The BBC is constitutionally more independent in Belfast than in London,' Barnes continued, 'yet its fear of making a mistake, where the consequence is a fighting matter, has prevented it until very recently from using the microphone as widely as in London or other regions. There is little sense of a "strong, independent BBC" either among the staff . . . or the Advisory Council.' He recommended a string of changes, including more talks, a good regional service for farmers and support for the cultural programmes which he believed showed great promise.

Stewart was eager to implement improvement and, in spite of considerable opposition from London, he succeeded in creating the Northern Ireland Light Orchestra and in enhancing musical standards in the region. Every producer was encouraged to use as much local talent as possible and he urged them to make more outside broadcasts and recordings. The quality and variety of radio programmes improved markedly. A fresh cohort of writers of original plays steered away from previous farmhouse kitchen stereotypes and their work could be relayed to the rest of the network with some sense of pride. The tape recorder and, later, the portable tape recorder helped to make feature programmes less stilted and more adventurous. Sam Hanna Bell eagerly took to the roads with the mobile recording unit, a cumbersome disc recording machine which was got into such places as the foothills of the Sperrins only with the greatest difficulty, for his series *Village Picture* and *It's a Brave Step*. Stewart's sustained search for indigenous scriptwriters of real talent began to produce results, including the most popular of all in this golden age of wireless, Joseph Tomelty. When audience research reached the Northern Ireland Region, Tomelty's *The McCooeys* was found to have an audience of half a million – in other words, this weekly story of working people in Belfast was listened to by at least one in three of the entire population of the region.

Stewart attempted in 1949 to get the politicians to agree to an arrangement for party political broadcasts but, like his predecessors, he failed. He did ensure that the very turbulent general election of that year – in the wake of the Dublin government's final severing of the last links with the British Commonwealth – was more thoroughly covered than any previous one.

TELEVISION: PROVINCE MUST PRESS FOR PARTICIPATION – this was the headline in the *Northern Whig* over an impassioned plea by George Marshall, retired but living in Belfast, in the autumn of 1949. Agreement in principle followed soon afterwards but it was not until the approach of Queen Elizabeth II's coronation in 1952 that a rather unseemly rush was made to put up a temporary transmitter, which sent out a weak signal and could not be picked up much beyond Belfast city boundary. A unit did shoot film for a locally produced fortnightly series called *Ulster Mirror* but, at first, reliance was almost wholly on relaying network programmes. The people of Northern Ireland moved to television more slowly than in the rest of the United Kingdom, partly because incomes were lower at a time when the cost of a set was relatively much higher than a good colour receiver today.

The irritation of having to share a wavelength was reduced somewhat by the start of VHF broadcasting in 1956 and as more and more people installed television sets. The completion of the Divis Mountain transmitter in 1955

Broadcasting a service from St Patrick's Memorial Church at Saul, County Down, in 1949 – A 'small ultra shortwave transmitter' sent a signal over two miles to the nearest telephone line, which was in the rectory. In this photograph the engineers are busy in the rectory, sending the live broadcast down the normal telephone line to Ormeau Avenue and from there on to Lisnagarvey.

BBC NI

ensured that 80 per cent of the region's land surface was covered and that around two-thirds of homes could receive the television signal. The construction of additional transmitters gradually eliminated areas where the signal could not be picked up.

Initially the production of local television programmes was tentative and underfunded. The region's film unit made six half-hour documentaries a year, some of which were shown on network, and a sound studio was adapted to produce each weekday evening *Today in Northern Ireland*, a five-minute programme of news and features. A purpose-built studio was not completed until February 1959 and there a magazine programme, *Studio Eight*, was put out each week with topical items and occasional documentary films. Viewers often objected to losing a national programme to make way for a local one but by October 1959 they were presented with a choice: Ulster Television began broadcasting and soon captured a larger local audience than the BBC. The arrival of independent television strengthened the hands of those inside Broadcasting House who felt that the region was too timid in tackling difficult local issues, especially as Ulster Television made it clear that it intended to foster intercommunity bridge-building. In fact, as coverage of news and current affairs increased, both stations often had to cope with strident criticism. As the Controller, Robert McCall, explained to the Board of Governors:

The majority of our listeners are quick to take offence if the BBC attempts to 'inform or educate' on the problems of the partition of Ireland. Even Irish music has become suspect to the Unionist part of the population . . . In the circumstances, with an audience quick to take offence – suffering perhaps from rather stretched nerves – the BBC in Northern Ireland has tried to preserve a sense of balance . . . It is not easy, when tempers are high, to induce a sense of proportion in an audience anxious to find some way of expressing its irritation.

After many attempts the BBC did at last get the political parties to agree to election broadcasts in 1958. Brian Faulkner, government Chief Whip, insisted on six out of eight broadcasts being allocated to the Ulster Unionist Party, and, following extensive negotiation, the Nationalist Party leader, Eddie McAteer, and the Northern Ireland Labour Party secretary, Sam Napier, accepted one each. Though in retrospect this was an inequitable arrangement, the 1958 Northern Ireland election was the high point in the fortunes of NILP and perhaps explains why the UUP refused to come to agreement on broadcasts for the 1959 Westminster general election. That was the last occasion on which agreement was not reached, however, and election broadcasts have been transmitted ever since. A fairer apportionment was accepted in 1961: four UUP, two Nationalist Party and one NILP on both radio and television (Ulster Television also carried the BBC broadcasts). These arrangements prepared the ground for more discussion of local political issues on both radio and television.

Northern Ireland was still a much-ignored backwater of the United Kingdom and many in Britain would have had difficulty in finding Belfast on the map. Network BBC was developing a more probing and questioning style of investigative journalism – would this approach be applied to the special problems of division in the region? On 9 January 1959 Alan Whicker presented the first of his reports on life in Northern Ireland for *Tonight* the network current affairs programme. A storm of protest followed, especially in the unionist press. The *Northern Whig* reported that as soon as the programme was over complaints began pouring in to Broadcasting House: 'a spokesman there said the Corporation had to deal with "millions" of these throughout the evening'. Eventually the Regional Controller apologised to the people of Northern Ireland, explaining that Belfast had no part in the editing or presenting of the programme. The end result was that Northern Ireland rarely featured in network programmes, except in news bulletins. Later in the year, the BBC broadcast the first of two American programmes, *Small World*, in which Ed Morrow interviewed British celebrities, as well as actress Siobhán McKenna, who took the opportunity to denounce partition and to refer to

J.G. Devlin and Elizabeth Begley during a recording of the successful radio soap opera *The McCooeys*.

BBC NI

All hands were needed to keep the cart carrying the recording unit and cable on an even keel on the way to the Marble Arch caves in County Fermanagh, 1946. This was for an edition of *Ulster Mirror*, a monthly magazine produced by Charles Freer.

BBC NI

IRA activists as 'idealists'. Again the protests flowed in and Brian Faulkner resigned his membership of the Northern Ireland Advisory Council of the BBC. Lord Brookeborough, the Northern Ireland Prime Minister, also intervened and, before this pressure, London decided not to show the second programme. The consequences were that network broadcasters were discouraged from examining the Northern Ireland 'problem'. As a result, when Northern Ireland suddenly became the centre of media attention towards the close of 1968, the British public had been given little explanation of the issues at stake.

Even if London backed away, programme-makers in the region during the 1960s were beginning to explore controversial issues more critically in current affairs programmes such as *Inquiry* and *Topic*. Gaelic football and hurling finals were shown and, from 1965, there was more cross-border co-operation, facilitated by a permanent link between Belfast and Dublin and regular monthly meetings between BBC and Radio Telefís Éireann executives.

Co-operation included coverage of horse racing, rugby, Twelfth parades, the funeral of Cardinal John D'Alton and the enthronement of Archbishop William Conway. Schools broadcasting had begun in the region in 1961 and from 1965 the series *Two Centuries of Irish History* for secondary schools tackled controversial episodes from the past in a manner which would have been unthinkable a decade earlier. The mould-breaking meeting at Stormont between Northern Ireland Prime Minister Captain Terence O'Neill and Taoiseach Seán Lemass in January 1965 inaugurated a period when gestures of reconciliation were to the fore and a belief that the region was putting ancient quarrels aside was becoming more widespread. Certainly broadcasters emphasised the positive and sought to cover topics which united rather than divided viewers and listeners.

The determination to find consensus and to strengthen it was nevertheless challenged by events. In 1966 Waldo Maguire was appointed Controller. An experienced News Editor with roots in Northern Ireland, he set about strengthening his news and current affairs team, reducing items which he thought 'too soft and whimsical' and providing viewers and listeners with more hard news, covered in greater depth. These changes were timely, for Northern Ireland was about to become the most continuously disturbed and violent part of western Europe in the second half of the twentieth century.

The BBC recording unit visiting the Marble Arch caves. The equipment had been taken from the road up a winding track by donkey and cart and then, on the last stages of the journey, the machinery and cables had to be carried on previously constructed stretchers. This was for the July edition of *Ulster Mirror*, in which Professor Estyn Evans of Queen's University described to listeners the extraordinary limestone formations ornamenting the dark and silent caverns 160 feet below the ground.

BBC NI

2

NEWS
AND CURRENT AFFAIRS

UNTIL THE SECOND WORLD WAR the people of Northern Ireland depended overwhelmingly on newspapers to tell them what was happening both in their region and across the world. From the outset of radio broadcasting, newspaper proprietors and editors succeeded in imposing severe restrictions on how the BBC covered the news – as a communiqué from head office informed the Station Director in September 1924:

> By an agreement with the news organisations, we may not broadcast any narrative which can come within the category of news, except such as is provided in the nightly news bulletins. This means that should you decide on a weekly review of sport, that review may not contain a description or criticism of any event that has occurred on the day of the broadcast . . . the line of demarcation seems to be provided in a time period possibly of twenty-four hours – at any rate sufficient time to have enabled the press to have published the narrative in question . . . two local news bulletins will be provided nightly by a Belfast journalist, Mr John Sayers of the *Belfast Telegraph* (a nominee of Central News).

The Director of Programmes added that the bulletins should be scrutinised to 'give but the barest publicity to tragedies and other sordid happenings' and to limit 'information useful to gamblers'. Nor was there to be much opportunity for current affairs broadcasts: in another letter, Major Scott was told that 'local talks must not contain any material that can be classed as direct or indirect advertising, and under no circumstances may they contain political matter'. Reith was soon able to break out of this straitjacket, but the staff in Belfast, most of whom were not from Northern Ireland, proved to be timid in dipping their toes into the local waters of clashing political aspirations and local cultural traditions.

Gerald Beadle arrived from South Africa as the new Station Director in 1926. Despite nurturing a close relationship with the Unionist government, he became steadily more dissatisfied with the news bulletins supplied by the *Belfast Telegraph*, the newspaper then most hostile to the BBC, and in 1930 got permission to appoint a News Editor to vet and redraft the bulletins as they arrived. The first appointee stayed only a few months and his place was taken

Opposite:
Larry McCoubrey, anchorman for evening news programme, *Scene Around Six*, in the 1960s and early 1970s.
BBC NI

21

in 1931 by Henry McMullan, who was to remain an employee of the BBC for the next forty years. Regular daily news bulletins, in fact, had been broadcast only from 8 July 1928.

In his trenchant 1936 analysis of the Belfast operations of the BBC, Charles Siepmann provided a searing summary of the local climate in which programme-makers were expected to broadcast to a divided community:

> Politics and public administration conditioned by religious faction have about them an Alice-in-Wonderland-like unreality. A system of government developed by and for a great nation has been imposed upon a province the size of Yorkshire and a population a little larger than that of Glasgow . . . A civil authority special powers act makes possible the arrest and indefinite imprisonment of any citizen without trial at the discretion of the authorities. Ministers of State commit themselves in public statements to partisan provocation of the Roman Catholic's religious susceptibilities. More than one responsible person told me that the recent riots were not unconnected with such provocative outbursts by Cabinet Ministers.

Although the 1935 riots had led to the deaths of fifteen people, local news bulletins had provided only the barest outlines of this violence. As reported in the *Northern Whig,* one Unionist politician believed that this timidity justified a government takeover of local broadcasting:

> During the recent disturbances they all had an example of the attitude adopted by the BBC in regard to riot news, when they had been told in a description of the occurrences on the Twelfth of July that 'a riot had arisen', no mention being made of the fact that the Orange procession had been attacked. Thereafter the BBC was almost silent on the subject. How much better it would have been if the Inspector-General or the Commissioner of Police had been able to come to the microphone every three hours and reassure people as to the real position.

A student speaking in a debate on whether education should be provided free of charge. This programme came from Queen's University in 1949 for the series *Your Questions*. Such discussions were pre-recorded, partly to edit out any comments which would be considered too extreme or otherwise inappropriate for broadcasting.

BBC NI

In his report Siepmann did praise talks for farmers and felt that there was scope for programmes 'on a strict factual basis of the conditions of Ulster in the sphere of health, education, etc'. He did, however, acknowledge the limitations brought about by 'the ban on controversy necessitated over a wide field by the political–religious issue'.

After the Second World War, when Henry McMullan became Programme Director, he pressed for extended news and current affairs coverage. He would be starting from a low base, as the *Irish Times* critic pointed out in November 1945:

Although the quality of the programmes is of the very highest standard, one feels that much good radio material is going to waste because of the excessive canniness of station policy . . . there is no sign of the Northern Ireland station serving as a forum for the discussion of social, political and religious problems . . . with a little courage the Northern Ireland station could make a great contribution to the solving of Ulster's problems.

McMullan probably sympathised with this view, but George Marshall, still Controller at this time, had striven for thirteen years to keep controversy out of regional broadcasting. In 1948, however, Marshall was replaced by Andrew Stewart who believed passionately that Northern Ireland was part of the United Kingdom and therefore, as in other regions, political debate on air should be encouraged.

The association of John Sayers with the BBC went back to 1924; then a journalist with the *Belfast Telegraph,* he supplied the Northern Ireland news for broadcast in full knowledge that it would not be edited or vetted. After the war, Sayers was the sole contributor to *Ulster Commentary.* The *Irish Times* radio critic regretted that he never said anything about the South (not knowing that he was forbidden to do so) and thought Sayers 'a little dazzled by the glory of the Empire'. John Boyd, the talks producer, 'contested McMullan's judgement that the commentaries were objective commentaries on the Ulster political scene. Indeed I considered them as merely extended first leaders of the *Belfast Telegraph* . . .' Boyd eventually got his way and invited J.J. Campbell, a nationalist and liberal-minded Catholic, and J.U. Stewart, a radical Protestant, to broadcast commentaries to counter-balance Sayers. Sayers, Boyd wrote later, 'told me he approved of the change, confessing he found the chore of writing

The fortnightly *Your Questions,* begun in 1954, became even more popular in Northern Ireland than the network version *Any Questions.* The audience asked the questions but left the discussion to a panel carefully chosen to avoid the expression of extreme views. The editor of the *Belfast Telegraph,* John E. Sayers, answering the question here in this June 1955 broadcast, had prepared BBC news bulletins for the Belfast station since 1924.

BBC NI

scripts more and more of a strain'. J.U. Stewart, the son of the caretaker of May Street Presbyterian church and eventually principal of the Belfast College of Commerce, had blunt, outspoken opinions and he delivered them in a no-nonsense, unaffected style. Campbell, a former hairdresser who had to work his way through Queen's University, was a classical scholar with a warm, engaging manner which listeners appreciated. With the help of such men and facing considerable opposition, Boyd was widening the scope of political debate. The arrival of Andrew Stewart removed many of the shackles of the Marshall regime and whole programmes of *Ulster Commentary* were eventually devoted to the subject of partition.

Boyd also produced Northern Ireland's variation on *Any Questions*, entitled

Maurice Shillington, the announcer and newsreader, whose voice was heard regularly delivering the local radio news bulletins. Shillington also became the first BBC Northern Ireland television newsreader on 30 September 1957.

BBC NI

Your Questions, which became even more popular in Northern Ireland than the network programme. Regular participants were J.C. Beckett, Professor of History at Queen's University, Charles Brett, solicitor and architectural historian, J.J. Campbell and John Sayers, and they discussed questions such as, 'How do you get sectarianism out of politics?' The series was so successful that a television version was tried but the response it drew was poor.

Cecil Taylor joined BBC Northern Ireland in the mid-fifties as its first television news journalist. He had no doubt at this stage that the BBC in the region was a service for the Protestant section of the population; the Catholic minority did not identify with it and tuned their radios instead to Radio Éireann's station, Athlone. Listeners and viewers were not made aware that Northern Ireland had religious and political problems, or problems about identity. Taylor, who had worked as a reporter for the *Larne Times*, the *Belfast News Letter* and the *Irish Times*, was interviewed by a panel which included the Northern Ireland Civil Service Commissioner and the Controller Richard Marriott, whom he describes as 'dark, severe-looking, staring'. Asked what he thought of bulletins put out by the region, Taylor replied that they sounded 'as if they were written night by night by the Northern Ireland Press Office in Stormont' and added that they were 'being broadcast by the BBC for the benefit of the Protestant and Unionist population, ignoring the minority'. The fact that he got the job indicated a new determination to prepare television news bulletins which would be more objective than before. Taylor's job was to organise film camera coverage for a five-minute news bulletin at 6.10 p.m. All other regions had ten-minute bulletins – it was decided, he remembers, 'that nothing ever happens in Northern

Ireland'. At first Taylor's equipment and support were completely basic and he had to operate the camera himself. There was virtually no help or advice available locally, for Northern Ireland then had no television film industry, no film crews and no film processing. Nevertheless, he relished the opportunity to create a fully professional local television news service. By the time he left the post in 1970, the five-minute opt-out after the London news – two-and-a-half-minute news and two-and-a-half-minute feature – had gradually expanded to the twenty-minute *Today in Northern Ireland*. Meanwhile, facilities improved and more staff were recruited: in particular, Taylor was able to draw on the expertise of Eric Waugh as industrial correspondent and W.D. Flackes as political correspondent, two men who were rapidly winning the respect of the viewing public.

McMullan and Taylor were determined that controversial topics should be tackled. One of the first was on the acute housing shortage in Londonderry. Alan Reid was sent to do a piece on Springtown camp, a place of acute deprivation and an eloquent illustration of official neglect. Reid got no co-operation from Londonderry Corporation, so Taylor drove up to see the town clerk, Gerry Glover. 'You're wasting your time,' Glover snapped, and when

Cameras are at the ready and Cecil Taylor, the editor, has a last-minute consultation with the newsreader, Michael Baguley, before 'going live' on *News From Northern Ireland* in the 1960s. On Baguley's left is Ann Chambers, television news secretary. The cameraman on the right is David Hanna.

BBC NI

Taylor indicated he intended the report to get an airing, Glover responded: 'I'll make sure it doesn't.' Next morning Glover was on the telephone to McMullan. 'I sent him away with a flea in his ear,' McMullan told his colleagues with some satisfaction. When asked if he would give an interview on this issue, the Nationalist leader, Eddie McAteer, said to Taylor, 'Good God! Miracles will never cease.' In the end, Glover felt he had no choice but to agree to attempt a defence of the corporation. The feature on Springtown did much to establish the BBC's credibility amongst all sections of Northern Ireland's divided community. From then on it became noticeably easier to cover controversial stories.

In 1963 Lord Brookeborough was forced to resign and was replaced by Captain Terence O'Neill. O'Neill was the first Prime Minister to make reconciliation a central plank of his platform and to make gestures of friendship to the minority, such as visiting Catholic schools and taking care to be photographed in the company of nuns. Stormont House, however, continued to assume that the BBC would faithfully reflect its slant on events. The Controller, Robert McCall, summoned Taylor to his office for a special meeting with the Cabinet Secretary, who made 'a clever speech', the gist of which was that the Prime Minister was determined to change Northern Ireland but he had problems, not everybody in his party shared his opinions, he was finding it difficult to get his views across and it would be a great comfort to him if he knew he could rely on the co-operation of the BBC's news department. Taylor knew his first duty was to run a professional and impartial news service and turned to McCall: 'Well, Controller, what the Prime Minister of Northern Ireland can

The IRA attacked the BBC transmitter in Londonderry on 12 January 1956. Here an engineer is assessing the damage.

BBC NI

rely on is that we will supply a news service for all the people of Northern Ireland and be fair to all politicians to the best of our ability.' The Cabinet Secretary returned to Stormont knowing that he was going to get no favours out of the BBC.

Even as late as the beginning of the 1960s there was still only a sparse diet of current affairs broadcasting. News bulletins were brief and film of, for example, violent incidents during the IRA campaign of 1956–62, was shown with the minimum of comment. McCall reported to the governors that the 'majority of our listeners are quick to take offence if the BBC attempts to "inform or educate" on the problem of the Partition of Ireland . . . and the reflection of some factual news has been described as propaganda for the Republic'. Indignation could be at its most intense if outsiders reported critically on Northern Ireland, as was the case when Alan Whicker looked at life in the region for the network *Tonight* programme in 1959. London was discouraged from examining Northern Ireland in any depth for many years thereafter. Locally, the BBC refused to be pressurised into blandness and on 10 October 1962 broadcast a thirty-minute discussion on discrimination in employment, following the publication of *The Northern Ireland Problem: A Study in Group Relations* by Denis Barritt and Charles Carter, two distinguished Quakers who worked closely with government agencies.

The current affairs programmes *Topic* and *Inquiry* adopted a probing investigative style on topics, such as housing, cross-border co-operation and the planners' neglect of Derry. Though men such as Nationalist John Hume and Unionist Brian Faulkner took part, care was still taken to sidestep sectarian and political aspects of problems. *Scene Around Six,* the news and features magazine television programme, shown each weekday between 6.00 p.m. and 6.20 p.m., began by being fairly light and non-threatening. Broadcasters were keen to cultivate the middle ground and were apt to congratulate themselves for doing much to help an integrated society to develop. At the same time microphones and cameras were covering news events which were showing that political tensions and intercommunal divisions were not being dissipated by O'Neill's liberal approach.

Those news events which increasingly were featured on network included the Divis Street riots in Belfast and direct action housing protests in Dungannon, County Tyrone, in 1964; the 1966 commemoration by nationalists of the fiftieth anniversary of the Easter Rising; the controversy over the naming of a new bridge over the Lagan, and the Ulster Volunteer Force murders in the same year; missiles thrown at the Queen's car during a royal visit in 1967; and the Caledon incident over the unfair allocation of a Tyrone council house in June 1968. Incidents of this sort had alerted the Director-General, Hugh Carlton Greene, to the region's particular needs in news gathering, which had led to the appointment of Waldo Maguire, a seasoned newsman, as Controller in 1966. When some members of the Regional Advisory Council argued that coverage of certain events projected an unfavourable image of Northern Ireland, the new Controller responded that 'regrettably it was one's

W. D. Flackes on *Scene Around Six* interviewing Bill Craig, one of Northern Ireland's most controversial politicians of the era. Craig held various ministerial posts in Terence O'Neill's government and he was probably Minister of Home Affairs when this photograph was taken. In 1968 he banned the Derry Civil Rights march on 5 October which brought Northern Ireland's problems to the attention of the world. Malcolm Kellard is sitting to the right.

BBC NI

duty to report what was happening and if there were riots the world wanted pictures of them'. *Scene Around Six* under his rule acquired a harder edge, though this was partly due to the outcome of events.

Local issues were being investigated more critically and extensively in *Inquiry* and a monthly version, *Gateway*, concentrated on political events and developments. Such programmes attracted continuing criticism, particularly from unionists, and the Imperial Grand Registrar of the Royal Black Institution asserted that both the BBC and UTV showed 'a veiled sympathy with the anti-Partition conspiracy and in a subtle way colour news items in a manner which cannot fail to impair the Unionist image at home and abroad'.

Taylor was appointed News Editor in 1965 and soon became anxious that the resources of his department were insufficient to cope with major stories or crises which might emerge in the near future. At a senior management meeting in 1967 he said that the region was crying out for current affairs programme space to 'reflect the tensions swimming beneath the surface'. 'What tensions?,' the Controller responded. Taylor replied that there was 'a real possibility that people will be killed on the streets'. Few others shared his views: at that time most liberal members of the educated middle classes sincerely believed that tensions would ease and that steady economic progress would ensure the eventual success of O'Neill's declared determination to reconcile the minority to the regime.

After 1966, news items and reports on Northern Ireland rarely featured on network and therefore the listening and viewing public in the rest of the United Kingdom and beyond was given little preparation for the explosion of unrest towards the end of 1968. That year the first civil rights march, in which around 2,500 protesters marched from Coalisland to Dungannon on 24 August, attracted little outside attention, even though it was halted by a loyalist counter-demonstration and a police barricade. About only four hundred demonstrators turned up at Waterside station for a civil rights march to the centre of Derry on 5 October 1968. Minister of Home Affairs Bill Craig had banned the march, however, and Gerry Fitt, Republican Labour MP for West Belfast, had three Westminster MPs with him, brought directly from the Labour Party conference then in session. As the marchers moved down Duke Street the police assaulted them with batons; Fitt, with blood streaming from his head, had to be taken to an ambulance; and, as parties of police chased after fleeing demonstrators, water cannon arrived. Both the UTV and BBC cameras were sprayed but RTÉ cameraman Gay O'Brien succeeded in filming the scene very fully and this was shown on BBC network. Those few hundred feet of film changed the course of Northern Ireland's history. Images of unrestrained police batoning MPs and other unarmed marchers, 'without justification or excuse,' as the Cameron Commission judged later, flashed across the world. At a stroke television coverage of the events of 5 October 1968 destabilised Northern Ireland, and as the sectarian dragon was fully reawakened, the region was plunged into a near-revolutionary crisis, characterised by bitter intercommunal conflict and protracted violence and destruction.

At Westminster, Harold Wilson, the Prime Minister, acknowledged the new power of the media: in response to an observation by Captain Willie Orr, leader of the Unionist MPs in the House of Commons, that questions about the handling of the march were 'mischief making,' he said: 'I say to the honourable and gallant Member that he is entitled to his view on the matter which he has just expressed. Up to now we have perhaps had to rely on the statements of himself and others on these matters. Since then we have had British television.'

Wilson insisted on a series of reforms, threatening both Faulkner and Craig with the imposition of severe financial penalties on Northern Ireland when they resisted O'Neill's pleas to accept root-and-branch change. After a series of very large civil rights marches and counter-demonstrations, marked by ugly scenes of destruction and confrontation, the region calmed in December in response to O'Neill's announcement of reforms and his impassioned television appeal beginning with the words 'Ulster stands at the crossroads'. 'Your voice has been heard, and clearly heard,' he said to the civil rights leaders. 'Your duty now is to take the heat out of the situation.' O'Neill's appeal was heard by the leaders and the principal civil rights organisations called off further street protests. The People's Democracy, however, determined to go ahead with its march, modelled on that led by Martin Luther King from Selma to Montgomery in 1965, between Belfast and Derry, starting on New Year's Day. That march, culminating in the notorious attack against marchers at Burntollet bridge and violence in Derry, demonstrated how ephemeral the peace was to be. Once again television footage vividly recorded history in the making and not only vied with reports of the Vietnam War but also played its part in giving Northern Ireland a sharp push towards the precipice.

There followed explosions at major installations, including water pipelines and an electricity substation, subsequently shown to be the work of the UVF; the fall of O'Neill; intense rioting in Belfast as the summer approached; the Apprentice Boys' march and the Battle of the Bogside in Derry; outright inter-communal warfare in Belfast and the first deaths of what soon became known as 'the Troubles'; and the deployment of British troops on active service in the streets. 'Let's make no mistake about it,' the *Irish News* concluded, '. . . the marches would not have mattered two pence if the TV cameras had not been there.' The truth of this comment caused much agonising in Broadcasting House: should the BBC attempt to calm the situation by holding back some of the news garnered in?

'The agony of Ulster is the agony of our own listeners and viewers,' Waldo Maguire told the Regional Advisory Council, and he continued:

> In the present atmosphere of hatred and fear, we have to recognise that the broadcasting of violently opposed views, passionately and offensively expressed, could have direct and immediate consequences on the streets of Belfast or Londonderry.
>
> This, then, is the dilemma. While taking account of the fact that network news bulletins and programmes are being seen and heard in Northern Ireland, the BBC must not fail in its duty to the rest of the United Kingdom, to present the news fully and fairly, to explain the background to the violence, to provide a platform for the expression of all significant opinion.

He suggested two possible ways of getting round this dilemma: to make 'uninhibited' programmes for network which would not be carried on Northern Ireland transmitters; or to keep those people likely to make inflammatory comments out of the studio, 'to modify to some extent' broadcasts, and so avoid extreme provocation. As a result, only sanitised news reports seem to have been broadcast on 15–16 August 1969, amid violence and the deployment of troops. Later, Martin Bell, a network reporter in Belfast at the time, said, 'that was probably the only time when I was stopped by the powers above from saying what I wanted to say'. He explained:

> We made a mistake . . . in 1969, in the August of that year when Catholics were burned out of their homes in the Falls by Protestants

who attacked them from the Shankill. The BBC reports then gave no indication of who these refugees were. They just spoke of refugees. The public was not to know whether they were Catholic or Protestant or who was attacking whom.

Keith Kyle was one of those 'parachuted in' by the BBC to prepare reports for the *Tonight* programme. Ten years earlier he had been in Ireland as political and parliamentary correspondent for *The Economist* and was therefore better informed than most other network reporters. In 1969 he wrote:

> It was a climate of anger, anguish, reproach and deputation in which every news bulletin and current affairs programme produced a minimum of 40 to 50 telephone calls and each brought into the building its quota of overwrought citizens exercising their privilege of shouting at the BBC in person.

More than a quarter of a century later he remembered:

> The atmosphere at Broadcasting House, on the corner of Ormeau and Linenhall Streets, in the whorl of demonstration and counter-demonstration, was understandably tense; the local broadcasters, drawn from both communities, plus, of course, the ever-increasing numbers of us invaders, found themselves directly involved in the constantly shifting street scenes.

He, like Martin Bell, recalled the internal censorship imposed in August 1969:

> At a special meeting in the Director-General's office on the third day of the disorders, and before the British troops actually arrived, the Corporation decided on what was termed 'a temporary departure from normal journalistic considerations'. What was happening was to be explained but not shown. Street interviews, in which members of the public were given to expressing themselves in an extreme way, were temporarily banned; and two individuals in particular, Ian Paisley and Bernadette Devlin, were to be kept off the screen.

The bans on Paisley and Devlin were soon lifted and the repetition of self-censorship, which Kyle feared, did not, in fact, occur.

As passions ran high, so the BBC, as Kyle observed, was inundated with abusive telephone calls and critical letters. The great majority of these were from loyalists, and at this stage all threats of violence came from the Protestant side. At a civil rights march in Armagh on 30 November 1968, for example, loyalists preparing the counter-demonstration warned cameramen and reporters that they were in danger if they filmed what happened. An ITN crew was attacked and a loyalist wielding a lead-filled sock knocked a cameraman unconscious.

The news and current affairs staff in Belfast found themselves supplying lead stories for the network almost every night of the week. Journalists were so hard-pressed that film was frequently transmitted on network without anyone in London seeing it beforehand. It was only eighteen months into the Troubles that stories were regularly recorded, as well as going out live. 'How are you coping?' John Crawley, Head of Network News, enquired over the telephone. 'You'd better come over,' Taylor responded. When Crawley arrived, Taylor had been up all night. 'Show him the worst,' news reporter David Capper said, and Taylor took him to the roof to show him smoke rising from several points in the city. 'What's needed?' Crawley asked, and three additional reporters were appointed almost straightaway. If the BBC was to be credible to the minority, Catholics had to be recruited and the increase in staff provided the opportunity to begin rectifying an imbalance that had been there since 1924. Passions were running so high that virtually all local news and current affairs broadcasters were liable to vilification in their own communities. Catholic reporters were branded 'Castle Catholics' and Protestants were denounced as traitors to their own kind, who gave aid and comfort to the enemy.

Local news reporters found their numbers augmented by network journalists. Maguire required incoming reporters at all times to consult with him, as his predecessors had done, a requirement backed by a London directive. In fact, Maguire was much more accommodating than Controllers before him, but occasional friction was inevitable. As 1969 drew to a close the BBC charted the emergence of the Provisional IRA and in the following year *Nationwide* filmed a secret PIRA camp in the Republic, where it claimed two thousand men were undergoing training. Unionist MPs at Westminster expressed their outrage, but that protest was muted by comparison with that which greeted a *Twenty-Four Hours* programme in January 1971 in which masked members of the Belfast Brigade of PIRA were interviewed by Bernard Falk, and admitted responsibility for recent attacks on the army post in Ballymurphy. Falk was not only reproved for failing to follow all necessary consultative procedures, he was brought to court and asked to identify Patrick Leo Martin, charged with membership of the IRA, as one of the men he had interviewed. Falk said he had given his word never to identify those he had interviewed and served four days in jail rather than break his journalistic code. As a result, BBC management issued a directive to programme staff prohibiting all interviews with PIRA without the prior permission of the Director-General. One consequence of the requirement to consult was that scoops could be rendered valueless because of delay, as other media – newspapers in particular – were able to reveal fresh news more rapidly.

Northern Ireland had now entered the most violent phase in its history. Faulkner, having ousted Major James Chichester-Clark as Prime Minister, imposed internment without trial in August 1971, which was followed by the biggest enforced movement of population in Europe since 1945 and an alarming upsurge in violent deaths and bombings. BBC staff were often in peril. On 9 February 1971 two BBC engineers, Bill Thomas and Malcolm Henson, and three construction workers were killed by a landmine as they approached the Brougher Mountain transmitter on the Tyrone–Fermanagh border. Cameramen and reporters were attacked and beaten up during riots. In September 1971 the BBC staff magazine, *Ariel*, described what happened to local cameraman Cyril Cave:

> 'I've been hit by just about everything,' he said, 'petrol bombs, paving stones and nail bombs.' He has been in hospital twice – once after a riot mob clubbed him over the head with a piece of wall and two weeks later after being knocked cold in a riot. He was dragged to shelter by the police behind an overturned burning lorry.

The article then went on to list other injured staff, including Eric Pollen and sound recordist Frank Gray, beaten up by a crowd; Dick Macmillan, dowsed by a water cannon; Peter Biggin and Bob Williams, who sustained severe head injuries from bricks and paving stones thrown at them; and recordist Roy Benford, attacked while covering the shooting of a sentry. Journalist Don Anderson was chased out of Portadown – where he once lived on the Garvaghy Road – with a man clutching his trailing legs as his driver drove off at speed. In Dungannon he was confronted by an elderly man pointing a shotgun and, immediately afterwards, was shot at by another: the bullet missed and shattered a shop window behind him.

While republicans often welcomed media attention, loyalist mobs were almost always hostile to television and radio reporters. Protestants, in general, felt that coverage was skewed against them and in August 1971 a petition with 33,000 signatures was presented to the Controller, which included these words: 'We question the right of the mass media to continually distort the news in favour of the terrorists and the politicians whose loyalties are to subversion and not to the constitution of the country.' Television and radio reporters found Protestant mobs more threatening than Catholic ones because Protestants believed the media would always show them in a bad light. Some journalists, such as Anderson, worried that the refusal of loyalists to engage

BBC Northern Ireland news cameraman Cyril Cave films armed members of the IRA at a roadblock in the Bogside in June 1972. Cave and his soundman, Jim Deeney, became known as being amongst the most intrepid of newsgatherers.

BBC NI

with the media, and their comparative incoherence when they did, diminished broadcasters' appreciation of their position. It was not until the Ulster Workers' Council strike of May 1974 that loyalists began to pay more attention to public relations and to recognise the value of stating their case in a lucid and reasoned fashion.

Broadcasting House was the object of direct attack in May 1972. A delivery van, belonging to a well-known local firm, was hijacked by PIRA, loaded with a large bomb and parked against the wall of the main radio studio. A warning was given only just in time to prevent anyone being injured. The explosion wrecked offices, flying glass lacerated tape recordings, and two reels – sucked out of shattered windows – were never seen again. The massive walls of the studio block were only scarred, however, and broadcasting was not interrupted. Staff in Broadcasting House were frequent witnesses to bombs at close quarters, as the Provisionals destroyed the neighbouring motor taxation offices in Ormeau Avenue and many warehouses, stores and offices in nearby Bedford Street and Dublin Road. James Hawthorne, appointed Controller in 1978, recorded in his diary:

The topping out ceremony was for the extension to the Broadcasting House complex and, not surprisingly, was held on the flat roof area. A senior visiting engineer was in the middle of his speech and had just said something like: 'It's nice to be in Belfast on a day like this . . .' when there was a no-warning explosion about 500 yards away.

The BBC's versions of events sometimes were at variance to those issued by the British army, which led to some disquiet in the ranks of the Conservative Party, and, at a time when staff were already becoming anxious about levels of internal censorship, a meeting was called, in December 1971, between the Home Secretary, Reginald Maudling, and the Chairman of the BBC, Lord Hill. In the end, while editorial procedures were strengthened, the BBC successfully asserted its independence and transmitted a controversial programme, entitled *The Question of Ulster*, to a very large audience, despite Maudling's appeal not to show it.

While on holiday in Donegal, Waldo Maguire went missing for twenty-four hours. He was found gravely ill on board a boat on a lough and though he made a good recovery, he retired early and in 1973 his place was taken by Richard Francis. The executive producer of *The Question of Ulster,* a former editor of *Panorama* and later Director of News and Current Affairs, Francis held

Broadcasting house had a narrow escape on 25 January 1973 when a Provisional IRA bomb set fire to an adjoining warehouse and offices belonging to the BBC. Prompt action by the Belfast Fire Brigade probably saved the studios but there was considerable flooding as well as broken windows and damage to metal work. Though the building was evacuated for almost two hours, engineers and presentation staff remained at their posts and programme output was not interrupted.

BBC NI

firm views on the role of broadcasters in maintaining an open society, opinions he was to articulate more thoughtfully and eloquently than perhaps any other member of BBC senior management since Reith's time. In a speech he made to the Broadcasting Press Guild in July 1979, Francis said:

> The media have a very real contribution to make, in particular a contribution to the maintenance of the democracy which is under threat, both by providing a forum where the harshest differences of opinion can be aired and by reporting and courageously investigating the unpalatable truths which underlie the problems of the Province. I have no doubt that if and when the communities of Northern Ireland reconcile their conflicts, it will be by understanding them and not ignoring them . . .
>
> The experience in Northern Ireland, where communities and governments are in conflict but not in a state of emergency or a state of war, suggests a greater need than ever for the media to function as the 'fourth estate', distinct from the executive, the legislature and the judiciary.

Francis was in post for less than a year when his philosophy was put severely to the test in what can be regarded as the most acute crisis faced by the BBC since the General Strike of 1926. This was the Ulster Workers' Council strike of May 1974. Following the Sunningdale Agreement in 1973, a power-sharing Executive had been formed on the last day of the year. However, the general election of 28 February 1974 demonstrated the hostility of the Protestant majority to the arrangement: eleven out of the region's twelve seats were won by members of the United Ulster Unionist Council, a loyalist pact opposed to power-sharing. On Tuesday 14 May a group of Protestant workers calling themselves the Ulster Workers' Council began a loyalist strike which for fifteen days brought Northern Ireland close to paralysis. Power generation was almost exclusively in Protestant hands and, as the strike progressed, electricity supplies were cut ever more severely. The newly elected Labour government made no attempt to suppress the strike by force and little was done to curb widespread intimidation.

The newsroom in Broadcasting House, already the busiest outside London, became a centre of intense activity twenty-four hours a day. Newspaper distribution and then production were brought to a halt and the region's population – marooned by the cessation of public transport, the seizure of filling stations and intimidation – depended as never before on the provision of news by the broadcasters. Radio came into its own again and the region rose to the occasion by more than quadrupling its output almost overnight. During the strike, there was little opportunity for reflection and analysis: the energies of the BBC staff were almost wholly devoted to gathering and broadcasting news. A stream of special bulletins provided up-to-date information on bread supplies, social services, transport, road blocks and on power supplies.

The UWC seized control of filling stations and dispensed permits for the purchase of fuel on its own criteria. At a crisis meeting in Broadcasting House it was agreed that to ask for petrol vouchers for staff reporters and camera crews would be to countenance the strike. RTÉ staff agreed to arrange for fuel to be made available south of the border and after fifteen minutes two men agreed to drive south to collect the petrol, on condition that a senior BBC executive accompany them. Taylor went with them. Two lorries drove down to pick up the petrol in forty-gallon drums on the north side of Dublin. Once back over the border, Taylor noticed that his driver kept his foot flat to the floor as they sped along the dark deserted road north of Newry. They were back at the BBC at 2 a.m. – the whole time, Taylor's wife assumed her husband was simply working late at the office.

Protestant feeling was rallied behind the strikers by Harold Wilson's self-indulgent broadcast on Saturday 25 May: the Prime Minister denounced the strike as 'a deliberate and calculated attempt to use every undemocratic and unparliamentary means for the purpose of bringing down the whole constitution of Northern Ireland' and referred to subsidies provided by British taxpayers 'without regard to cost'. Wilson continued: 'Yet people who benefit from all this now viciously defy Westminster . . . people who spend their lives sponging on Westminster and British democracy and then systematically assault democratic methods. Who do these people think they are?'

Following this speech, and the army takeover of petrol stations, the UWC ordered a reduction in electricity to 10 per cent capacity. The voice of Hugo Patterson, the official spokesman for the Northern Ireland Electricity service, became familiar in every home. On the morning of Monday 27 May he was interviewed for the BBC by Barry Cowan:

> Patterson: Let's be clear about this; this shutdown is on, it's complete, it's final, it's irrevocable. I don't think there's any going back on this one now.
>
> Cowan: In other words, as of two minutes ago, nine-thirty, the complete shutdown of power in Northern Ireland has begun and cannot now be stopped.
>
> Patterson: . . . you're right . . . We are past the point of no return.

At 1.20 p.m. Faulkner resigned and a loyalist demonstration at Stormont became a massive victory rally. That night flames leaped up from bonfires in Protestant districts to celebrate the end of one of the most successful general strikes in Europe since 1945.

'The BBC were marvellous – they were prepared to be fed any information,' one UWC leader observed. 'They fell into their own trap that "the public must get the news". Sometimes they were just a news service for us, we found that if the media was on our side we didn't need a gun.' If this was so, it was due to the failure of government ministers to respond to the Controller's repeated invitation to come forward and rebut the claims of the UWC and to give their own version of events. John Hume, Minister of Commerce in the power-sharing executive, felt that Hugo Patterson was doing the work of the UWC with the connivance of the BBC. Cecil Taylor, News Editor, approached the strike as an experienced newsman, with the firm belief that the public had a right to know. The staff, however, had also to avoid putting citizens in peril: businesses defying intimidation in difficult areas contacted Broadcasting House beseeching reporters not to say over the air that they remained open and at work. Merlyn Rees, the Secretary of State, was opposed to taking vigorous action to attempt to halt the strike and preferred not to push himself forward on the airwaves.

During fifteen days, when a self-appointed junta in league with loyalist para-militaries had made an entire region of the United Kingdom ungovernable, the people of Northern Ireland had become extraordinarily reliant on the BBC in Belfast as the source of reliable and up-to-date news and comment. This source overwhelmingly was radio rather than television. Northern Ireland radio bulletins and pro-grammes were opt-outs on pro-grammes from BBC RADIO 4. The events of May 1974 gave a new urgency to plans already well advanced to provide BBC listeners in Northern Ireland with their own wavelength, transmitting pro-grammes originating in Belfast. The regional service was therefore great-ly augmented by the launch of BBC RADIO ULSTER in January 1975. Now listeners were provided with a fifth wavelength broadcast from

Belfast and, unlike local radio stations in Britain, it was set up to be the BBC's principal radio station in Northern Ireland. Like BBC LOCAL RADIO, however, instead of departing from the national schedules, BBC RADIO ULSTER planned its own schedules and could draw on programmes made elsewhere to meet local tastes and interests. It was not long before this mixture won it by far the largest daily patronage of any radio service available in the province. The con-tinuing violence and political instability ensured that news bulletins and cur-rent affairs programmes attracted some of the largest audiences.

Merlyn Rees was not critical of the BBC; at most he would reveal his con-cern by his constantly furrowed brow, by his characteristic hand-wringing and by drawing anxiously on a cheroot. Roy Mason, appointed Secretary of State in 1976, by contrast, was bombastic and pugnacious, theatrically affecting the style of a paternalistic colonial governor, appearing for photo opportunities clad in a tweed safari suit made for him in Belfast and smoking a pipe resolutely clenched between his teeth. He showed his contempt for politicians of all parties by refusing for some time to see them at Stormont. He showed even greater contempt for local broadcasters.

On 5 November 1974 members of the Loyalist Women's Action Group invaded Broadcasting House for a 'sit-in' protest against what they believed was partial news reporting by the BBC. They argued that the BBC gave too much publicity to terrorists and failed to represent the views of Protestants.
BBC NI

The BBC Board of Governors visited Belfast in November 1976 to mark the opening of an extension to the BBC's premises in Ormeau Avenue and held a private dinner party in the Culloden Hotel. Guests included the Secretary of State, the RUC Chief Constable, Kenneth Newman, the Lord Chief Justice, the British army GOC and the Vice-Chancellor of Queen's University, and as the meal drew to a close they were invited to speak on the role of the BBC in the region. Sir Michael Swann, BBC Chairman and an avid follower of cricket, turned to Mason and said: 'Secretary of State, may I invite you to open the bowling.' Stung by a programme on the weekly current affairs series *Spotlight*, which had profiled him in spite of his refusal to take part, Mason launched into a vehement denunciation of the corporation, asserting that the BBC did not behave 'like a public service organisation', that its coverage was 'appalling' and that it gave the Provisional IRA a 'daily platform'. The other guests joined in the chorus of denunciation, with the notable exception of the Chief Constable. The visiting governors and senior executives present were aghast at this assault and were grateful to Cecil Taylor, now Head of Programmes, for his trenchant, point by point, rebuttal of the charges. Robin Walsh, the News Editor, found the dinner 'a shocking experience' and as the company rose from the table he observed to a colleague, 'Herewith the Second Battle of Culloden' – a title which was swiftly applied generally to this episode, and which was leaked to the press two months later.

Mason's ire was provoked again in March 1977 when *Tonight* broadcast Keith Kyle's interview with Bernard O'Connor, a schoolteacher and driving instructor in Enniskillen, County Fermanagh, who alleged inhuman treatment by the police who had held him for 168 hours. Harry West, UUP MP for Fermanagh–South Tyrone, spoke for many when he described the programme as 'murderously irresponsible'. The *Evening Standard's* cartoonist Jak showed a man spreadeagled on the pavement and a BBC reporter thrusting his microphone to masked gunmen inviting their opinion. Kyle had been careful to follow the consultation guidelines and Richard Francis, the Controller, resolutely defended the programme. The Attorney-General read the script of the film and immediately realised that, regarding the treatment of prisoners, there was an apparent breach of undertakings he had given the Council of Europe; he asked to see Kyle, who remarked that it 'made me feel that he was as good as offering his legal advice to O'Connor to press the suit'. Eventually the High Court awarded O'Connor exemplary damages of £5,000 and costs. However, the long-term danger for the BBC was that its network staff could be discouraged from making similar investigative programmes about Northern Ireland in the future.

James Hawthorne, who had been the region's first schools producer and had been appointed to launch a television service in Hong Kong, was appointed Controller in 1978. An early duty was a lunch in the Crawfordsburn Inn with the Secretary of State. Mason seized the opportunity to elaborate on the criticisms he had made at the Culloden Hotel. The new Controller's notes vividly convey the tenor of the meeting:

BBC 'stirs things up'. Northern Ireland BBC bad enough, but London BBC totally irresponsible. 'They don't care about Northern Ireland, about soldiers – being maimed and killed' . . . Journalists who 'want to make their names in Northern Ireland' don't give a damn about the trouble they inflict.

'You've joined the BBC (Jimmy boy) and it's just about to crack.' 'Bloody gentlemen of the BBC think they are above criticism . . . Airey Neave and Margaret Thatcher have come to see me and we're absolutely agreed that there should be no increase in your licence fee unless you put things right . . . De Gaulle knew how to handle the media.'

Hawthorne recalled that 'except for several moments of incandescence' Mason was 'friendly in a blustering sort of way'. 'I am convinced,' he continued, 'that the real purpose of the sermon was to persuade me to play down the Ulster

W.D. Flackes rapidly established himself as the authoritative voice of the BBC to whom viewers and listeners turned for clear and balanced explanation and analysis during the most turbulent years of the Troubles. In this photograph he stands outside the Parliament Buildings at Stormont for a 1977 edition of *Inside Politics*.

BBC NI

coverage and at all cost to avoid interviewing extremists or the smaller "critical" groups.'

If the BBC in London sometimes hesitated to embark on examining stories on Northern Ireland in depth, local broadcasters showed no such inhibition. *Spotlight* began as a weekly discussion on current affairs, with Harry Thompson in the chair in the Balmoral studio, and developed to become one of the most courageous and professional investigative programmes shown anywhere in the United Kingdom. Turbulent Northern Ireland was the place to be for ambitious journalists starting out on their careers and one of those was Jeremy Paxman. 'Paxman could get to the meat of the story,' Taylor remembered; he sealed his reputation in a *Spotlight* programme when he said that the Irish National Liberation Army, not the Provisionals, were responsible for murdering the Conservative spokesman for Northern Ireland, Airey Neave. The purpose of the programme was to point to the emergence of a new terrorist organisation, a movement the RUC had denied was in existence. Taylor went through the script line by line with Paxman

Gillian Chambers and Jeremy Paxman reporting from a classroom for the BBC Northern Ireland *Spotlight Special* on secondary education in January 1977.

BBC NI

and the producer – 'I don't think I changed one word,' he remembered.

Don Anderson recalls that there was always 'a slight interface between the Young Turks and our local people'. Network broadcasters who dropped in, such as Martin Bell, were known as 'visiting firemen' and staff in Broadcasting House sometimes felt that after the visitors had got their stories they were left to pick up the pieces. Wise network journalists sought local advice: indigenous broadcasters knew the local patois and how to ask a searching question in a way that did not cause affront. Much time was taken up in Broadcasting House accommodating those from further afield, reporters from United States networks in particular. The Americans were acutely aware that labels are libels and much management time was taken up in Broadcasting House scrutinising political labels and language. Was it right to refer to 'the mainly Catholic SDLP' when no reference was ever made to 'the mainly Protestant Unionist Party'? When was it appropriate to use the terms 'loyalist' and 'nationalist'? Should Londonderry be called Derry?

Though Mason had criticised the region's output, network programmes rather than local ones were more often the objects of attack by politicians and the press. In November 1979 the *Guardian* revealed that a *Panorama* team had been making a programme in the Republic when it had received a tip-off about Provisional IRA activity in Tyrone and subsequently filmed masked men checking traffic in the village of Carrickmore. Although the programme was never broadcast, questions were asked in parliament and Prime Minister

Margaret Thatcher said that the BBC's filming in Carrickmore, together with an interview of a member of the INLA, would be referred to the Director of Public Prosecutions. The Attorney-General, Sir Michael Havers, later announced that the BBC television journalists would not be prosecuted, but he did write to Sir Michael Swann, pointing out the implications of the 1976 Prevention of Terrorism Act. The BBC's response was to avoid the possibility of breaching the law by refusing to interview terrorists or to respond to invitations to film their activities.

Because Broadcasting House in Ormeau Avenue was so often relaying and analysing momentous events, it nurtured some of the most experienced and accomplished broadcasters in western Europe. Above all, they could respond rapidly to the unexpected. For example, in May 1978, with two minutes to go before a transmission of *Scene Around Six*, a single fuse blew, putting out of action all but one of the studio microphones, all the sound in the studio, the Autocue and the slide scanner. As engineers struggled to rectify the situation for five agonising minutes into the programme, Barry Cowan demonstrated his professionalism in conducting an interview with the Bishop of Derry in Dublin without being able either to see the bishop or to hear a single word he said. Minister of State Lord Melchett, who was in the studio and witnessed the whole affair, later wrote to Cowan, expressing his admiration for the way the proportions of the disaster were concealed and eventually overcome. Skilled broadcasters from Northern Ireland could be lured away – indeed Cowan joined RTÉ for a time – and it was a constant challenge in Belfast to nurture new talent.

Services to listeners were extended further by the launch of BBC RADIO FOYLE on 11 September 1979, an opt-out service from BBC RADIO ULSTER which started broadcasting for twenty hours a week on VHF only. In the first six months of its existence its Derry premises were hit by bombs directed at nearby buildings. There was a second explosion in the early hours of Sunday morning, 8 June, and despite extensively damaging the offices housed on the second floor of the Northern Counties Building, no output was lost. Temporary premises were found in a building belonging to the University of Ulster's Magee College and, within four weeks, a garage in the grounds was converted to a studio with adequate sound insulation and communication links.

The bloodiest day of 1979 was Monday 27 August when members of the south Armagh Provisional IRA commando unit assassinated Earl Mountbatten and three others by blowing up his boat at Mullaghmore, County Sligo, and, later in the day, killed eighteen soldiers at Warrenpoint, County Down. Robin Walsh, who was News Editor at the time, immediately chartered a plane to take his crew to the west of Ireland. ITN was off the air, so the BBC was the sole source of pictures, and Belfast was the base for the processing, editing and transmitting of all film, as well as providing facilities for broadcast journalists flown in from North America and the European mainland.

Spotlight, now the longest-running current affairs television programme in

BBC Northern Ireland, broadcast the first in-depth programme on the 'dirty protest' by republican prisoners in the Maze prison which began in 1978 and followed the 'blanket protest' two years before, when prisoners refused to wear prison clothes, in protest at the removal of special category status. Following brawls with warders over the emptying of chamber pots, prisoners smeared their excrement over their cell walls. A hunger strike begun in the prison in 1980 collapsed but the BBC followed developments in the 'H-Blocks' closely. Some – including the National Governor, Lady (Lucy) Faulkner – worried that too much prominence was being given to the prisoners' actions. When she wondered whether the BBC had 'gone over the top' in interviewing Ciaran Nugent, the recently released prisoner who had initiated the 'blanket protest', Hawthorne responded:

> H-Block has become a sizeable political controversy whether we like it or not. Clearly his release from prison is a matter which must be covered by any competent news medium. If we were not to cover such an event – or for any technical reason fail in our coverage – we should be culpable. Granted that news conferences can be a source of propaganda for the Provisional IRA, nevertheless they provide a means for us to ask searching challenging questions and this we did.

Little did the Controller realise the extent to which the Maze prison would dominate the news in 1981.

Bobby Sands, the PIRA prisoners' officer commanding, began refusing food in the Maze prison on 1 March 1981. As more prisoners joined the hunger strike and Sands, close to death, was elected MP for Fermanagh–South Tyrone on 9 April, passions ran very high across Northern Ireland. Supporters of the hunger-strikers complained that their demonstrations were often ignored or given insufficient attention, while unionists of almost every hue were incensed because coverage was, in their view, excessive. When, at 1.17 a.m. on Tuesday 5 May, Sands died on the sixty-sixth day of his hunger strike, coverage by visiting journalists was on an unprecedented scale. Broadcasting House was the focus of up to forty international broadcasting organisations and the demand for engineering support services and for editorial consultation was immense. Hawthorne recorded in his diary:

> Though the intrinsic editorial problems were straightforward, the pressure on the BBC in Northern Ireland to 'manage the news' was excessive. Events determine the content of news, and whether or not the events of the Spring of 1981 were astutely stage managed by the republican movement, the fact was that a drama of unique journalistic interest had been unfolding every day for a long and sustained period.

In the House of Lords, on 15 May 1981, Lord Ellenborough opened a debate on the motion that 'BBC news items seemed oriented towards the IRA rather than their victims'. Sir Ian Trethowan, the Director-General, felt obliged to respond to the outpouring of criticism, on 4 June 1981, in *The Times*:

> When last did an elected MP starve himself to death? When last did someone starving himself to death receive a procession of eminent international emissaries? The irritation of many viewers at being shown so much about Sands was entirely understandable, but however much they disliked it, the Sands affair became an international event which had to be reported to the British public.

There was little doubt that the hunger strike was a propaganda victory for the PIRA, bought though it was by ten men starving themselves to death. In a region polarised more than ever by these events, the unionist community felt that the BBC had been used to deliver this propaganda triumph. *Scene Around Six* invited six viewers to put their points to Sir Richard Francis, the BBC's Director of News and Current Affairs and the former Northern Ireland Controller, and Roy Lilley, the editor of the *Belfast Telegraph*. It was evident that feelings about the role of the media were running high. There were some seven hundred angry calls to Broadcasting House between 22 April and 22 May 1981, which Hawthorne felt were best summed up by one caller who said: 'Sands, Sands, bloody Sands . . . that's all we get.' Broadcasters, other than the BBC, were subject to similar criticism: John Armstrong, Church of Ireland Archbishop of Armagh, attacked radio and television in general for 'a wicked inversion of priorities' and Harold McCusker, a UUP MP, claimed that the media had been commandeered by the republican movement. Criticism of BBC regional management was accompanied by 'constant personal threats' to the Controller, Hawthorne recalls, 'to the point where my own family had to be taken out of Northern Ireland for about six weeks. I remained in the Province but at the height of the pressure moved to a "safe house" and drove daily to work in a variety of battered "Minis".'

By 1984 the BBC News and Current Affairs Department in Northern Ireland had no fewer than fifty-five professional journalists, operating the only news-room outside London serviced twenty-four hours a day, every day. The demand for local news was greatly increased by the launch of BBC RADIO ULSTER, which became largely the responsibility of Don Anderson, who joined the BBC in 1968 and had been the first to report the events of the Derry march of 5 October of that year. As a network reporter, he had witnessed the fall of South Vietnam and escaped only by trekking miles across country to Thailand. Anderson became the first programme controller of Downtown Radio, the first broadcaster to provide regular local news bulletins through the day. He brought some of the culture of a local independent station to Broadcasting House, attempting to diminish excessive formality.

Towards the end of 1984, Paul Hamann, a BBC documentary and features producer in London, contacted Belfast to say that he had in mind a programme in which he would probe the psyche of extremism within the 'normality' of Northern Ireland for his *Real Lives* series. Hamann had made several highly acclaimed programmes about various aspects of the Troubles and was careful to keep in constant touch with Broadcasting House in Belfast. The pro-gramme, eventually entitled *At the Edge of the Union,* was about two young men, republican Martin McGuinness and loyalist Gregory Campbell, both from Derry City, who had, through the central tragedy of Northern Ireland politics, gone their separate ways and become irreconcilable. Unknown to the BBC, Barrie Penrose of the *Sunday Times* had been preparing a major feature, in which he would charge the BBC with interviewing 'the IRA Chief of Staff' (a reference to McGuinness). In addition, Penrose hand-delivered letters to the Home Secretary, Leon Brittan, the Northern Ireland Secretary of State, Douglas Hurd, and the Prime Minister's press secretary, Bernard Ingham. Margaret Thatcher, commenting on a hijack crisis in the Middle East, had observed with disapproval that the media had been 'providing terrorists with the oxygen of publicity'. A few days later Mark Hosenball of the *Sunday Times* asked the Prime Minister how would she react if she were to learn that 'a British TV company' were to interview the 'IRA Chief of Staff'.

There followed, in Hawthorne's words, 'a row of gargantuan proportions'. Leon Brittan demanded that Hamann's programme should not be shown. The Board of Governors, encouraged by the retiring Northern Ireland Governor, Lady Faulkner, voted to ban the programme against the firm recommendation of the BBC Board of Management. 'For myself,' the Controller confided to his diary, 'I had only one all-consuming question. How could such a decent piece of programming, from so reliable and professional a producer as Hamann, be causing so much mayhem?' BBC journalists, including those in Belfast, went on

Sean Rafferty interviewing
Margaret Thatcher about her
memoirs.

BBC NI

strike and picketed the BBC buildings. Hawthorne observed later: 'However they put it, the Governors had made a decision under pressure from the Home Secretary and against the most experienced and senior editors of the BBC. They had banned the programme because they disliked it.' Hawthorne threatened to resign but was eventually persuaded to change his mind.

Probably the most serious internal crisis the BBC faced in its history, this episode was of most interest to those fascinated by the politics of the BBC in London and concerned about the independence of the organisation. The *Real Lives* programme had not been made by regional staff; no political party in Northern Ireland had lobbied to stop transmission; and when it was subsequently shown it did not provoke an outcry.

The government's broadcasting ban of 1988 – similar to that operating in the Irish Republic – stopped the transmission of interviews not only of 'terrorist' spokesmen but also of representatives of political parties, such as Sinn Féin, associated with them. For years the voices of people like Sinn Féin president Gerry Adams could not be heard over the air, though their words could be spoken by actors. 'The ban was an enormous encumbrance – it made our lives terribly difficult,' remembered Keith Baker, Editor of Television News and later Head of News and Current Affairs.

For those outside Broadcasting House towards the end of 1985 the crucial event of interest was the Anglo-Irish Agreement. Signed at Hillsborough on 15 November, this accord between London and Dublin was to the liking neither of republicans, who objected to the copper-fastening of partition, nor to unionists, who were alarmed by the new say that Dublin was to have in

Northern Ireland's affairs. The agreement was designed to be immune to loyalist protest, unlike Sunningdale, but Protestant anger was intense and sustained because unionists had not been consulted. Reporters and camera crews felt themselves under more threat than at any time over the previous ten years. Four members of staff were injured in a demonstration outside Belfast; a vehicle hired by a London crew was burned out in Derry; and at Castlewellan in County Down a cameraman was fortunate that his camera deflected a blow to the head. 'In addition,' the BBC Year Book reported, 'our staff were warned that their presence would not be welcomed at certain demonstrations and death threats were received from paramilitary organisations . . . the immense difficulty of broadcast operations in Ulster was underlined at Easter with direct death threats to our crews.'

The early 1970s had been the most violent and terrifying years of the Troubles. Thereafter, there was a significant reduction in the annual death toll, but peace was far from returning to Northern Ireland. In addition to the vicious weekly round of sectarian murders, ambushes, shootings and bomb attacks, horrific incidents and atrocities continued periodically to grab the attention of the world. The atrocity which stirred the emotions more than any other in these years was the Remembrance Day bomb in Enniskillen.

Just before 11 a.m. on Sunday 8 November 1987, as the annual wreath-laying at the war memorial in Enniskillen was about to begin, a bomb was detonated and the three-storey gable end of St Michael's Reading Rooms crashed down. Gordon Wilson and his twenty-year-old daughter Marie were buried beneath several feet of rubble. Marie Wilson, a nurse, was one of eleven people killed. That evening her father gave a BBC radio interview to Mike Gaston and was subsequently interviewed for BBC television by Chris Moore. He described in a tone of quiet anguish his last conversation with Marie as they lay beneath the rubble, and he went on to say:

> I have lost my daughter, and we shall miss her. But I bear no ill will. I bear no grudge. Dirty sort of talk is not going to bring her back to life. She was a great wee lassie. She loved her profession. She was a pet. She's dead. She's in Heaven, and we'll meet again. Don't ask me please, for a purpose. I don't have a purpose. I don't have an answer. But I know there has to be a plan . . . And we shall meet again.

No words uttered in more than a quarter of a century of violence have had such a powerful, emotional impact. He had spoken for all the bereaved and injured, and over the next few days millions across the world were to share his grief. Journalist Charlie Warmington telephoned Gordon Wilson from Broadcasting House to tell him that he saw apparently hardened reporters in tears when they heard the broadcast. Keith Baker, who comes from Enniskillen, was telephoned by his sister that Sunday morning to tell him of the explosion and he recalled the profound effect of the interviews on his staff. 'Professionalism carried you through,' he added, 'the urgency of events has its own momentum'.

Keith Baker talked of the oppression of the constant day-to-day drip of violence and the feeling that the Troubles would go on for ever. As midnight approached each New Year's Eve, a most common time for a soldier or a policeman to be killed, he dreaded the telephone call which necessitated once more sending a reporter and a cameraman into the unknown. His staff did this 'willingly, nobly and bravely'. Baker was determined that his colleagues would never come to regard a murder as a normal act and that, if someone was killed, there had to be a very good reason why it should not be the lead story.

One tragedy followed another with such relentless regularity that desperately sad events which would be major stories anywhere else were often down the bulletin items. Every day sensitive decisions had to be made about what images to show. It was important not to shock people unduly and at the same time not to minimise the horror, Baker said. Lasting images could be chosen without showing mutilated bodies: a shoe beside the road where an explosion had taken place may have been mundane but it added poignancy because of the context. On Friday 17 January 1992 a minibus carrying construction workers drove into an elaborately prepared bomb trap at Teebane Cross near Cookstown in County Tyrone. The resulting explosion killed seven men, mortally wounded the driver, and injured six others. To allow the cameras to linger on the carnage would have been too horrific, it was judged; the tragedy and violation was movingly portrayed by filming a workman's lunch box blasted onto the verge. It had to be remembered always that the victims' families were watching the bulletins telling of the killing of their loved ones. A very high proportion of bereaved families asks for video copies of news reports and of the funerals which follow, and these are always provided.

During the first years of the 1990s, it looked as if the spiral of violence

Barry Cowan being given a final make-up check before the start of *Scene Around Six*. The other journalist is David Capper, the make-up artist is Kath Carruth and the fourth person is floor manager, John Ardrey.

BBC NI

was sinking to the dreadful levels plumbed two decades earlier. During this escalation of bombings and tit-for-tat killings, criticism of the BBC by the general public became more muted as viewers and listeners turned to political analysts such as Jim Dougal and Brian Rowan for explanation and for signs of breakthrough. The announcement of the PIRA 'cessation' on the last day of August 1994 and then the loyalist ceasefire in October of that year inaugurated the first sustained period of peace since 1968. This encouraged new thinking in Broadcasting House on the need to give more space in news and current affairs to items addressing other issues, such as threatened hospital closures and amalgamations, the growing problem of drug abuse and road deaths. In fact, major news items on the security and political situation continued to push forward. Coverage of President Bill Clinton's visit in November 1995 was a massive operation; PIRA ended its ceasefire by bombing Canary Wharf in February 1996; contentious Orange Order parades, particularly at Drumcree in July 1996 and July 1998, demanded full reports not only for the region but also for the network; and as the 'peace process' gained momentum, culminating in the Good Friday Agreement of April 1998 and the referendums which followed it, the accumulated expertise of reporters, commentators and engineers was required as never before. Sir Kenneth Bloomfield, the National Governor, described the coverage of the presidential visit in 1995, which involved thirteen hours of transmission, as 'almost certainly the most protracted and extensive programming challenge we have ever faced'.

The BBC and independent broadcasters constantly compared their output and vied for the attention of Northern Ireland's viewers and listeners. This healthy competition was most apparent after the launch of UTV's *Good Evening Ulster* in January 1979, with Gloria Hunniford (who had moved from the BBC) as its first presenter, and the programme steadily increased in popularity. In November 1984 it was reported that *Inside Ulster* had lost one-third of its audience directly to the ITN *News* at 5.45 p.m. and to UTV's *Good Evening Ulster* at 6 p.m. Lighter elements were introduced into *Scene Around Six* but attempts to find the perfect slot for news and current affairs in the early evening – particularly with the growing popularity of Australian soaps – proved elusive.

BBC RADIO ULSTER, at a stroke, gave the corporation the opportunity to provide the listener with much more extensive coverage and analysis of news, so often urgently needed. *Good Morning Ulster* and PM *Ulster* had audiences less liable to fluctuation and presenters such as Seamus McKee, Wendy Austin, Paddy O'Flaherty and Maggie Taggart almost seemed like members of an extended family in many homes. *Good Morning Ulster* provided essential briefing for the day with a lively mix of regional, national and international stories, and the segment between 8.00 a.m. and 8.30 a.m. became the most listened to half hour of radio in Northern Ireland. Its team of presenters conducted in-depth and incisive interviews with major public figures and at the same time discussed local items in a relaxed but informed manner. Hourly news bulletins and *Newsbreak* kept the audience updated throughout the day.

Good Evening Ulster began as a blend of news and light-hearted magazine. In

A remarkable day for BBC RADIO ULSTER on 31 August 1994, as Mark Carruthers brings further news of the reaction to the IRA 'cessation'.

BBC NI

the autumn of 1996 the programme was revamped and renamed *Evening Extra* between 5 p.m. and 7.p.m. this 'drive home' programme served as a radio newspaper, including features on sport, business, the cinema, arts events and agriculture. It had more pace than its predecessor and, when Sean Rafferty took up a new post with BBC RADIO 3 in September 1997, Mark Carruthers rapidly endeared himself to the audience. As the schedules of BBC RADIO ULSTER and BBC RADIO FOYLE continued to expand, so more slots became available for news bulletins and current affairs and discussion programmes. *Seven Days*, following the Sunday lunchtime news, took a look back at the week's events and developments in the company of public figures, politicians, clergy, writers and academics in a relaxed atmosphere under the sure-footed chairmanship of Barry Cowan who, in September 1996, won a Sony Gold Award for his interview with Sir Hugh Annesley, the RUC Chief Constable. *Inside Politics* on Saturdays provided a specialist analysis and the opportunity for longer interviews of leading politicians. Those still hungry for news in the small hours were able to listen to the BBC WORLD SERVICE when BBC RADIO ULSTER closed down for the night.

Fresh thinking on early evening television programming resulted in the launch of *Newsline 6.30*, which was designed to provide an authoritative survey of the day's events at a time which audience research indicated was more

BBC Northern Ireland newsroom staff pictured monitoring the 1997 general election results coming in. In the forefront is Brian Rowan, Northern Ireland's Chief Security Correspondent and behind him is Stephen Grimason, BBC Northern Ireland's Political Correspondent. Other members of the team from left are Gemma Cunningham, Irene Kirkpatrick, Marie Irvine and Chris Kelly.

BBC NI

appropriate for viewers. More space was devoted to news items outside the security and political field than in the programme's predecessors, but it took time for the new format to settle down, partly because of stiff competition from network programmes and its counterpart on UTV, not to speak of a greater choice of channels available to the growing number of households with satellite and cable television. Well-researched, accurate and succinctly delivered reports by specialist correspondents, however, not only showed that the BBC was remaining faithful to its public service remit but also ensured a faithful and steadily growing viewing audience. The programme attracted praise, in particular, for the balance and integrity of its coverage of elections, the tensions surrounding Drumcree and the crisis in the beef industry following the export ban prompted by fears over BSE.

The Political Editor, Jim Dougal, was appointed Head of the European Commission office in Belfast, but other strong talent was on the way up. Dougal's successor, Stephen Grimason, confidently disentangled the Byzantine intricacies of local politics and, after fifteen gruelling hours of live broadcast, was the first to reveal the contents of the Good Friday Agreement; Brian Rowan in his lucid conversational style relayed fresh information on security matters revealed to him by his network of contacts; and there were noteworthy scoops on significant inward investments by firms such as Seagate, National Westminster Bank and IBM. *Newsline 6.30* won a BROADCAST Production

Award in 1999 for its coverage of the Good Friday Agreement.

Tensions and hatreds were not suddenly removed by the Good Friday Agreement and there were still grim news events to report. After a horrifying night of violence in Ballymoney, County Antrim, in 1998, it was on *Good Morning Ulster* that a police officer first revealed that the terrible deaths of the three young Quinn brothers were sectarian murders. A BBC reporter and cameraman were the first broadcast journalists on the scene of the explosion in Omagh on 15 August 1998, which killed twenty-nine men, women and children in the crowded town centre and mutilated many more − the highest death toll from a single incident in all the years of the Troubles. Once again there was evidence that journalists, while maintaining their professional duty to bring the news to the screen and the radio, were themselves deeply affected by a violent tragedy as it unfolded.

Spotlight proved such an enduring formula that there was no thought of replacing it. Instead, attention was directed towards improving its quality and sharpening its bite − knowledge that it had to compete with UTV's *Counterpoint* did much to concentrate minds. The weekly programme aimed to be a regional equivalent of *Panorama*, with structured films, often prepared for months in advance, on current affairs topics receiving only superficial coverage elsewhere. At the same time it had to be Northern Ireland's equivalent of *Newsnight* and respond quickly to explore major events happening earlier in the day. The programmes included the first comprehensive interview with John DeLorean about his sports car manufacturing plans for Belfast, the first in-depth investigation of punishment shootings by paramilitaries, an early detailed inquiry into the shoot-to-kill controversy, which became known as the Stalker Affair, and an analysis of a split in the Ulster Defence Association. Several *Spotlight* films were shown later in the evening on *Newsnight:* one of these, shown in part both on the *Nine O'Clock News* and *Newsnight,* was a documentary on the Gibraltar shootings of 6 March 1988, when the SAS shot dead three unarmed PIRA activists. The Foreign Secretary, Sir Geoffrey Howe, made an unsuccessful appeal to the BBC not to show the film and seldom has a regionally produced programme been given so much network exposure.

Noel Thompson presented *Hearts and Minds,* which became the liveliest and most appealing political series ever to have been made in Northern Ireland. This success was not the result of gimmicks or trivialisation, but the weekly programme certainly held the attention of the viewer by an ingenious mix of items and styles. With enormous charm, Thompson subjected politicians to searching inquisition and strove to keep debates between diametrically opposed politicians from lapsing into disorderly acrimony. The Royal Television Society awarded Noel Thompson the Best Regional Presenter Award in both 1998 and 1999. Seasoned by the peppery wit of Ian Knox's cartoons, trenchant essays were read from Autocue by some of Ulster's most outstanding journalists, notably Fionnuala O Connor and Malachi O'Doherty. Assembly members (MLAs), previously little known beyond their constituencies, became more familiar to viewers through potted film biographies and

Noel Thompson waiting to interview David Trimble, John Hume and Gerry Adams for *Hearts and Minds*. This weekly programme, with its mix of discussion, satirical cartoons, critical analysis, biographies of Assembly Members and searching questioning, delighted viewers with the freshness of its approach to current affairs. Thompson won the Royal Television Society Best Regional Presenter award in 1998 and in 1999.

BBC NI

interviews. *Hearts and Minds* was successful in recruiting younger viewers to a political series, who particularly appreciated the late night repeat and the final piece showing local comedian Tim McGarry as a Belfast taxi driver expressing his homespun wisdom on the latest political developments.

The Good Friday Agreement was followed by agonising delays and disappointments. A devolved administration began to govern in January 2000, and after a hiatus precipitated by the issue of the decommissioning of arms, resumed work in May. In response to the advent of devolution in Scotland, Wales and Northern Ireland, the BBC Board of Governors provided additional investment from London. This made possible the expansion and enhancement of existing programmes, including *Spotlight*, *Hearts and Minds*, *Let's Talk* – a vigorous community debate programme with David Dunseith – and *Straight Up*, a compelling discussion programme with young people, chaired by Jim McDowell. Conor Bradford reported debates every Tuesday on BBC Northern Ireland in *Stormont Live* and BBC RADIO ULSTER provided further coverage on Mondays and Tuesdays at 10 p.m. That the debates proved good listening and viewing was primarily due to the new ministers and MLAs themselves, who, despite some inevitable flashes of acrimony, proved to be as fluent – and often a great deal more entertaining and witty – as the MPs at Westminster.

3

TALKS, FEATURES
AND DOCUMENTARIES

T
HE EARLY OUTPUT OF 2BE was dominated – some listeners thought
interminably – by music, and most talks programmes were to come
from London. The regional station was to produce some talks of its
own, however, and these were intended to respond to and stimulate local interests. The problem was that no member of staff had any intimate knowledge of
the potential audience and so Major Scott formed an Educational Advisory
Committee to suggest topics and speakers. Tyrone Guthrie had responsibility
for drama, features and talks; he recalled:

> I was supposed to be in charge at the age of twenty-three of all the spo-
> ken word that went out and had advisory committees to tell me what
> to do and not to do. Well, of course, they didn't know anything, and they
> assembled Bishops, Archbishops, Moderators, grand people of all kinds
> but they really knew nothing about it and they left it in my own twen-
> ty-three-year-old hands.

The committee's recommendations for young listeners early in the evening
could just as easily have been prepared in London. Professor R.M. Henry and
Dr R.W. Livingstone gave a series of lectures on aspects of Greek and Roman
civilisations.

At the end of 1924 the Ulster Association offered to put forward speakers
and, Guthrie reported to the Station Director, these talks 'would be delivered
by prominent public men and would be absolutely free of political bias'. Topics
suggested included: the building of an ocean liner; Ulster's contribution to the
breakfast table; Ulster's contribution to the empire; the romance of a flax seed;
and aspects of Ulster's past and present. A series along these lines was approved
and, after the first lecture, drew this response from George Russell (AE), the
Portadown writer and social improver, in the *Irish Statesman:*

> It is surely unwise for a Company which seeks the support and aims at
> the sympathy of all sections of the community to broadcast the address
> which Mr Pollock, the Northern Minister of Finance, delivered as the
> first of a series of addresses on Ulster, arranged by the Ulster Association.
> Mr Pollock has not formed his style upon the principle of conciliation,
> and large parts of his address must have seemed controversial (to say the
> least of it) to those who do not share his political opinions.

Opposite:
Charles Freer, editor of the radio
magazine programme *Ulster Mirror*,
interviewing Mina and Ruth Atwell,
two members of a family
woodworking firm, in business for
over seventy years. This programme
was broadcast in 1949.

BBC NI

Less controversial was a series on Ulster's antiquities and other talks drew this favourable review on 1 June 1925 in the *Irish Radio Journal*:

> There is no mistaking the call of 2BE, and we in Dublin, denied the privileges of our own, appreciate the one Irish broadcasting station in existence. Last week we listened to Mr Sam Henry on Ulster Folk Songs, and the item was a fitting answer to those who suggested that 2BE is merely a pocket edition of the British stations.

Broadcasting in the Irish Free State did not begin until 1 January 1926, when the Dublin station 2RN came on the air.

The Belfast station was intended to meet local needs but its staff was not drawn from Northern Ireland. John Sutthery, the Programme Director for Northern Ireland, sparked off a controversy in 1935 when he gave an interview to the *Northern Whig*. 'Ever since I came to Belfast,' he said, 'I have been looking for someone with the London announcer type of voice . . . I don't want any intrusion of personality.' 'There is practically no one in the Northern Ireland studio,' he added, 'who has not . . . an "Ulster idiosyncrasy".' The *Northern Whig* wireless correspondent followed up the interview with this observation:

> Northern Ireland has always been somewhat doubtful about the 'London announcer' type of voice extolled in my interview last week . . . Ulster folk are not quite certain if there is not some personal slight in such a recommendation, and the new, monotonous reading that comes from London is not very popular here.

The letters pages of the *Northern Whig* were soon crowded with the comments of those eager to give their opinion on the issue. A Lisburn correspondent said that 'flat, inexpressive voices' were 'not to the pleasement of the Ulster people, whose own speech is naturally vigorous'. Another asked: 'Why have an Ulster station at all? I suggest that one or two Ulstermen at least should have some say in the selection of the Northern Ireland programmes.' From Coleraine came this letter:

> The sweeping assertion of the lack of talent in Ulster is as unreasonable in its inclusiveness as that of David that 'all men are liars'. It is not the function of the BBC to impinge its cultural eccentricities on the people of Ulster, but it is their duty to find out what the people want and supply that which will cater for every laudable desire in the cultural world.

While this correspondence was in full flow, the station was already meeting most of the criticisms which were being made. The Reverend W.F. Marshall was giving talks on dialect, entitled *Ulster Speaks*, and these proved so popular that they were published and sold very well for years afterwards. Marshall followed up this success in June 1936 with selections from Shakespeare's *A Midsummer Night's Dream* spoken in a Tyrone dialect. It was the Belfast station which first brought the eminent poet W.B. Yeats to the microphone for the first time in 1931.

Although the Belfast station became the Northern Ireland Region in May 1934, eighteen months were to pass before the Lisnagarvey transmitter became operational to enable listeners all over Northern Ireland to hear the broadcasts. In anticipation of a genuine regional service *Provincial Journey* was launched as a series in which each programme would be about a different town in Northern Ireland. Marshall informed the governors that the first, on Portadown, 'although not of great programme value . . . brought forth a considerable volume of appreciative letters and was a clear indication of its value from the point of view of licences'. The series was careful not to go beyond the reach of the Belfast signal until the new transmitter at Blaris was ready, as the Regional Director explained to listeners:

> There are few things more irritating than for the people of the district to know that their countrymen are broadcasting, and to be unable to hear them. So you will see a steady reaching out in this direction, and the same policy will be pursued in talks and in feature programmes . . . A diligent search for talent will be made in those districts in the West which have had so little representation up to the present, and we shall try to present to you the lore and the remote existence of those in the Province who live in such places as the Sperrin mountains and Rathlin Island, which have remained so little affected by the march of industrialism . . .

Some years were to pass before these assurances were to be implemented. It was hoped that *Six Men Went Forth* would be of interest to the whole region, but of the famous Ulstermen featured in the series – Lord Castlereagh, Colonel Edward Ross, John Dunlop, Lord Lawrence, Lord Dufferin and Lord Kelvin – four were builders of empire and none were Catholics.

Ensconced comfortably in the Ulster Club, Marshall was on easy terms with the Unionists and – within the strict limits laid down by Reith – members of the government were able to come to the microphone when they desired. The Minister of Commerce, James Milne Barbour, gave a talk with the title *The Ulster Yet to Be* in March 1932 and in 1935 Lord Craigavon made this announcement on air:

> It is with deep emotion I have to record the death of Lord Carson at the advanced age of eighty-one. His long and distinguished career at the Bar, in politics and on the Bench is widely known, but to few has the privilege fallen of such intimacy as I have enjoyed with him the past thirty years. One of the most brilliant men of the century and a great patriot, the outstanding characteristics of his remarkable personality were indomitable courage, coupled with a charming simplicity, transparent honesty and a passionate love of country in its widest interpretation. His birthplace was Ireland, his sphere of activities largely in England, his greatest triumph saving Ulster for the Empire.
>
> I know from his oft-expressed desire that he wished to be laid to rest in the land for which he fought so long, so valiantly and so successfully. The Government of Northern Ireland have offered a State funeral and the Dean and Chapter of St Anne's Cathedral, Belfast, have

intimated their willingness that that sacred building should shelter his remains which will be conveyed from Liverpool in one of His Majesty's ships, a tribute to an ex-First Lord of the Admiralty.

Sutthery saw opportunities for BBC Northern Ireland Region and the South's Radio Athlone to share their output and travelled to Dublin in December 1935 to speak to Dr T.J. Kiernan, Director of Broadcasting in the Irish Free State. Both men were enthused by the possibilities presented and Sutthery had the support of London. 'We have had very friendly relations with Dr Kiernan since his appointment,' he was told, and the Programme Director was encouraged to develop 'as much co-operation as Kiernan is ready to accept.' However, this was a period of strained relations between Eamon de Valera's government and Westminster and not long after the worst sectarian strife Belfast had experienced since 1922. News of these negotiations was leaked to the press and in the wake of indignant reaction in Northern Ireland, Sutthery stifled his initial enthusiasm, as he informed the Director of the Empire Service in February 1936:

> There is the difficulty that there is a section of the public on both sides of the Border, which will make all the trouble it can at the first sign of programme interchange and friendly relations generally between the two broadcasting systems. It is my personal belief – not official – that this is more likely to be very much stronger in Northern Ireland than in the Free State.

A week later Sutthery added further explanation:

> The real trouble arose when these articles were read by the more rabid type of Ulstermen, who have no desire whatever for better relations. Reading between the lines, you will see that the more contact there is between Dublin and Belfast, can be read by the nationalist as a step nearer the co-ordination of the whole of Ireland on a Free State basis, and that anything which might tend in this direction is as the proverbial rag to the bull, from the Ulster point of view.

The possibility of exchange was not pursued again for many years.

Meanwhile, Charles Siepmann was preparing his searching report on the BBC in Belfast. Talks was the only part of the output exempt from his criticism, much of it excoriating:

> TALKS Here there are further possibilities despite the ban on controversy necessitated over a wide field by the political–religious issue. Sutthery is very sensible of the possibilities of talks development. The talks to farmers are already popular and a genuine public service. The recent series on dialect provoked extraordinary interest and there is in my view scope for a great deal of constructive social work by the discovery on a strict factual basis of the conditions of Ulster in the sphere of health, education, etc, to the people themselves.

His observations on features were distinctly unflattering:

FEATURE PROGRAMMES Here there is great scope both for programmes from the studio and extensive OB work. This indeed is the most promising field for programme development and the resources of the region are not at the moment being exploited to the full, partly through what seems to me a maladjustment of the staff, partly pending the arrival of the recording vans. Even here, however, it is likely that we shall have to draw on our own resources for the drafting of scripts. There is a serious shortage of writers and as in other departments a depressing shortage of people who are suitable as narrators or for intelligent reading.

He added that 'Provincial Journey, a series of OB feature programmes, has hitherto been of doubtful standard but it has provoked local enthusiasm and is good propaganda'.

Even as Siepmann was giving his report, the Northern Ireland Region was preparing its most ambitious programme so far, *Lillibulero*. Siepmann had not recommended an increase in staff but the Dublin playwright and lawyer, Denis Johnston, had been engaged as a researcher and scriptwriter to help augment output. Johnston combined his dramatic and feature-writing skills to produce a 'diorama', the region's first dramatised documentary. *Lillibulero* was mould-breaking because it tackled a contentious episode from Ulster's troubled past, the 105-day siege of Derry in 1688–9, an event which continued to arouse party passion. The Apprentice Boys' demand to see the script was refused and when they got a Unionist MP to make the same request, he was also turned down. As Marshall reported to the governors:

It appears the trouble with Derry is not the usual one of two opposing

The Fintona Horse Train was one of the features recorded in the programme *Belfast – Enniskillen*, broadcast in November 1937.

BBC NI

factions, namely the Protestant and the Roman Catholic, as there is no disputing the fact that the Protestants were besieged and held out till they were relieved, but, on the contrary, some sort of quarrel between the beleaguered Episcopalians and the Presbyterians, each of whom claim to have taken the most important part in the siege itself . . . It was pointed out that the author had made a very exhaustive and careful research into the history of the siege, had examined contemporary documents, etc . . . and Mr Johnston says the real trouble is that the Protestant elements in Derry are afraid that their siege may be 'debunked' and lose forever its glamorous political significance.

Long afterwards, Johnston recorded his memories of making the programme:

It was highly inflammatory so far as the subject matter was concerned. And it really faced me with a problem – a kind of problem which I always enjoyed very much – of writing a historical programme which is based upon facts which is not going to send people off in a fury. It put the Belfast station to the pit of its collar.

Well, it was a very elaborate programme. I had very, very fine music written for it by 'Bandy' O'Donnell. He wrote an orchestrated version of the celebrated tune, Lillibulero, which is the most delightful version of it that I know. It had a lot of other tunes in it but it had the lambegs, the great fat drums of Ulster, being played in the studio. And when one came down Linenhall Street and heard the 'bump! bump! bump!' of the lambeg drums inside this building, you said 'What on earth is going on in the BBC?' because, again, they'd never been heard of before.

Actors were brought over from England to take part, including Jon Pertwee, who later won renown as Doctor Who, and a 'bass' narrator and a 'baritone' narrator. Two well-loved local actors, J.G. Devlin and Graeme Roberts, later recalled the final rehearsal:

DEVLIN: I think we made radio history because we were the first people in a radio play where the critics were brought in to get a special performance before we did it live the following night.

ROBERTS: And probably the first cast to have police protection on the way out.

DEVLIN: Absolutely!

The precaution of inviting journalists to the rehearsal was rewarded by a sheaf of favourable reviews. 'The fears of the BBC,' the *Belfast News Letter* remarked, 'that the Siege of Derry might be a dangerous and controversial subject for a radio programme were clearly without foundation.' In its glowing preview, the *Irish News* observed:

Whether our forefathers were on the side of those that defended Derry or those who besieged it, and whether we think that the version does or does not do justice to the besiegers, we must in the first place applaud the directors of the Northern Ireland Station for giving us in good radio-dramatic form an interpretation of one of the outstanding events in Irish history.

The technique of the piece is excellent. Inside an hour we are given a representation of a siege which lasted for several months, and in more vivid form than could have been done in the most detailed history . . .

No Irishman North or South of the Border who tunes in to it will regret having done so, and many of us look forward to the day when the BBC will give Mr Johnston a commission to write another diorama from Irish history.

Johnston stayed on, not only to write radio plays, but also to produce many features in 1937–8, including: *Stentor*, a celebration of the bicentenary of the *Belfast News Letter*; *The Parnell Commission*, which drew on the transcripts of the trial of the Irish Parliamentary Party leader, in which it was proved that letters associating him with assassins calling themselves the Invincibles were forgeries; *Weep for Polyphemus*, on the troubled domestic life of the author of *Gulliver's Travels*, Jonathan Swift; and *Death in Newtownstewart*, a documentary on the murder of a bank clerk in County Tyrone in 1873, which transferred so well to the stage that it remained popular with amateur dramatic societies for years afterwards. During the summer of 1937 the national programme came to Northern Ireland to make recordings of the Lammas Fair for its series *Summer Over the British Isles*. Johnston was able to borrow the van for a couple of features, for example, to collect authentic sounds from the shipyard for *The Birth of a Giant*. When the microphone was taken out, around and about, the programmes were still subjected to the BBC studio-based discipline of scripts, which tended to remove all spontaneity and were characterised by an artificiality of speech, as can be observed in this extract recorded in London: 'Ulster *Express*: a description in sound of a daily routine which links London with the north of Ireland, arranged by H.L. Fletcher from records taken with the BBC mobile recording unit on the London, Midland and Scottish Railway.'

> *[Engine whistle]*
>
> PASSENGER: I'm on the *Ulster Express* and I saw the microphone here and I'd thought I'd like to say a word or two before departing for Belfast via Heysham. The *Ulster Express* is now gathering their passengers together and they are taking their seats, so that they may have comfort and peace going home. I very often come this way as I find I have great convenience in travelling via the *Ulster Express* and via Heysham.

The hapless programme-maker may have had no choice but to accept this deathless prose, possibly because there was no space left on his recording disc. This next extract from Cushendall in County Antrim may seem a little contrived but at least there is some attempt at spontaneity:

> 'But, I say, there's Robert sittin' over there in the corner and he's not saying a single word.' 'Oh no, not a wan.' 'But before these "Talkies" and

tennis took these young people away from the good old-fashioned amusements of the countryside, well now, in those days I heard Robert supply the music often enough, and he wanted no rosin for his bow either.' 'Aye.' 'Heth, Robert was considered the best lilter from here to Derry.' 'So he was.'

'I say, Robert, I say, Robert, supposin' we ax the young people to take their partners for a four hand reel, would ye give them a wee lilt just to let the young people hear what music is?' 'Aye.' 'Aye.' 'Are yez listenin' over there?' 'Now Robert here is goin' to lilt yez a four hand reel.' 'Go on.' 'Go on, Robert, ye boy ye – fill the house with it.' 'Go on.' [*Lilting follows*]

This overwritten script is characteristic of the 1930s:

We have only one more journey for you. We go to where the great line of cranes and gantries stretch out above the city like gigantic black arms. Here the staccato rattle of the riveter's hammer is heard day and night while ship after ship slides down from the yard into the waters of the River Lagan and so out into the Seven Seas.

All round the urgent voice of the shipyard beeped upon your ears, striking dissonant chords, too fantastic for the visitor to unravel. To the shipyard worker, each voice is articulate, each note has its meaning. Listen . . .

Even though the mobile unit had been taken to Queen's Island, its microphone only recorded the machines and hammers and not the men themselves – who, no doubt, dearly wished, in the depths of the Depression, that ship after ship *was* sliding down the ways. The recording van was taken back across the Irish Sea and Northern Ireland did not get another one until American troops arrived in 1942.

When, on the outbreak of war, regional broadcasting closed down for over four months there was no output from Belfast whatever. The few staff remaining were keen to have Northern Ireland featured on the Home and Forces programmes and got their opportunity early in 1940. Both Lord Craigavon and his successor, John Andrews, gave talks. Most of the output was variety, revue and light entertainment, but there were talks such as: *In and Out of Uniform* by Freda Macauley, which dealt with work done at home in Northern Ireland; Gerald McCreesh on rural industries revived by the war; a talk by A.J. Tulip on American presidents; a discussion entitled *Planning, both Town and Country in Northern Ireland*; and a 'rousing feature programme', *The Fighting Men of Ulster*, which paid tribute to the valiant deeds of four Irish regiments.

George Marshall used all his influence to stop items about Éire. The Regional Director's obstructiveness may have discouraged programme-makers in London but the Ministry of Information was eager to supply programmes for the tens of thousands of southern Irish who had joined the forces or had crossed the Irish Sea to work in the factories and mills. Some programmes suggested by Ursula Eason, the acting Programme Director, were ruled out by London. She proposed a special talk by Andrews to mark the twentieth

anniversary of the founding of Northern Ireland but this was turned down – 'I'm inclined to leave the Ulster–Éire stew alone for the minute' and 'I do not think in these we want to stress the tragic division in Ireland itself' were remembered as examples of comments made at head office. Denis Johnston, now BBC war correspondent in Dublin and Belfast, was reprimanded by Marshall for referring to Dublin as the 'Irish capital' in an Overseas Service programme inadvertently played on the Home Service. The exasperated Johnston responded that what he had really said was, 'It is the Eirish capital.' Johnston survived this experience to be asked by Marshall to write a special feature, *Atlantic Bridgehead*, on the role of Northern Ireland's ports during the war.

'Of the entire staff engaged in Ulster broadcasting, how many are Ulster born?' This question was asked, and by no means for the first time, by a contributor to the letters page of the *Northern Whig* in 1943. Steps were taken to rectify the situation when regional broadcasting was restored at the end of July 1945. Henry McMullan returned from war service to become Programme Director; Sam Hanna Bell became the features producer; and John Boyd was appointed talks producer. Bell and Boyd were the first members of the BBC programme staff not to be drawn from the upper middle classes. Both were

The talks producer, John Boyd (left), with the Belfast-born playwright, novelist and biographer of Lord Craigavon, St John Ervine. Ervine spoke on George Bernard Shaw for the 1948–49 series, *Irish Writers*.

BBC NI

'scholarship' boys from comparatively humble origins – Boyd was the son of a steam locomotive driver and Bell had spent part of his childhood in straitened circumstances on a small farm in County Down. Both men were socialists and chafed against the stuffy, establishment atmosphere that prevailed in Broadcasting House. Both were to bring a freshness and vitality to broadcasting in the region which it had not experienced before. Highly innovative craftsmen and accomplished writers, they set new standards in Broadcasting House.

Boyd began to learn his trade in the company of Horace Fleet, the gardening expert. In *The Middle of My Journey* he describes the preparation of a talk for broadcasting. After typing, editing, timing, redrafting and retyping the script, three hours before transmission

> Horace and I would go down the corridor to the small studio with its double doors and its soundproof walls, and there in front of a microphone placed on a table like an icon to be worshipped I was obliged to listen once, twice, thrice and more until Horace almost knew his fifteen-minute talk by heart and so did I. It had been timed by my stopwatch to last exactly fourteen minutes and ten seconds; the remaining time would be used by the announcer for his opening and closing announcements.

The announcer arrived, voices were balanced, and Boyd joined the technician in a cubicle adjoining:

> I would sit by his side, both of us following the broadcast with our scripts, my responsibility being to keep my eye on my stopwatch. If Horace slowed down – and he had been timed minute by minute on the page – we would depress a small key which flashed a red bulb on the table, and his speed of delivery would promptly accelerate. The cardinal crime, I learned, was to allow a talk to overrun its time and be chopped off before it had reached its final sentence.

The restriction which most irked Boyd was that he was expected to find short-story writers exclusively from Northern Ireland, even though the music department was given wider scope:

> The BBC governors in London seemed to imagine that Irish literature could be sliced up like ham to suit the political needs and appetites of the time. This stupidity, which was not confined to London, had the backing of Belfast. It was one of the cultural effects of partition.
> I found it impossible to stomach. Of course it was right to broadcast the stories of Michael McLaverty, Joseph Tomelty, Brian Friel, Sam Hanna Bell, John O'Connor, Lynn Doyle and a few more, but what justification, other than political, could be advanced for ignoring the rich tradition of short-story writing throughout the whole island of Ireland? It was a form of literary apartheid and like all apartheid it was ugly and ultimately unworkable. There were simply not enough good writers in the North to satisfy the needs of the BBC; just as there were simply not enough dramatists and poets.

Sam Hanna Bell was determined to bring ordinary people to the microphone for the first time. He and Boyd welcomed the arrival of Andrew Stewart
as the new Controller in 1948, who gave them encouragement and more up-
to-date equipment. Bell's first programme was to feature the Antrim port of
Larne in the *Provincial Journey* series and was appalled at the way the contributors were brought to the artificial and often intimidating environment of a
studio in Ormeau Avenue. From then on, he took to the countryside to gather material for series such as *Village Picture* and *It's a Brave Step*. Conversations,
memories, music and song, picked up by the microphone, had to travel down
a lead connected to a cumbersome recording unit to be transferred onto large
shellac discs. As Sean McMahon observes in his biography of Bell: 'The
machine used by Bell took up most of the back of the sturdy Humber car
which came to know every loanen, boreen and casan in Northern Ireland.' On

Sam Hanna Bell (centre)
meeting local people prior to
recording a programme in the
series *It's a Brave Step*. Bell, who
also became one of the greatest
novelists Northern Ireland ever
produced, meticulously kept his
programmes and most of these are
now in the BBC Sound Archive in
the Ulster Folk and Transport
Museum.

BBC NI

hill slopes it was sometimes necessary to take the equipment up tracks with a donkey and cart. In 'The Microphone in the Countryside', written for the BBC 1949 jubilee publication, Bell described how he got his recordings:

> Some months ago, I went with a recording unit to the remote and lovely country west of the village of Killeter in County Tyrone. Houses were scattered on the braeside and men and women were out working at the corn harvest, but, apart from passing the time of day with us, they weren't anxious to stop their work and talk. I climbed up to a tall grey house at the side of the glen and knocked at the door. It was opened by a man in his shirt-sleeves with a flat-iron in his hand. I'm not quite sure how I explained my predicament to Denis (that was his name) apart from the tentative suggestion that he should introduce me to the progressive farmers, the blacksmiths, the coopers, the surfacemen, the ballad singers, the old men who told tales. Anyway, Denis laid down his iron (he was a tailor), pulled on his jacket, and for the next three days gave the BBC every spare minute of his time. He introduced us to men and women who, when the work was done, told us of bygone days in the district, sang songs, and explained the difficulties peculiar to

Bill Graham, BBC recording engineer, setting up his apparatus in a leafy glade at the entrance to the Marble Arch caves in County Fermanagh for an edition of *Ulster Mirror* in July 1946.

BBC NI

farming in the Derg valley. During those three days as we tramped the loanens and fields from house to house, I listened to Denis, followed his pointing finger, and built up a picture of the district that I would never have got otherwise.

The programmes were far from being mere recordings linked together. Finely crafted scripts painted word pictures to enable the listener to visualise the place, with the effect heightened by music and recorded sound. Bell wrote many of the scripts himself, including *This is Northern Ireland* (1949), *Rathlin Island* (1950), *In Praise of Ulster* (1951), *The Islandmen* (1953), *Kist o' Whistles* (1960) and *The Orangemen* (1967). *Kist o' Whistles*, researched by Reverend Professor Jack Barkley, was about the fierce dispute in the Presbyterian Church over the introduction of the organ or harmonium into churches in the late nineteenth century; this apparently dull subject was brought to humorous life by dramatised scenes, precise sound effects and a masterly script. The fact that *The Orangemen*, researched by Aiken McClelland, caused no hostile reaction and was well received across the spectrum demonstrates how Bell had become universally admired as a programme-maker.

A government White Paper of July 1946 recommended the setting up of a representative advisory council in each region. Out of an Advisory Council of twenty members, the appointment of three Catholics was hardly representative of the Northern Ireland Region. However, this body proved a good deal more liberal and progressive than might have been expected. In 1948 one of the first programmes of a series called *Free for All* was *The Future of Derry*. Since the city was the most depressed urban centre in the United Kingdom, with a scandalous housing problem, the discussion naturally included sharp criticisms of government policy. Marshall reported to the governors:

> Much of the discussion naturally ranged over the constitutional question, and this was deleted in the recording. What was left, however, was sufficiently critical in tone to displease both the Unionist minority in Londonderry and the Government of Northern Ireland.

The council, however, gave its full support to the programme (not being aware of the excisions) and concluded that 'if uncomplimentary remarks about any locality were made during a recording of these public and unscripted debates, then it was no function of the BBC to suppress them'.

The Advisory Council – and the veteran ex-internee and Nationalist MP for Fermanagh Cahir Healy, in particular – was responsible for initiating a series called *Fairy Faith*. Andrew Stewart summoned Bell to his office, as he recalled to Rex Cathcart, author of *The Most Contrary Region: The BBC in Northern Ireland, 1924–84*:

> One day he called me into his office and said, 'I've got hold of some money and I want you to go out and look for the heroic tales and myths of Ulster.' We were lucky in having the folklorist Michael J. Murphy about and so we went off to ask him about the suggestion. He said that the heroic myths were pretty dormant and what survived was so

corrupted that they were not worth collecting. 'But,' he said, 'there are the fairies.'

Bell and Murphy toured the remote parts of Ulster and found that the elderly people, from whom the lore was collected, were delighted that the stories would not die with them. 'We met men and women who could hardly tell their stories for laughter,' Bell wrote in the *Radio Times* in March 1952, 'but we politely stared the laughter out of face and got the story.' Seamus Delargy, who had set up the Irish Folklore Commission in Dublin in 1935, described the resulting archive as 'the most important work in Irish Folklore in modern times'. Sam Hanna Bell and those who worked with him had preserved on their shellac discs and tape recordings a priceless record of a rural society which was fast disappearing.

A great deal of what Boyd produced was sent out into the ether and was not preserved. 'Is there anything you'd like brought up?' J.J. Campbell and David

E. Estyn Evans, Professor of Geography at Queen's University and a distinguished archaeologist, historian and writer, giving one of his regular talks on the BBC Northern Ireland Home Service.

BBC NI

Kennedy asked Boyd, before going to a meeting of the Advisory Council. Boyd suggested stepping into the treacherous waters of Ulster's past and the proposition was subsequently backed by the council. Very little Irish or local history was taught then in Northern Ireland's schools — even in Catholic schools, as a survey by the educationalist Jack Magee subsequently proved. A revolution had been taking place in the writing of Irish History (later described by critics as 'revisionism'), in which there was an emphasis on avoidance of propaganda, on examining the evidence impartially and on strict scholarly standards. The result of the work of this generation of Irish historians was often somewhat rarefied and beyond the reach of the general reader. Boyd persuaded the most distinguished historians, led by T.W. Moody and J.C. Beckett (both 'scholarship' boys from Belfast), to present the results of their researches in a series of accessible talks. These were widely acclaimed and subsequently published as *Ulster since 1800: A Political and Economic Survey* (1954). A second series followed and was published as *Ulster since 1800: A Social Survey* (1957). A decade later, a yawning gap in local history was filled by talks on the history of Belfast, with sparkling contributions by Estyn Evans, J.L. McCracken and Charles Brett, in particular, published in book form as *Belfast: The Origin and Growth of an Industrial City* (1967).

Boyd finally persuaded his superiors to allow him to record writers from south of the border, starting with Frank O'Connor, with whom he struck up a special rapport. Boyd and O'Connor agreed that rehearsals 'killed' a story:

> The most important thing was that I should have complete faith in him to tell his story in the allotted time, but like a musical conductor I would guide and control him to that end by gestures. If I wanted him to increase the pace I would make a circular motion with my right arm,

rotating it very slowly if the pace was to be quickened slightly, and increasing the speed if I judged the pace was dragging seriously. If, however, the story was being delivered too fast I would slowly open my arms in a gesture of benediction.

'No, dear boy, not again,' Guthrie responded to Boyd, when asked to give a broadcast on drama. 'Jam, jam, jam! Let me broadcast about the making of jam.' Guthrie had turned the disused railway station at Newbliss, County Monaghan, into a jam factory to provide work for the unemployed. 'I don't intend to advertise, dear boy, merely to eulogise.' 'It was a superb talk,' Boyd remembered, 'delivered with all his brio.' The seasoned seafarer, Captain R.H. Davis, gave a popular series of talks about his days on sailing clippers setting out from Ulster to cross the oceans (the texts now form a valuable archive in the Public Record Office of Northern Ireland): he always insisted on a stiff tot of rum before each talk – and another after. Boyd booked a studio and came to London to record a talk by Louis MacNeice on his childhood in Belfast and Carrickfergus, only to find that MacNeice had not written a script. Boyd insisted on going ahead. Despite his reluctance, MacNeice gave a fluent extempore talk. Boyd picked up the sparse notes at the end: '1st House: 2nd House; Dramatis Personae; Church and Castle: Walks: Houses: Books: Titanic and War.' MacNeice died shortly afterwards and this broadcast, *Early Memories*, is the only extant recording of the poet talking about his life.

Slowly, the BBC in Northern Ireland opened itself up to the whole community in the region. Boyd wrote in his autobiography:

> The great demerit of the place during most of my time there was the exclusion of Catholics from the senior staff: not a single producer belonged to that faith. Once, in a casual conversation with Richard Marriott, the Controller from 1953 to 1956, I mentioned this as a fact. He was incredulous. 'I don't believe you,' he said. 'It can't be true.' I repeated that it *was* true. He left me, a worried look on his face. Soon afterwards a Catholic was appointed to the news department, and from that time onwards I think religious discrimination began to disappear.

Denis Johnston, Sam Hanna Bell and John Boyd played a unique role in helping to open up the BBC, but they chafed against the restrictions imposed by their superiors. In an appreciation written after Bell's death in 1990, former schools producer Douglas Carson wrote:

> He fought his corner with determination . . . The struggle, however, distracted and angered him. He had joined the tabernacle which preached public service, and was treated like a heretic because he believed . . .
>
> For most of his twenty-five years in the Region, the only active athletes were himself and John Boyd. Despite that, they kicked with skill and scored goals. And Sam became a local institution. In the creative life of Ulster he carried the banderol. As well, his voice was known in every home. He introduced his neighbours to themselves – an antiphon of voices round the hearth.

Sam Hanna Bell (right) with Alan Gailey, Keeper of the Ulster Folk and Transport Museum, during the making of a programme for *Country Window* in November 1968.

BBC NI

The Divis Mountain transmitter began to put out a television signal in 1955, and since equipment was vastly more expensive than that required for radio, most of the programmes came from the network. The initial demands on Northern Ireland were modest enough: six silent films – with commentary and music added later – each year. Some of these, including *Family Farm* and *Rathlin Island*, were shown on network. At the end of October 1959 Ulster Television began broadcasting from Havelock House and soon its weekday magazine *Roundabout* was getting good audiences. As more and more people in Northern Ireland bought television sets, competition between Broadcasting House and Havelock House intensified. Most television programmes received from both the BBC and independent television originated in London and viewers became accustomed to seeing a more adventurous approach to the tackling of difficult topics. Robert Coulter, who was responsible for the Northern Ireland Region's television output, later reflected:

> in the first instance subjects which had been relatively taboo became more easy to tackle and in the treatment of them one was freer . . . Partly this came about because of the very fact that the whole population in Ulster was receiving network television in a new flood and it became used to seeing the harder line of questioning, the deeper inquiry, across the water.

Because Alan Whicker's *Tonight* programme on Northern Ireland in 1959 caused such a storm of protest, network television tended to avoid returning to the region to examine its problems for almost another decade. Meanwhile, in Ormeau Avenue there was – in contrast – a new willingness to look at topics which had previously been studiously avoided. Nevertheless, broadcasters were anxious to encourage the middle ground and not to put on air or on the screen those people likely to express extreme views. Indeed, the Advisory Council took the view that this was the right approach and a comfortable assumption was made that old wounds were healing. The arrival of the experienced newsman Waldo Maguire as Controller coincided with alarming portents of future violence in 1966 as nationalists celebrated the fiftieth anniversary of the Easter Rising and the UVF carried out its first killings. Maguire sought a more fearless and less relaxed approach in news coverage and in features screened on the evening magazine programme, *Six-Five*. However, during the relative calm which preceded the storm of autumn 1968, features and documentaries only occasionally looked hard at issues which would shortly tear Northern Ireland apart. The main television features in 1966 were profiles of the Prime Minister Captain Terence O'Neill, and Cardinal Conway, the Archbishop of Armagh, and *For Valour*, a documentary on Ulster and the Battle of the Somme. Radio documentaries included *Lough Neagh Bounty*, on the eel-fishing industry; *A Hundred Hits*, a feature on the Ulster songwriter Jimmy Kennedy; *The Light Fingered Brigade*, on shop lifting; *Lyric Theatre* on Mary O'Malley's venture in Derryvolgie Avenue; *Somme Anniversary*; and *Bombs over Belfast,* a recollection of the German air raids on Belfast in 1941.

Even in 1969, as Northern Ireland plunged into violence, the principal features and documentaries hardly grappled with the state's acute difficulties. On television the two main documentaries were *The Fate of the Armada*, on the wreck of the *Gerona* off the north coast, and *Highway of Progress*, a fifty-minute programme on the career of the inventor of the tractor, Harry Ferguson. Amongst the radio features were *Youth in Search of a Fix*, on the province's comparatively insignificant drug problem; *Debt is a Four-Letter Word*, on hire purchase; *Somebody Else's Baby*, on adoption; and *The Man who Made the Headlines*, on the educational philanthropist, Vere Foster. The burning issues of the day *were* being dealt with in news reports, on *Scene Around Six*, and on the weekly television discussion programme *Speak Your Mind*. The documentaries on the Troubles, however, were being made by network, partly because London had superior resources.

The installation of new film processing and telecine facilities, together with an increase in staff, enhanced the ability of Broadcasting House to make features and documentaries, though Northern Ireland's problems were still left largely for the attention of news and current affairs. *Dusty Bluebells*, a colour film on the traditional pattern of children's street games in Belfast won an international Golden Harp Award in 1972 in competition with films on folk-lore from twenty-four countries. Another documentary attracting wide praise in the same year was *You Can't Make Money Ashore*, most of it filmed at sea with the men of the County Down fishing fleet. Television documentaries in 1974 and 1975 included *The Mitred Earl*, on the extravagant, art-collecting, radical Frederick Hervey, eighteenth-century Bishop of Derry and Earl of Bristol; *Virgo, Geraldine and the Lunar Wall*, on rock climbing in the Mourne Mountains; *A Trotting Man*, on the enthusiasm for horse-trotting in the Shankill

Road and other parts of Belfast; *Rock of Fergus*, a history of Carrickfergus Castle in words and music; BBC *Northern Ireland*, an impression of a day in the life of the BBC in the region. *Oh To Be in Ulster*, a programme reflecting children's views of the Troubles, screened in 1975, was a rare example of a documentary on the upheavals in Northern Ireland not produced by current affairs staff. *Surgery of Violence* in 1977 was an uncompromisingly realistic and moving documentary on the Royal Victoria Hospital, an institution in the front line of Northern Ireland's suffering.

The launch of BBC RADIO ULSTER in 1975 created space for documentaries which did tackle issues arising out of the Troubles in programmes such as: *The British Army in Ulster* and *Sunningdale and the South* in 1974; *In the Name of God*, about violence-torn Belfast; *Portrait of an Ulster Town: Forum for the Foyle*, on Londonderry's problems; and *I Don't Want the Moon and the Stars*, in which teenagers from a deprived area of west Belfast take part in a play about themselves, written by a community worker.

The task of making documentaries and features on current issues fell increasingly to the *Spotlight* team and included two programmes on the role of the army in Northern Ireland, a special programme on the RUC, an interview with the Secretary of State, Douglas Hurd, by Roisin McAuley; and a feature on attitudes in Northern Ireland, based on an opinion poll. *Spotlight* often turned aside from the Troubles to investigate subjects such as infant mortality, mentally handicapped children, teenage joy riding, the plight of farmers, epilepsy, abortion, the reorganisation of Northern Ireland's secondary schools,

Bridie Gallagher, the popular ballad singer, talks to Denis Franks for an edition of *Other People* in the early 1960s. Adjusting the tape recorder in the background is the producer Maurice Leitch, who later became a writer of powerful broadcast dramas and novels.

BBC NI

pollution, and marriage. One of the most remarkable investigative documentaries produced by the *Spotlight* team was *Fowl Play*, a look into the dark and secretive world of cock fighting in mid-Ulster, which included riveting, and at times hilarious, exchanges between journalists and the illegal participants and punters. Screened in 1994, it won the Royal Television Society Award as the Best Regional Current Affairs Documentary. *Spotlight*'s *The Black Catch*, on the fishing industry, won the European Journalism Award the following year.

The output of television documentaries on many aspects of life in Ulster steadily increased and some were taken by network, including *Hobby Horse Man*, a charming story of an old Belfast character and his horse-drawn merry-go-round, known as 'Mickey Marley's Roundabout', constantly travelling the poorer and more troubled parts of the city and giving delight to children everywhere, shown in the *Look Stranger* series on BBC TWO. *Goliath Go to Sea!* was a film about the Harland and Wolff shipyard; *Catch as Catch Can*, on the north coast fishing industry, was highly praised; *The Bold Bad Baronet*, about a celebrated legal case, was shown on BBCTWO, as was *The Man America Forgot*, the story of Charles Thompson, an Ulsterman who designed the Great Seal of America and was secretary to the Revolutionary Council; *God's Frozen People* was a film about Iceland and its links with Ireland; and *Transport of Delight* celebrated a hundred years of railways in Ulster.

Home Truths, launched in 1994 as a major new series, put on screen some of the finest in-depth documentaries to have been made by the region. The two programmes, *More Sinned Against than Sinning*, on the mystery surrounding the murder of Patricia Curran in 1952 were so absorbing that the case once again became a common topic of conversation and renewed speculation in the press as to whether justice then had been done. The body of the nineteen-year-old daughter of Lance Curran, a High Court judge, was found with thirty-seven knife wounds in a lane near the family home in Whiteabbey, County Antrim, by her brother Desmond. The murder was followed by the largest-ever manhunt carried out by the RUC, carrying out 4,000 interviews and taking 900 statements. At the trial Iain Hay Gordon, a twenty-year-old aircraftman serving at Edenmore RAF base, confessed to the murder but avoided the noose by pleading insanity. Gordon spent eight years in Holywell Mental Hospital and was released in 1960, insisting he was innocent of the killing. Desmond Curran, converted to Catholicism, became a priest and went to South Africa to work in the townships. The programmes looked at how the murder affected the lives of the two men. The producer, Bruce Batten, said:

> We spent 18 months investigating all aspects of the case and travelled to Scotland and South Africa to carry out interviews. Many people speak publicly for the first time, some voicing concern about Gordon's conviction, others recalling the tragic event as if it happened last week.

Home Truths was a major series which looked at a wide range of familiar aspects of life in Northern Ireland and gained large audiences, particularly for a retrospective evaluation of the comedy genius, James Young – a programme which, though appreciative and sympathetic, pulled no punches.

The 1990 Broadcasting Act required that the BBC commission one quarter of its television output from independent companies. This presented new opportunities for companies such as Chistera, which made two fifty-minute television programmes to mark the bicentenary of the United Irishmen rebellion of 1798, *The Patriots Fate*, presented by Brian Keenan, the former Beirut hostage and author of *An Evil Cradling*. Included in programmes made by Flying Fox Films were: *Frank Orr – Lambeg Drummer* (1987), the story of the drum and the cult surrounding it; *A Space for Dreaming* (1990), a tribute to the archaeologist, geographer, anthropologist and local historian Estyn Evans; *Hidden Ground: Thomas Flanagan* (1989), the story of an American academic's affair with Ireland; *Reels and Yarns* (1991), the story of the linen industry in Northern Ireland, told by the workers; *Where Your Face is Known* (1992), the cultural diversity of Ulster as seen in the microcosm of the Lecale district of County Down; *Hidden Pursuits* (1992), on local historians and the importance of their work; *Mountain Fen and Lake* (1992), a programme on the landscapes of counties Down and Fermanagh; '*Ye Barbarous Mountaines . . .*' (1994), an examination of the last residual source of native Irish in the north of Ireland; and *Braid Scots* (1996), a look at the Lallan tongue in the north-east of Ulster.

A major factual series on BBC Northern Ireland in 1997–8 was *Lives of Our Times*, which told the story of Northern Ireland through the voices of those

who lived throughout the twentieth century. The BBC production team was assiduous in tracking down old film and stills to illustrate the memories of those who spoke of the horrors of the Battle of the Somme, the blitz on Belfast, the excitement when American troops were stationed in Northern Ireland in 1942 and 1943, working in the shipyards and factories, dancing at the Floral Hall, Portrush and elsewhere, and of love, marriage and children. A series in the same vein was *The Century Speaks* on BBC RADIO ULSTER, part of the biggest project in the history of radio. Some forty BBC producers across the UK searched for thousands of people who would be willing to be interviewed about their lives, with the aim of capturing the experience of the twentieth century through the voices of those who lived through it. Over six thousand people of all ages and backgrounds came forward. The sixteen programmes on BBC RADIO ULSTER began in September 1999 at weekly intervals to put on air those who often spoke with surprising frankness about the intimacies, the sorrows, the joys, triumphs and struggles of their lives.

The Maternity, broadcast for five weeks on Mondays at 9.30 p.m., starting on 15 January 2000, was an absorbing fly-on-the-wall documentary on the Royal Victoria Hospital, made for BBC Northern Ireland by About Face Media. This look behind the scenes featured the highs and lows of the lives of the doctors, nurses, ward staff and patients over a six-month period. Liam Fay of the *Sunday Times* described the series as the 'world's first stork-on-the-wall documentary' and felt that he would have liked more blood and guts: 'There was a determination throughout to avoid any sight or mention of gore and pain. This is childbirth for the queasy, the Ladybird book of easy labour.' Most viewers, however, were thankful for that and the series generated a huge amount of interest, particularly in the fate of the babies, including Owen McTaggart, who had hydrocephalus when he was born and had to undergo a serious operation six weeks later, and Linus Gilbert, born weighing only 2 lb 6 oz during his mother's trip home from New Zealand to attend her mother's funeral. Both babies were restored to complete health. The fixed cameras recorded the tears and fears of patients and staff, and drew protest from domestic staff when the programmes went out because their bosses could be seen upbraiding them for the poor quality of their work. The star of the series was the consultant paediatrician Professor Garth McClure, who agonised about the fate of every baby and pointed out that during his working lifetime the mortality rate among babies in Northern Ireland had fallen further and faster than anywhere else in western Europe.

The Maternity was screened just when the debate on whether maternity services should be centred in the City Hospital or the Royal Victoria Hospital was at its height. Bairbre de Brún, the Health Minister, decided in favour of the Royal Victoria Hospital, and many believed the programmes had done much to tip the balance in its favour. The series was another demonstration that major changes within the BBC nearly a decade earlier had led to the emergence of a strong cohort of locally based independents capable of making programmes of high quality.

4

COMEDY, VARIETY
AND LIGHT ENTERTAINMENT

THE EARLIEST COMEDY TURNS and variety acts were born of the need to find material to give the listener a break between music pro- grammes. One of the station's part-time actors, Richard Hayward, was also establishing himself as a writer and he scripted a series called *Double-sided Records* made up of two vignettes. These were dialogues in Belfast dialect, depicting city life in, for example, *At the Cinema, In the Tram* and *Seeing Them off at the Liverpool Boat*. Some of these productions were the most innovative attempted by 2BE. The *Irish Radio Journal* in July 1925 had warm praise for Hayward's *A Trip to the Isle of Man*:

> This was partly broadcast from the open air – a yard adjoining the sta- tion – where a real taxi, bands and unlimited paraphernalia were used. In the studio the equipment included barrel organs, Punch and Judy shows, etc, etc. The author and producer, with his knowledge of the legitimate stage acquired from his very creditable work with the Ulster Players, has set himself the task of solving the problems of radio drama, and perhaps his greatest achievement as a producer is the skilful manner with which he weaves into his broadcast suggestive sounds which do lit- erally take the place of scenery as it is known in the theatre.

The real credit for the production should have gone to the Station Director's junior assistant, Tyrone Guthrie, who later would demonstrate in his radio plays the skills he had acquired during his two years with 2BE.

Special telephone lines were laid to relay public concerts in the Ulster Hall and it was not long before they were taken further to cinemas, hotels, dance halls and the theatre. *Hip, Hip, Hooradio*, a revue relayed from the Empire Theatre in Belfast on 13 December 1927, was the first broadcast to be made from an Irish theatre. Broadcasts from the Hippodrome followed in 1931. 'Ulster has a drama of its own and a humour of its own,' the BBC *Year Book* for 1930 enthused, ' . . . Many original revues have made their first appearance at Belfast, among which *Four-in-Hand, Le Cabaret au Lapin Qui Saute* and *All Right on the Night* are worthy of special mention.' In his internal report of 1936, Charles Siepmann found the quality of the region's light entertainment very uneven:

> Use is made exclusively of amateur artistes. Auditions have hitherto revealed a low standard among applicants. Within the Province, there are

Opposite:
PK Tonight: Patrick Kielty, the comic from Dundrum County Down.

BBC NI

77

two or three reasonably good syncopated turns, a single syncopated pianist – half a dozen turns shall we say in all and then a lapse to gloomy depths. There is but a single good author of light Belfast material. On average one real show is put on a fortnight . . . the overall output within a year amounts to about 120 shows. Very few indeed are fit for export.

A high proportion of the plays were comedies, such as E.A. Bryan's *Enter Mrs. Grundy* and J.H. McIlveen's *A Rift in the Lute,* described in 1931 as 'a County Antrim comedy', and these also attracted Siepmann's scorn. When the Blaris transmitter became operational in 1936, the challenge posed by the fast-increasing audience in the area of light entertainment was one that Linenhall Street found particularly difficult to meet. The best of the offerings seem to have been: *The Ballymagraw Gazette*, with sketches by Harry S. Gibson; *Winnie's Hour*, 'devised' by Harry Hemsley; and *Linenhall Blues*, billed as 'a sophisticated and satirical review'.

War summarily closed down regional broadcasting but also inaugurated the golden age of wireless variety entertainment. When the BBC in Belfast began to make programmes again in the spring of 1940 for the Home and Forces Services, the overwhelming demand was for light music and entertainment for war workers and those serving in the army, navy and air force. David Curry's *Irish Rhythms* met the first requirement so magnificently that the programme was probably the most distinctive contribution the BBC in Northern Ireland ever made to network radio. Meeting the demand for light entertainment proved more difficult, partly because the appeal of Ulster humour and regional dialect was highly localised.

During the darkest days of the war, the London government nursed hopes that Éire could be cajoled out of neutrality. It is now known that the the day before France signed an armistice with Germany in 1940 that Churchill's Cabinet agreed to offer de Valera, in return for his state's participation, 'a declaration of a United Ireland in principle, the practical details of the union to be worked out in due course'. When he heard of this proposal, Craigavon made vehement protests but de Valera refused the offer on 7 July and the crisis was soon over.

Whether or not George Marshall, the Regional Director, picked up hints of these secret negotiations in the Ulster Club is impossible to say. Henceforth, none the less, Marshall implacably opposed broadcasting co-operation with Éire and turned down requests from Dr T.J. Kiernan, appointed Director of Broadcasting in the Irish Free State in 1932, for studio facilities in Belfast. The London government, on the other hand, was aware that thousands of southern Irish men and women were engaged in vital war work in Britain or had joined the forces. The Ministry of Information and the Dominions Office urged the BBC to include items of special Irish or Catholic interest, including some in the Irish language. 'Will you consider,' the Ministry of Information asked the Controller of Programmes, 'whether there is anything the BBC can do which it is not now doing to attract Irish listeners, i.e. Eire listeners . . .' Marshall resisted, declaring in 1941 that any 'St Patrick's Day feature should be confined to

Northern Ireland from which we present something appropriate to the occasion', but he was overruled. The *Northern Whig* fulminated in its leader headed 'More Appeasement':

> We invite the attention of our readers to the curious programme for St Patrick's Day which has been specially arranged by the BBC. It is to consist of a joint entertainment from Eire and Northern Ireland and will ignore the political frontier. There is no sort of hint that Ulster is fighting side by side in the War against Germany and Italy while Eire is nominally neutral, but is actually aiding the Empire's foes in a number of ways . . .

The Controller of Programmes reported that the Northern Ireland government had been complaining that the programme had been tantamount to 'shaking hands with murder'.

Much of the work in arranging and producing such programmes for Irish listeners at home, in Britain and in the forces fell to the BBC correspondent for Belfast and Dublin, Denis Johnston. Johnston later recorded this memory:

> I used to bring people up from Dublin to play in programmes of this kind and very often strong republicans came without any qualms whatsoever who seemed to be quite prepared to take part in these things. I did also a thing which I don't think has been done since: a St Patrick's Day programme in which both Radio Eireann, as it was then, and the north took part. We went from entertainments in the north to the Abbey Theatre. We had songs from the north and songs from the south and, apart from technical difficulties which cropped up (we came up with an interval which required some explanation) . . . it was an interesting experiment . . .

Johnston helped to set up *Irish Half Hour,* which was made in the BBC's wartime production centre in north Wales. Radio Éireann's popular broadcaster, Joe Linnane, was engaged as compere and Harry O'Donovan agreed to provide the scripts. Jimmy O'Dea was by far Ireland's most popular comedian and drew large audiences during his frequent appearances on the stage of Belfast's Empire Theatre. His radio monologues as 'Mrs Mulligan' were enormously popular in Northern Ireland with those who could pick up the signal from Athlone. He agreed to take part in *Irish Half Hour* with alacrity. Here is a sample of O'Dea's humour which was heard across the world:

> ANNOUNCER. Ladies and Gentlemen, *Irish Half Hour* is on the air again. Here is Joe Linnane.
> LINNANE. Here we are again, setting out for Ballygobackwards, the only place with an all purpose station – railway, petrol and fire. Yes, Jimmy O'Dea has recently taken on the captaincy of the Ballygobackwards fire service, a private venture of his own, in competition with the local fire brigade. He's burning to get crackling, so put on your fire-proof suits, take your place on the engine and so – off we go! [*Sound of steam engine, music and fire bell*]
> MAGGIE. What is it? What is it? Who's ringing the fire bell?

LINNANE. It's fireman Jimmy O'Dea and here is – Jimmy O'Dea!

O'DEA. Here I am, here I am. Ask me why. I climb the ladder. Me
hose is slippin'. The suspense is awful. A beautiful girl is leaning
out of the window. What will be her fate? Will I turn the water
on her face? No, I'll turn it on meself and dampen me ardour. It
will never be said that O'Dea never put out the old flames. A brave
man, I see him dash up the escape, his helmet gleaming in the
ruddy glow, his helmet . . . holy fly fixer! Me helmet's in pawn.
Where's the ticket?

ASSISTANT. Where's the fire?

O'DEA. Sure there's no fire at all. Sure I was just rehearsin' in case,
you know. Where's me Sunday helmet?

ASSISTANT. Well, I took it into the kitchen to keep it dry.

O'DEA. So that's what. Maggie was cooking the stew in it. Now we
can't have a fire until after dinner.

ASSISTANT. Now, that's very incendiary.

O'DEA. Would you say so?

ASSISTANT. Jimmy, look, that new fire gadget's arrived from Dublin.
It's called a stirabout pump.

O'DEA. Stirabout pump! A stomach pump you mean, ye ignoramus
– it's for puttin' out insanitary bombs.

Irish Half Hour was a runaway success in Éire, Britain and with the forces overseas. Sir John Maffey, the United Kingdom's representative in Éire, gave his
warm approval and John Betjeman, the British Cultural and Press Attaché in
Dublin, judged it a series which would keep alive among soldiers serving away
from home 'the sense of Irish nationalism in the broadest meaning of the
term'. Marshall, however, was furious that he had not been given the scripts in
advance. 'Had I done so,' he wrote to the Controller of Programmes, 'I should
have certainly deleted the compere's words at the beginning, "It's all yours
Ireland".' He continued:

> Several people have complained recently that the programme is called
> *Irish Half Hour* instead of 'Eire Half Hour' and only last week the Prime
> Minister wrote to me to the same effect. Eire is the official name of the
> twenty-six counties and I think that as the programme is intended for
> loyalists in the British Forces whose homes are in Eire and not in
> Northern Ireland, it should be given the correct title.

The Regional Director obstructed Johnston as much as he could, limiting the
number of southern artistes he could bring north and he refused to allow Dr
Kiernan's wife, the much-loved singer Delia Murphy, to be broadcast from
Belfast on the unfounded belief that she and her husband were pro-German –
in spite of the fact that Delia Murphy famously continued to sing all night in
the Ulster Hall throughout the Easter Tuesday air raid on Belfast in 1941, during which nearly a thousand citizens lost their lives.

Marshall, no doubt, was mollified when the British Forces Overseas Service
invited Belfast to contribute a variety, news and music programme for
Ulstermen serving in the Middle East and in North and West Africa. When the

programme first went out as *Six Counties Half Hour,* the Northern Ireland government was appalled and used its influence to have the series title changed to *Ulster Half Hour.* Broadcast on shortwave, the programmes were not heard in Northern Ireland. Val Gielgud, BBC Head of Drama, was not impressed with the quality. After listening to a programme he observed: 'This example would have done no credit to broadcasting in the year 1925 . . . apart from its possible stimulation of local patriotism, in the worst sense of the word, I see no justification for this programme in any circumstances.' Marshall was able to persuade the Controller of Programmes not only to save the series but also to put it on air on the Home Service in 1943 and it continued until 1946. The quality of the programmes was constantly criticised: the *Irish News* thought the BBC had gone 'all broth of a boy' and that 'the old Punch cartoons of Irishmen, tailcoats, shillelaghs, and all, are being refurbished, translated into terms of electrical frequencies, and pumped out through a transmitting station known by the good Irish name of Lisnagarvey'. The programmes certainly did not please the Unionists who wanted to press the BBC 'to have that programme more truly reflect the life of Ulster'.

Much of the best of Belfast's contribution to the Home and Forces Services came from performances of variety, comedy acts and popular music relayed from the stage. Sheila Hughes, who toured with Fossetts Circus and learned to walk the tightrope, and later became a dancer at the Empire Theatre, recorded her memories to Owen McFadden for the 1999 BBC Northern Ireland series *The Century Speaks.* She and her friend Norma Barry, head girl of a dancing troupe, remembered that the Empire never closed and 'whenever the Blitz came, she said there were only three people the night after that . . . But we kept going and then it built up and built up and built up . . . So that again, as I said, every night then we had packed houses.' The Empire was a favourite venue for the BBC's Forces programmes. For example, part of the one-hundredth edition of the revue *Come to the Show* was relayed from the stage between 7.00 p.m. and 7.30 p.m. on 8 July 1943.

The first Americans, 362 'civilian technicians', arrived in Londonderry in June 1941, six months before the United States came into the war. Then from January 1942 American troops began to pour in and by 1943 there were around 120,000 United States personnel in Northern Ireland. Theatres, cinemas, ballrooms and halls were packed with off-duty visitors. On the eastern shore of Lough Neagh a new town sprang up at Langford Lodge; here the Lockheed Overseas Corporation, on behalf of the American government, repaired and maintained aircraft. Ulster men and women were working side by side with Americans here, at aerodromes and at Derry, where the United States invested seventy-five million dollars developing the largest anti-U-boat base in the Atlantic. A special edition of the BBC Home Service's immensely popular *Workers' Playtime* was produced in Belfast late in 1943 to be broadcast in America. It was introduced by the first Northern Ireland Prime Minister at ease in front of a microphone – Sir Basil Brooke:

Matt Mulcaghey, 'the oul' besom
man from Tyrone', made his first
broadcast on 16 March 1927 and
remained a regular broadcaster
for the next twenty-five years.
Essentially he was a writer and
actor who adopted a permanent
character role. His real name was
Wilson Guy.

BBC NI

I can imagine no happier name for this short period of recreation than
Workers' Playtime. A break for a meal and a few minutes' bright entertainment sends our workers back to their jobs in this Ulster factory with
cheery hearts and quickened enthusiasm. I visited many war factories by
day and by night and I would like you in the United States to know that
our people are in fine fighting fettle.

Most have husbands, sons, brothers and sweethearts in the front line
of battle. They know that the lives of their men in the Services depend
on an ever-increasing flow of arms and supplies. In the early days of the
war the output of munitions was a mere trickle; now it has become a
mighty flood. We shall go on turning out ships, planes, tanks, fighting
equipment of every kind until we have smashed the foe and he is utterly routed. In this great enterprise you and we are comrades. The day of
final victory is not yet but it is coming, sure as tomorrow's dawn. In the
hands of the United Nations the future is safe. It is our common privi-
lege to help in shaping it now. In the name of the war workers of Ulster
I send you heartiest greetings and wish you good night and God speed.

Denied a wavelength of its own after the war, Northern Ireland Region
had to share with the North East England Region. During the time the
Home Service allocated to local broadcasting, the transmitter on the
Cumbrian Mountains beamed out programmes that were often well-nigh
incomprehensible to one region or the other. This was particularly the
case in comedy broadcasts and listeners in Newcastle upon Tyne were wont to com-
plain to the BBC in London that they could not understand a word being said
in Belfast. A performer most likely to upset the English listener was Wilson
Guy, who took on the character of Matt Mulcaghey, 'the oul' besom man from
County Tyrone'. He and others like him, such as 'Mrs Rooney', were middle-
class performers giving impressions of humble people 'respectable' citizens

might expect to enjoy in the theatre or the drawing room. At a time when Raymond Glendinning and Sam Hanna Bell were bringing authentic voices from the countryside and the town to the microphone, such broadcasts sounded rather stagy. A new era dawned with *The McCooeys*, first broadcast on 13 May 1949.

When he had been Director of Programmes in Scotland, Andrew Stewart had seen the success of a serial called *The McFlannels* and he suggested to Henry McMullan that a similar series based on the life of an ordinary family could be produced for Northern Ireland. McMullan, in turn, consulted his talks producer, John Boyd, who recommended an actor and writer he had known for many years, Joseph Tomelty. Tomelty agreed to their offer and proposed *The McCooeys*, a working-class Belfast family. Care was taken to ensure that the family could not be identified as Catholic or Protestant: the telephone book was consulted to ensure the name was not listed – in fact, there were McCooeys living in Ulster (thirty were listed in the directory in 1999 and seven with the name McCooe) and several contacted Tomelty soon afterwards to register their enthusiasm. 'It ran for two months,' McMullan wrote in the 1949 jubilee book, 'was "rested" during the high summer, and came back to the air in October. Within a month of its return it had proved the most popular and most discussed programme ever broadcast in Northern Ireland, and for seven months the McCooey family were listened to and quoted in thousands of homes all over Ulster. Their temporary departure from programmes to allow everyone, including the author, to draw breath, has been greatly deplored.' He continued:

> What is the secret of 'The McCooeys'? Probably the answer is their normality. The author knows and loves the people he is writing about. The cast find his lines 'read themselves', and the problems and anxieties to which he exposes them are largely the ordinary problems and anxieties which afflict us all. There is a warmth and humanity in the McCooey family which has reached the listener and brought him back week after week to his loudspeaker.
>
> Attendance at a performance of 'The McCooeys' is an odd experience. The artists taking part have found that the characters they play have become part of them . . . When one member of the cast married, the rest of the McCooeys were there . . . when Mina Dornan, who plays the Mother, had her appendix taken out at short notice the 'family' saw to it she lacked neither flowers nor visitors.

Listeners would write in if they felt a favourite character was being neglected. On one occasion, when the parlour of the McCooey family was redecorated, worried listeners telephoned to protest that the family had failed to fix a price for the work beforehand and letters arrived to offer advice on what a fair rate should be. Catch phrases from the serial were to be heard repeated all around Northern Ireland, including 'Oh now', 'You're a comeejan', and 'shloup with vegabittles'. McMullan once got a telephone call from Lord Brookeborough:

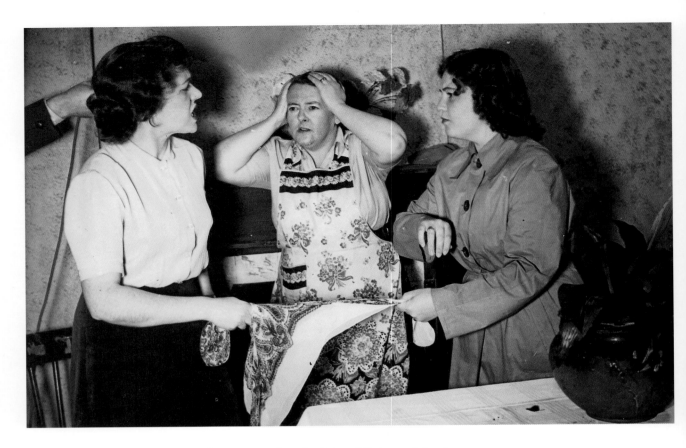

The McCooeys

BBC NI

On one occasion the Prime Minister of the day rang me up, on a personal basis, saying could I put *The McCooeys* on at half past seven because they were having frightful trouble, because they all said firmly 'No dinner until *The McCooeys* is over' and this was Saturday night? 'And as well as that, you do it on Monday,' he said. I said very firmly: 'It's got its placing and that's where it's going to stay.'

The McCooeys ran for seven years until in 1957 Tomelty suffered a severe motorcar accident and was unable to continue the series. It proved impossible to fill the void. *Mrs Lally's Lodgers,* written by Jack Loudan, did acquire a good following but nothing like that won by *The McCooeys.* Derek, the window-cleaner in *The McCooeys,* was played by James Young, who was given a programme of his own, *The Young Idea.* Young proved to be a comic genius, capable of taking on an extraordinarily wide range of roles, such as the Cherryvalley lady recently risen in the world and the street urchin. He poked fun – harder on air than anyone had done before – at the entrenched attitudes on both sides in Ulster and, while members of the Advisory Council might on occasion be scandalised, most of his audience appreciated his vulgarity. The problem in Broadcasting House was that Young did not write his own material and, in the years to come, it was to be demonstrated that the success of comedy and light entertainment ultimately depended on scriptwriters possessing unusual talent. It could be argued that it was not until the emergence of The Hole in the Wall Gang in the 1990s that Tomelty was to find his match.

The arrival of television did not immediately offer the region the opportunity to present light entertainment on the screen – the cost of production was too high and, in any case, the necessary technical equipment was limited. When Ulster Television made its first broadcast and commercial radio came on air, the BBC in Belfast was presented with a dilemma: should it attempt to compete head to head with the independents in the area of light entertainment, where they seemed strongest? As the sole provider in the past, the BBC in Belfast, since the early days of 2BE, had always scheduled helpings of comedy, variety and light entertainment and the region now had no hesitation in deciding that it should continue to do so. Nevertheless, the relaxed, chatty and unscripted approach of commercial radio, and the fact that the rapidly expanding number of viewers were becoming used to fresh styles in programmes from both BBC network and independent television, demanded significant cultural changes in Broadcasting House.

The McCooeys
BBC NI

Light entertainment was first provided as items slotted in to magazine programmes such as *Studio Eight*. As the Ormeau Avenue facilities were limited for large productions, the BBC rented Balmoral Hall in the Royal Ulster Agricultural Society's grounds in south Belfast and set up a mobile four-camera unit there mainly for entertainment programmes. Good audiences were gained for shows such as *Half Door Club* and *Ceili*. Variety acts frequently were screened for the lively community magazine programme presented by Kate Pratt, *Kate at Eight*, and on the nightly regional magazine on television, *Six-Five*. *Six-Five*'s successor, *Scene Around Six*, continued to include a wide selection of lighter items and in *Look Who's Talking*, on Thursdays between 9.55 p.m. and 10.20 p.m., Harry Thompson gave a platform for local entertainers. As Northern Ireland began seizing the world's attention from the autumn of 1968, however, hard news items pushed lighter ones off *Scene Around Six*. Most journalistic and production energy in Broadcasting House was naturally devoted to news gathering and current affairs.

The local comedian who towered above all others on television during the 1960s and the darkest years of the Troubles was James Young. Members of The Hole in the Wall Gang remembered how, as children, they begged to be allowed to stay up to see him. Young ridiculed both communities but his humour was rarely threatening. He knew the Protestant community best and most of his triumphantly successful portrayals were of Protestants, such as

Orange Lil. He tended to put a southern inflection in his voice when taking on the persona of a Catholic. Perhaps it was too early for hard-hitting satire and, at a time when much of Northern Ireland was convulsed and fear stalked the streets from nightfall, Young's gentle but often extremely funny sketches were what were needed.

James Young, an Ulster Group Theatre actor, first made familiar to the listener as Derek the window cleaner in *The McCooeys*.

BBC NI

Other light entertainment series on television included: *Date with Derek*, featuring Derek Marsden; *The Melody Lingers On*; *You're On*, a five-programme series which gave amateur talent throughout Ireland a competitive opportunity to become better known; and *Clubsound*. Created by George Jones, *Clubsound* was in many ways an updated version of the pre-war *Eight Bells* – a blend of popular music, sketches, patter and renditions. The programme was one that was safe enough to let small children watch unattended and, indeed, Jones was later to demonstrate a special talent for talking to children and getting them to talk back.

Local competition from UTV was keenly felt and no more so than on Friday nights, when Gerry Kelly's chat show – a northern equivalent of RTÉ's *Late Late Show*, hosted by Gay Byrne – was becoming an institution. In 1989 BBC Northern Ireland planned an ambitious series called *The Show*, largely devised by Martin Dillon, with the intention of making a special bid to win the adherence of younger viewers. The programme was to be a mixture of satirical sketches, novelty acts, music and straight discussion, broadcast from the Balmoral Studios. The audience was to be invited to the Joker Club, an elaborate set which was a commercially run bar with customers moving about freely during transmission. Eamonn Holmes, already established on network television, was to be the presenter and Rhonda Paisley, daughter of Democratic Unionist Party leader, the Reverend Ian Paisley, was engaged as an interviewer. *The Show* was first screened on 10 November 1989. Reaction was swift.

'A TV presenter, Eamonn Holmes, quit a BBC satirical programme last night,' the *Yorkshire Post* reported next day. 'He resigned after one edition of *The Show*, which led to fierce protests in Northern Ireland when it was shown live last Saturday. Outraged viewers accused it of being smutty, blasphemous, vulgar, obscene and insulting.' Rhonda Paisley, in fact, resigned just hours after the programme ended: she had conducted a straight interview with Seamus Mallon, the SDLP MP, and had only seen the sketch satirising her father recorded on video when she got home. 'She described it as lewd and offensive and bad satire,' the *Yorkshire Post* continued. 'Ulster-born Mr Holmes said that he was also going, as nine Ulster Unionist MPs backed a Commons motion denouncing the show. They demanded that senior BBC staff be reprimanded.' Anderson and McAuley cancelled their engagement with Holmes to open their refurbished store in central Belfast. The offending sketch showed the writer and rock singer Tom McLaughlin playing a clergyman, the 'Reverend Elvis Kyle McCracken' of the 'Fundamentalist United Church of Carnality', preaching from a pulpit, crafted like a ship's figurehead which resembled Margaret Thatcher, and throwing off his clothes and calling on the congregation to 'gyrate for Jesus'. Frank Delaney, who had launched his broadcasting career in Belfast, gave his opinion in the *Independent*:

> An unmelodious song about abortion, contraception and menstruation has also given offence, and the surreal abounds. Bands with names like Four Idle Hands sing Cajun music for which the nasal flats of the Ulster accent seem freakily suited . . . This crazy salad has provoked what may have been the largest public reaction ever experienced by broadcasters in Northern Ireland.

Some two thousand indignant calls were received by the BBC and on the Saturday afternoon before the second transmission around a hundred hymn-singing fundamentalists protested outside Broadcasting House. One of their prayers was: 'Oh, God, if Thou art just, Thou wilt not let this blasphemous programme be transmitted this night.' Norman Jenkinson in the *Belfast Telegraph* wrote that watching *The Show* was 'like looking through a keyhole into Hell'. The Controller, Colin Morris, a Methodist minister who regularly contributed inspirational and eloquent contributions to BBC RADIO 4's *Thought for Today*, stoutly defended the skill and dedication of the producer Colin Lewis and his team but apologised for items which gave 'gratuitous offence' and promised changes. A couple of days later Gerry Stembridge resigned as director and was replaced by Martin Shardlow, who had previously directed *The Two Ronnies* and *Blackadder*.

Kate Pratt presenting *Kate at Eight* in 1968. This magazine-style programme introduced a new informality into television broadcasting in Northern Ireland by reaching out into the community and featuring local arts and cultural events.

BBC NI

Anderson on the Road. His fame was secured forever when on air he referred to the difficulty of naming Derry/Londonderry and suggested 'Stroke City' as a truly impartial title.

BBC NI

The second programme in the series was better received. Sinn Féin councillor Máirtín Ó Muilleoir said: 'It was effervescent, crackling and not completely neutered, thank God. The puerile show of last week came of age in seven days.' The BBC pressed ahead and altogether three series were screened between 1989 and 1991, with David Dunseith, Gerry Anderson and Sean Rafferty serving terms as presenters. The later programmes attracted more praise. The *News Letter* critic who had commented on the first programme, 'technically it was brilliant; in content it was diabolically bad', observed on 11 April 1990 that '*The Show* has been a resounding success.' Mary Kelly in the *Belfast Telegraph* regretted that soft drinks only were available but felt 'it wasn't a bad evening – the bands were good, the crack was mighty, and there's another series in the pipeline.' *The Show* continued to offend some viewers ('I just *hated* it,' Jim Kincaid, then the National Governor, recalled), but it had great appeal for a core of younger viewers – in some ways the series revealed that there was a generation gap in Northern Ireland, the previous lack of which, it could be argued, had helped to perpetuate ancient fears and resentments. *The Show* was the first television series to provide genuine satire on the Troubles and the attitudes which helped to generate them; many viewers, regardless of concerns about quality, found that too uncomfortable.

The early 1990s witnessed a decline in real terms of the BBC's income. The obvious benefits of pooling resources revived suggestions of co-operation between Belfast and Dublin, which had stirred up such storms in the past. The last decade of the century witnessed regular collaboration and this time the criticism was negligible. BBC Northern Ireland and RTÉ combined to produce a major series, *Go for It*, in 1992. In each of the ten programmes in the series five acts were introduced by the host and a celebrity guest, and points were apportioned to each participant for presentation, performance and potential. A thousand musical hopefuls were auditioned. The first series won a *Belfast Telegraph* EMA Award and the final winner, singer Peter Corry, went on to achieve professional success in London and Berlin. In the 1993 series, in which the host was Marty Whelan and the resident judges Rose-Marie and Bill Hughes, the winner was a surgeon from the Adelaide Hospital in Dublin, Dr Ronan Tynan. With a rendition of 'Torna a Sorrento', Tynan won maximum points; he described how he felt just before his performance: 'I put on a lovely new shirt and covered it completely in make-up. Then I tried to put my shoes on the wrong feet . . . the sweat was rolling off me, my hands were cold as ice and I was running to the loo every ten minutes.' He was launched on a highly successful singing career, issuing an album which was a runaway success.

Conleth Hill and Maria Connolly in a scene from *Out Of The Deep Pan*, a zany comedy, written by Tim Loane.

BBC NI

Another BBC Northern Ireland/RTÉ co-production of the same type was *Let Me Entertain You*, a series launched in January 1999. Gerry Ryan, one of the best-known broadcasters in the Republic, was the host. This form of popular entertainment – similar to *Opportunity Knocks* – was not for the fastidious. 'The format of the show is stomach-churning,' John Boland judged in the *Sunday Independent*, and Eddie Holt, writing in the *Irish Times* on 23 January, described the programme he had seen as follows:

> It sounds like a screamfest on speed and is full of fiercely orchestrated, manic merriment. The studio audience emits the sort of edgy delirium you might expect if the Nazis were running Butlin's . . . it's presented by Gerry Ryan, never a shrinking violet, but even the Montrose Motormouth himself seems barely adequate to the decibel levels required.

Gloria Hunniford had launched her broadcasting career with BBC RADIO ULSTER in the 1970s and went on to achieve network fame. She returned to Belfast on 17 January 1997 for one of the city's biggest social events – the official opening of the Waterfront Hall – to introduce the Ulster Orchestra and its soloists for BBC TWO. In the same month she hosted an edition of *Something for the Weekend*, a series designed to compete directly on the same night with *Kelly* on UTV, with a particular emphasis on winning the attention of older viewers who tended to stay in on Friday evenings. Interviewed on the first show were Caprice Bourret, the Wonderbra girl, and other guests included the veteran crooner, Val Doonican, the film critic Alexander Walker and David Soul of *Starsky and Hutch* US detective series fame. A different celebrity came each week to host the show, which was a mixture of chat, music and comedy, and it did win respectable audiences but was an expensive gamble which failed to knock Gerry Kelly from his perch.

Gloria Hunniford
BBC NI

In the 1980s the City Temple in Belfast's Botanic Avenue changed its allegiance from God to Mammon and became the Empire Bar soon afterwards. Here the Empire Comedy Club was set up by former BBC producer Jackie Hamilton in October 1992 and it immediately provided a platform for up-and-coming comic artists and satirists. Patrick Kielty began by doing stand-up gigs in the Students' Union at Queen's University when he was studying psychology there and he entered a competition at Billy Magra's club in Dublin and featured in the final, which was screened on *The Late Late Show*. He established himself as master of ceremonies at the Comedy Club, which was given a special programme to provide a major showcase for local talent by BBC Northern Ireland in 1994. Kielty was the star of *The Empire Laughs Back*, which won the Royal Television Society Award for Best Regional Programme.

Ever vigilant to find a Friday evening light entertainment slot, BBC Northern Ireland in 1995 offered Kielty his own show, *PK Tonight*. It was an immediate success, with a 43 per cent share of the audience, averaging 280,000 viewers, and won him the Royal Television Society Award for Best Regional Presenter. In 1999, when Gay Byrne retired from *The Late Late Show*, it was widely rumoured that Kielty had turned down the offer of hosting this long-running programme. Instead, he chose the BBC ONE half-hour comedy and chat show made for the region by his Green Inc company, *Patrick Kielty Almost Live*.

Kielty's father, a leading Gaelic Athletic Association official in County Down, was murdered in 1988 by the Ulster Freedom Fighters. Kielty was one of a new generation prepared to satirise the most uncomfortable aspects of the Troubles directly and savagely, and killers from both sides of the divide were equal targets. He quickly learned, however, that what was suitable for the Empire Club had to be tailored for television audiences. Here is a sample of his special brand of humour:

> Everyone is now talking about peace in the North, and building a future

in the North, and we're coming together and we're building this and we're building that . . . I don't mean to worry anyone, but the last thing we built in Belfast went down with Leonardo de Caprio and Kate Winslet hanging off the back of it.

and

What IRA are they talking about? There's so many of them now, isn't there? There's the Real IRA, the Surreal IRA, the Continuity IRA, the Provisional IRA, the Official IRA, Low Fat IRA, Diet IRA, I-Can't-Believe-It's-Not-The-IRA . . .

Damon Quinn, Tim McGarry and Michael McDowell met while they were studying law at Queen's University. They began by writing and performing one-act comedies to raise money for Oxfam, Amnesty International and for the Ethiopian famine in 1984. While they were practising as lawyers they continued to write and were given their first break by BBC RADIO ULSTER in 1990, when they contributed three-minute satirical pieces for *Talk Back*. Both the producers and the listeners were impressed and the following year they were given their own six-week show, *Perforated Ulster*. They called themselves The Hole in the Wall Gang and were joined by Nuala McKeever and Martin Reid. At a time when there was an alarming upsurge in bombings and sectarian murders listeners were presented with their exceedingly black humour, an assault on sectarianism and on where it was leading the people of Northern Ireland. The series won a Sony Award.

Paul Evans, Head of Production, gave The Hole in the Wall Gang their first broadcast break. Pat Loughry, then Head of Programmes and later Northern Ireland Controller, recognised their unique potential. He gave the team financial support and set a room aside for them in Broadcasting House, making it possible for them to take the risk of giving up their day jobs for a year to see if they could survive in broadcasting full time. The Hole in the Wall Gang was given a platform on television in what became *Two Ceasefires and a Wedding*. Tim McGarry said later: 'There's only one broadcaster on the island who's prepared to do anything vaguely risky, and that's BBC Northern Ireland.' Broadcast in May 1995 *Two Ceasefires and a Wedding* was given such a rapturous reception that it was given a network broadcast on BBC TWO. In one scene Billy, a Protestant policeman, is having a secret relationship with his Catholic girlfriend, Emer, and the two of them are up on Cave Hill getting passionate:

EMER [*Stops*]   Billy, do you not think you should be wearing some
                 protection?
BILLY   Yeah, right enough, good idea.
[*He puts on a bullet-proof vest and a flak jacket.*]

In another scene Emer has this exchange with her mother:

MA   I wish they'd take the UDA and the IRA and the UVF
                 and the INLA and put them all on an island and let
                 them shoot each other all they want.

EMER   But Ma – this *is* an island and that's *exactly* what they're doing.

The Hole in the Wall Gang's *Give My Head Peace* grew out of the serial on BBC RADIO ULSTER about a dysfunctional family entitled *Perforated Ulster*, highlights of which were subsequently used for a special programme for BBC RADIO 4. The main characters were: Da, eventually elected a Sinn Féin Assembly member (for which he gets his dole money stopped), who has a beard like Gerry Adams's and glasses 'like Gerry's' but for fear of the dentist has not got teeth 'like Gerry's'; Ma, who is a kind of one-woman Northern Ireland Women's Coalition and who has no time for her husband's antics; Billy is a policeman who lives with his Uncle Andy and enjoys eating pasties in the back of a Land Rover; Andy has become a loyalist fashion icon with Reactolite sunglasses and greasy, slicked-down hair; Cal turned down a cross-community holiday in Florida because he would miss the anti-internment riots but, despite his apparent stupidity, he constantly confronts Da with awkward questions; Emer is married to Billy ('a beacon of hope for our two divided communities') but eventually leaves him after an affair in Spain with the gorgeous Ronaldo; and Dympna, Emer's sister, with aspirations for a singing career, starts a relationship with Billy three minutes after they meet. In the introduction to *Give My Head Peace: The Book*, members of the Gang explain:

It was inspired as a satirical counterblast to two particularly pernicious

Spain beware: the Hole in the Wall gang on holidays in *Give my Head Peace*, considered the perfect antidote to that other famous Northern Ireland sitcom, Northern Ireland politics. The characters from left: Da, Ma, Cal, Dympna, Billy, Uncle Andy and Big Mervyn.

BBC NI

types of Northern Ireland play that seemed to predominate stage and screen in the 1970s and 1980s. The first type was what Stephen Rea has called 'balaclava' plays – the kind of *Harry's Game* nonsense where all terrorists are psychopathic twitchers played by English actors with dodgy Northern Ireland accents. The other type was what we call 'why can't it all be like Corrymeela' plays, which usually featured star-crossed lovers thwarted by the sectarian divide. Both of these types of play invariably end with, as Uncle Andy says in *Two Ceasefires and a Wedding*, 'the inevitable tragic denouement'.

Here is a typical sample of the series, taken from *The Long Marching Season:*

> DA   Cal, get up, you lazy scut, the march has started. Cal, if you don't get up now you're going to miss being offended.
>
> CAL   I'm ready.
>
> DA   Aw come on, Cal – you can't protest looking like that.
>
> CAL   This T-shirt is making an important political statement.
>
> DA   Barney?
>
> CAL   Aye – it's saying that Orangemen are political dinosaurs.
>
> DA   Go and get your 'Re-route the flute' T-shirt and stop your nonsense.
>
> CAL   I can't. Mammy put it in with the coloureds.
>
> DA   Come on we'll be late. Grab your placard.
>
> [DA *and* CAL *walk out of a living-room door*]

Give My Head Peace (words frequently uttered by Ma) was directed at a general audience and was, of necessity, less hard-hitting than much of the Gang's earlier work; nevertheless, southern humorists constantly asked them, 'How do you get away with it?' Ian Kennedy, who as BBC Head of Television in the region, long wrested with the problem of producing comedy programmes which directly addressed what actually was happening in Northern Ireland, observed that after years of violence and trauma:

> Every day life goes on, people have survived, and one of the mechanisms they use is humour. They will laugh, therefore, at things that other people would not find in the least bit funny. And it's a black humour – if they don't laugh they are going to cry, as the old cliché says. People here will laugh about things which outsiders would look at and say – that's not funny . . . you do not make fun out of the personal suffering, heartbreak, tragedy, but there are things on the periphery that you can laugh at.

5

DRAMA

IT WAS THE BELFAST STATION'S GOOD FORTUNE that Tyrone Guthrie, later one of the greatest directors of the English stage in the twentieth century, began his career as junior assistant to Major Scott. Guthrie had distinguished himself in undergraduate drama productions at Oxford and it was he who directed the first plays transmitted from Belfast. He had no previous broadcasting experience and, like almost everyone else, he was learning fast by experience at 2BE. One of his first productions was *Land of Heart's Desire* by W.B. Yeats and one of the station players, Graeme Roberts, recalled: 'I remember Norah Campbell put the microphone off the air with her scream.' He himself had a leading role in *The House in the Quiet Glen* by John Coulter and recorded his memory of a rehearsal in Linenhall Street:

> I remember going through it on a hot summer day on the top of the old building with our shirt sleeves rolled up. I was a fellow coming home from the fair with a girl I was supposed to be in love with . . . I had to start making love to her and I remember Guthrie saying 'More beastly, more beastly' to me.

Guthrie stayed only two years and resisted attempts to entice him back to Belfast.

The uncertain Post Office links across the Irish Sea meant that the Belfast station had to make the great majority of programmes it transmitted and this placed an almost intolerable burden on those responsible for producing drama at Linenhall Street. Indeed there were few indications during the first quarter century of the BBC's presence in Northern Ireland that the production of high quality drama would become a speciality of the region. The pool of versatile and able actors was tiny and, as the 1933 BBC Year Book frankly admitted, 'apparently the Ulster author has yet to be found who is master of the medium'. Plays submitted – and for lack of alternatives, often accepted – needed substantial adaptation and 'suffered from lack of action and from slow development requiring visual impressions to sustain interest'. The Belfast station at this time produced no fewer than seventy plays a year and the task of maintaining minimum standards in every one of them was all but impossible.

Gerald Beadle was keen to encourage locally produced radio plays. Although he failed to persuade Guthrie to return, he did succeed in enticing John Watt, later to become the BBC's Head of Variety Programmes, over in 1927. 'John Watt used to bring over a lot of artists from across the water,' veteran actor

The crew on location for the filming of the BBC Northern Ireland drama *Henri*, made for network in 1994. *Henri*, starring the young Sara Bowman, won three international awards.

BBC NI

Graeme Roberts recalled:

> One of the earliest I remember was Tommy Handley. In his first show
> he was ringmaster in a kind of circus and Jimmy Mageean and I took
> the part of clowns . . . there was no talk-back arrangement in the stu-
> dios and he had to come into the studio when he wanted to tell us what
> we were doing wrong. He used to say he knew nothing about local
> dialects. I remember at the end of the first act he'd come in and get up
> on a high stool and would say 'perfectly bloody', 'perfectly bloody'.
> Then he'd start and go through our various mistakes.

Watt's talent and enthusiasm were widely admired and when he left in 1930,
the *Irish News* regretted his going:

> I saw him conducting a play, just as a conductor directs the orchestra and
> singers in an opera. Wireless technique in plays is a comparatively new
> thing. When a play is being produced the actors sit round, scripts in
> hand. The producer gives the sign and conducts the small orchestra for
> the preliminary effects. Then, at the right moment, he points to the
> beginners to get ready, just as the conductor of an orchestra warns his
> violins. Then he points to the microphone, and off the play goes . . .
> Then the producer scans his script, gets the next players ready, points to
> them at the critical time, and gets them speaking. It was an extraordi-
> nary sight to see a play being produced like this . . . I am not surprised
> Mr Watt has gone to London.

The great majority of the Belfast station's plays were farmhouse kitchen comedies of a kind staged in church halls all over Ulster. The best of these, and ones
which attempted to move away from a stylised format, included: *Rolling the
Planet, Insurance Money* and *Tully's Experts* by George Shiels; *Neighbour's Childer*
and *The Wheat and the Chaff* by J.H. McIlveen; and *Apollo in Mourne* by Richard
Rowley. Actors from the Abbey Theatre Company were brought in to perform
some of Shakespeare's plays, including *A Midsummer Night's Dream, As You Like
It,* and *The Merchant of Venice,* Synge's *Playboy of the Western World,* and W.B.
Yeats's version of *Oedipus Rex.* George Marshall, who replaced Beadle in 1932,
firmly believed that Belfast could become a centre of excellence for wireless
drama and openly appealed to writers to come forward but warned: 'the
majority of authors who submitted works still have a tendency to confuse the
studio with the stage and their work is hampered accordingly'. The best plays
broadcast in Marshall's first year – described as 'dialect plays' – included J.H.
McIlveen's *The Leap Year Proposal; The Miracle Man* by Frederick Lyburn; *Enter
Mrs. Grundy*; a comedy by E.A. Bryan; and *Rose O'Neill,* a play on the Ulster
Plantation by Wilson Guy.

Programme Director John Sutthery, an Englishman, gave an interview to the
radio correspondent of the *Northern Whig* in October 1935. He made it clear
he did not approve of poetry and plays from England being read by Northern
Ireland artists – 'They are none of them accentless, to my ear' – and he
deplored the typical Ulster kitchen comedy:

When I first came to Belfast and read the so-called radio plays, which
were submitted to this station, I was amazed. I wondered if such characters really existed and thought how unpleasant a province this must
be, since they appeared in every play. Now I have come to realise that
these types are simply a convention, though why on earth such a convention ever obtained is more than I can understand. I do wish that
playwrights would get out of the rut. At first I wondered if they ever
would, it was so difficult to teach them anything of the requirements of
radio drama. Now I am becoming a little more hopeful . . .

A lively correspondence arising out of this interview ensued in the *Northern
Whig* and partly as a riposte to Sutthery, W.F. Marshall rewrote most of
Shakespeare's *Midsummer Night's Dream* in a Tyrone dialect and this was broadcast to an appreciative audience in June 1936. A few months later, however, the
rigorous report prepared in 1936 by Charles Siepmann recommended
that Belfast abandon wireless drama productions altogether:

> DRAMA There has been a considerable output in the past but the stan-
> dard has been poor and a small coterie of artists has been run to death.
> There is not much distinctive local material to exploit. A certain
> amount of kitchen comedy is available and popular but there are lim-
> its to its use. There is no repertory company equivalent to those work-
> ing in the North and in the Midlands. The Ulster Players were once
> good but are no longer so. There are a good many amateur societies
> but their performances are at such a crude level of efficiency as to be
> of little value to us . . . While ninety-two players were in fact used last
> year, it was freely admitted that not ten of them even approximated to
> the standard of London expectations. There are a few playwrights, very
> few. The most promising of these, as I understand, has recently thrown
> his hand in, not finding the inducements of our fees alluring.

Later in the report he added that 'the standards of performance and the
quality of the plays hardly seems justified as an indispensable contribution to regional culture'. He did, however, leave the final decision
on the fate of the drama department to the Regional Director.
Siepmann's recommendation that there should be more features and
talks led to the appointment of Denis Johnston as a scriptwriter and
researcher. Johnston had won acclaim as a dramatist in Dublin with plays such
as *The Old Lady Says No* and *The Moon in the Yellow River,* and his arrival in
Belfast gave an immediate fillip to drama output from Belfast. The range and
quality of productions increased under his influence and more plays were taken
by London, including Rowley's *Apollo in Mourne,* with the main character
played by Micheál Mac Liammóir of Dublin's Gate Theatre, *Cathleen ni
Houlihan* by Yeats, and Synge's *Riders to the Sea,* presented by the Abbey Theatre,
Not One Returns To Tell by Denis Johnston, and *In the Train* by Frank O'Connor,
adapted by Hugh Hunt and Johnston.

   Johnston became a BBC war correspondent in 1939 but the stimulus he had
given was still being felt in the drama department when regional broadcasting

Micheál Mac Liammóir from the
Gate Theatre who played Apollo in
Richard Rowley's play *Apollo in
Mourne,* broadcast in 1938.

BBC NI

resumed in 1945. A competition was announced for original plays and by August 1946 132 scripts had been received. The 1947 Year Book observed: 'In view of the controversy about the representative play being invariably set in a farm kitchen it was interesting to find that a good half of the plays submitted were much more broadly conceived.' The first prize was awarded to Graeme Roberts – already well known to listeners – and the second to Janet McNeill.

James Mageean, who had first performed in the Belfast station's first radio play in 1924, had been appointed drama producer in 1939 and he continued in that position until 1951. A play was broadcast almost every week. Many of these were by writers who had established themselves before the war and included St John Ervine's *Friends and Relations,* performed by the Ulster Group Theatre Company, *The Passing Day* by George Shiels, and *Light Falling* by Teresa Deevy. Mageean also succeeded in encouraging the new talent revealed by his competition: in 1947 Janet McNeill inaugurated a prolific period of writing for radio with her play *The Dear Ruin* and in the same year Joseph Tomelty's acute ear for ordinary urban speech was reflected in his play *Straw in the Storm.*

Not everyone welcomed the realism which characterised BBC drama after the war. 'BBC'S "SORDID" PLAYS – CRITICISM BY BELFAST ROTARIAN', ran a headline in the *Belfast News Letter* on 25 October 1949 and the report continued:

> Complaints that the BBC was broadcasting 'tragic and sordid plays of unhappy married life' during the great family listening time of *Saturday Night Theatre* were made by Mr. Robert Bell, past-president of the Belfast Rotary Club yesterday. He said he hoped that the BBC would get back to plays of the high standard with which the series had started. 'The answer might be to produce the type of plays we want in our own region,' he added.

Much of the regional drama output would have been very satisfying to Mr Bell and, indeed, while he was giving his speech, *Saturday Night Theatre* was broadcasting St John Ervine's *Boyd's Shop*: the cast from the Ulster Group Theatre Company included Elizabeth Begley as Agnes Boyd, R.H. McCandless as Andrew Boyd, Joseph Tomelty as the Reverend E. Dunwoody and J.F. Tyrone as John Haslett. This elicited an appreciative review from the *Belfast News Letter* critic, who observed, nevertheless, 'I have doubts if the

This photograph of Joseph Tomelty was taken in 1947 when he was already a prolific broadcaster. One of the most talented artists of his day, he was a leading actor at the Ulster Group Theatre and a writer of short stories for the BBC Home Service. Two years later he became one of the best-known figures in Northern Ireland following the dazzling success of *The McCooeys.*

BBC NI

subtleties of the dialogue would get across to English listeners.' Other new plays would, no doubt, have disturbed the Rotarian, particularly those by Janet McNeill, such as *A Child in the House* and *Search Party*, which exposed the tensions which could shake the stability of middle-class family life, and plays by John D. Stewart, which explored the hypocrisies and parochial narrowness of Ulster society. Bitterness and religious intolerance were more directly confronted in a powerful and innovative verse play by John Hewitt, *The Bloody Brae*. Brian Friel, to become the finest Ulster dramatist of his generation, made his radio début with his play, *A Sort of Freedom*.

By the late 1950s Northern Ireland Region had completely vindicated Marshall's decision not to close down the drama department in Belfast, as Siepmann had recommended in 1936. Northern Ireland's expertise in radio drama remained unquestioned in the ensuing decades. The BBC's network stations regularly took Belfast productions, such as Brendan Behan's *The Quare Fellow*, for *Monday Night Theatre* on the Home Service, J.P. McCrory's *The Sea Goat* for *Saturday Afternoon Theatre* on BBC RADIO 2, and *The Fleas and Mr Morgan* by Martin Waddell for *Midweek Theatre* also on BBC RADIO 2. The region was slow to make television plays and this was understandable. Television drama is, with some rare exceptions, the most expensive form of programme-making and in a part of the United Kingdom with a population of less than one and a half million it was difficult to justify the cost of production unless the plays would be transmitted on network.

The Last Hero, a play for broadcasting by Donagh MacDonagh, produced in Belfast for the BBC Home Service and broadcast on 12 October 1953. *Deirdre of the Sorrows*, the beauty jealously guarded by King Conor of Ulster, is played here by Siobhán McKenna and Naoise, her lover, by John Glen.

BBC NI

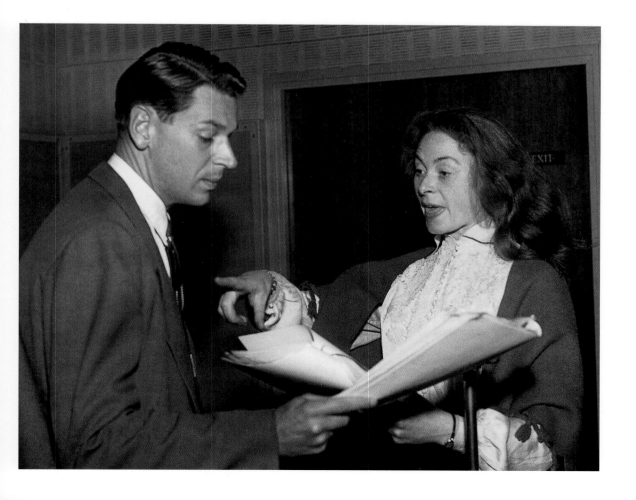

Ronald Mason directing
Tom Fleming in *The Enemy Within*.
Mason presided over the drama
department for many years and was
responsible for an impressive flow of
radio plays for network.

BBC NI

There was no television drama from Belfast until the middle of the 1970s. A few plays about Northern Ireland were produced in the 1960s, both by the BBC and Independent Television networks. Sam Thompson, a former shipyard worker and painter for the Belfast Corporation, had caused a furore with his stage play, *Over the Bridge,* written with the encouragement of the BBC features producer Sam Hanna Bell, and this direct assault on sectarianism was screened by Granada in 1961. The BBC in London produced another Thompson play, *Cemented with Love,* in 1965 and in the same year it broadcast probably the most powerful and far-seeing drama of the decade on Northern Ireland, *Progress to the Park* by Alun Owen, a writer who did not share Thompson's view that working-class solidarity would in time dissipate religious and political antipathies. Owen's play is located not in Northern Ireland but in Liverpool, and Teifion, the Welsh-Liverpudlian, observes that the Irish in the city 'are the best Catholics, the best Protestants and the worst Christians in the world'.

For most network viewers Northern Ireland was a little known backwater until, suddenly, it was projected centre stage by its turbulence and ensuing violence. Despite the obvious wealth of dramatic raw material daily made available to the playwright, the networks initially were somewhat nervous about authorising productions on such a volatile topic. Screened in October 1972, the BBC's first play since 1965 was *Carson Country* by Dominic Behan, on the Ulster campaign against Home Rule led by Sir Edward Carson. Senior staff in Belfast were sent the script beforehand and asked for their comments. Drama producer Ronald Mason observed:

> The induction ceremony still gives me some cause for concern . . . the author and his associations in the minds of the Protestant section of the audience will be enough to trigger off a considerable number of phone calls from the vociferous fringe . . . the extremists who feel affronted by the play *might* go so far as to stage a demonstration outside BH . . .

Cecil Taylor's judgement was unequivocal: 'It is an extremely bad play. The dialogue is an endless stream of clichés, the main characters are caricatures, and the situations are hackneyed . . .' He anticipated 'resolutions of protest from the lunatic Protestant fringe claiming that we have done a disservice to Carson's memory'. It *was* an extremely bad play and that might explain why the protests were less alarming than Broadcasting House expected.

Martin Dillon, the energetic BBC producer in Belfast who could claim that *Talk Back* was his brainchild and who wrote gripping books on the Shankill Butchers and other particularly grim features of the Troubles, wrote the script for *The Squad,* a thirty-minute drama shown on *Centre Play Showhouse* on BBC TWO in 1976. This was the region's first tentative step towards producing television drama for the network. It dealt with the viciousness which intense passions and violence in Northern Ireland make possible. Jill Weekes made this observation in her *Television Today* review: 'The problem of linking the atrocities in Belfast to ordinary human beings is probably insurmountable since it remains impossible to believe that ordinary sane people could generate such chaos.'

People living in the eye of the storm, however, were all too aware that ordinary human beings were often deeply involved in generating the chaos. The first full-length network drama from the region, Stewart Parker's *Catchpenny Twist,* a comedy with music which reflected the anguish of the conflict in Northern Ireland, was broadcast in December 1977. Equally at home on the stage, on radio and on television, Parker was one of the most innovative and prolific of contemporary playwrights. He wrote seven plays for radio and one of these, *The Kamikaze Ground Staff Reunion Dinner,* which won the Giles Cooper Radio Drama Award, was the *Play for Today* in February 1981. His bitingly funny *Radio Pictures* – a caustic behind-the-scenes play about radio drama production – was broadcast in 1985. Parker's *Iris in the Traffic* and *Ruby in the Rain* were both produced for *Play for Today* in November 1981, and his stage success, *Pentecost,* was screened on *Theatre Night* in July 1990, two years after his death at the age of forty-seven.

BBC Northern Ireland had to compete with other regions, as well as the

network itself, for the resources for drama production. The most important criterion was quality and during the final two decades of the twentieth century it was clear that London had developed a strong appreciation of Belfast's professional expertise in this area. Other early productions made by the region for network transmission included: *Bought and Sold* by David Hammond, directed by Bill Miskelly, with music by Paul Brady (February 1980); *My Dear Palestrina* by Bernard MacLaverty, set in provincial Ulster in the 1950s, with memorable performances by Eleanor Bron as the piano teacher and Ronan Downey as the young boy (December 1980); and *Cowboys,* a charming thirty-minute play by actor Harry Towb, based on his memories of childhood in Belfast (October 1981).

The breakthrough for television drama production in the region was *Too Late to Talk to Billy*, broadcast as the *Play for Today* in February 1982. The script was by Graham Reid, a former soldier, hospital worker, mature student and teacher, who had four successful plays staged in Dublin. Reid's first play, *The Death of Humpty Dumpty*, quickly established him as a writer with a distinctive voice. *Too Late to Talk to Billy* is set in the Protestant Donegall Road area of Belfast and concerns a lively and passionate family, the Martins. Norman, the father, cannot forgive his wife Janet for a past love affair and his refusal to visit her while she is dying in the City Hospital causes unhappiness to the four children. The play is about the shifting relationships within a family against the background of an area of the city where there is a visible Ulster Defence Association presence in the streets. The play is not directly about the Northern Ireland conflict: the Martins are simply too wrapped up in their private problems to think about the public Troubles outside. They are fragmented not by sectarian differences but by wounded, inarticulate love.

The director, Paul Seed, and the producers, Neil Zeiger and Chris Parr, went to extraordinary lengths to assemble a cast. Two young schoolgirls, Tracey Lynch and Áine Gorman, were 'discovered' as actresses after many auditions among young hopefuls, chosen from no fewer than 650 Belfast girls who wrote in to be considered for the parts. This play launched Kenneth Branagh on his career: he had moved from Belfast to Reading at the age of nine and was still a student at RADA when he was chosen to play the part of Billy. James Ellis, the Group Theatre veteran who two decades earlier had become familiar in every British household as Sergeant Bert Lynch in *Z Cars*, had a key role as the father; Brid Brennan played the oldest sister Lorna, who holds the family together; Mary Jackson was Billy's girlfriend, June; and Maggie Shevlin played the mother.

Stewart Parker a prolific writer of radio and television dramas, many of which were broadcast on network. He had a penchant for unusual titles including *The Kamikaze Ground Staff Reunion Dinner*, a well-received play on BBC RADIO 4.

BBC NI

No previous BBC drama made such a powerful impact on the viewing public as *Too Late to Talk to Billy*. The switchboard was jammed with calls. Typical of the many letters Reid received was this one from a woman in Shropshire:

> I thought it was really marvellous. It was incredibly real, your portrayal of the family was utterly convincing and full of strength. The atmosphere was perfect, too – the misty quality of being out in the streets, along the alley-ways, the friendliness and loneliness, the fear of alien forces lurking; then the feeling of despair hanging heavily in the hospital. The play had a deep effect on me.

An Englishman living in Portstewart, County Londonderry, dashed off this note: 'What can I say except – BLOODY MARVELLOUS – A REALLY WONDERFUL

James Ellis plays the father
Norman, and Kenneth Branagh is Billy
in *Too late to talk to Billy*.

PLAY — *FIRST* CLASS ACTING! . . . BLOODY GREAT IT WAS! P.S. This is my first letter ever to the B.B.C. or any T.V./radio/media for that matter.' 'Our living room
carpet is still wet with tears,' the novelist and playwright Maurice Leitch wrote.
The critics were generous with their praise: Chris Dunkley in the *Financial
Times* felt that it was 'a hugely powerful work . . . almost Lear-like in the inten-
sity and bleakness of its gaze'; Sean Day-Lewis described it as 'a powerfully
dramatic debut by Mr Reid' and referred to 'the touching performances';
Dennis Hackett in *The Times* found it 'as bruising a drama as I have seen:
unremitting gloom punctuated by violence and the sound of parting family
relationships'; and in the *Guardian* Nancy Banks-Smith thought the play 'had
great native vigour and a cracking part for Norman'.

Inevitably there were those viewers in Northern Ireland who were embar-
rassed by this gritty urban drama. A correspondent from Bangor, County
Down, wrote:

> Imagine my embarrassment and disgust when, on hearing the first few
> statements made on that programme, I had to switch off because of the
> filthy language used. If this is typical of a Belfast based programme please
> will you refrain from further degrading our beloved Province. I think
> we are entitled to more wholesome viewing — and without vulgar
> language.

Another viewer wrote: 'The language was crude, foul and atrocious . . . this type of play should be banned completely by the BBC and to allow young children to be involved in sordid plays of this nature is surely most degrading.' Though the Troubles had long familiarised viewers and listeners in the rest of the United Kingdom with the Ulster accent and dialect, local productions still proved problematic for some, particularly in radio and television drama. Hackett remarked about the play: 'The gritty, nasal Ulster accent gave it moments of inevitable incomprehensibility', and Banks-Smith observed:

> I should warn you it is not altogether safe to call him Norman on a Saturday night. 'Don't jew Norman me or I'll put your heid through that wall, jew and ya bloody Da'. (trans: 'call me Mr Martin').
>
> *Too Late to Talk to Billy* was like being stuck in a lift with W.D. Flackes, the BBC's durable Northern Ireland correspondent. After a while you get the tune of the voice but the lyrics seem to escape you.

Too late to talk to Billy, screened as *Play for Today* in February 1982, was acclaimed by viewers and critics alike. Written by Graham Reid, directed by Paul Seed and produced by Chris Parr, the play was about the shifting relationships within a family against a background of an area of Belfast in 1977 where there is a visible UDA presence. Billy was played by Kenneth Branagh (his first television role); Brid Brennan (centre) was his eldest sister Lorna who holds the family together; and Áine Gorman is the youngest sister, Maureen.
BBC NI

The public demanded more and got it. Two sequels followed: *A Matter of Choice for Billy* in May 1983 and *A Coming to Terms for Billy* in February 1984, which gave a splendid vehicle for the talents of Mark Mulholland, a regular radio drama actor, as Uncle Andy. Other Reid plays made by BBC Northern Ireland included *Lorna* in June 1987 and *Life after Life* in April 1995.

Writing in the September 1988 issue of *Broadcast,* in a debate with Graham Reid entitled 'Drama out of a Crisis', the journalist, critic and broadcaster Eamonn McCann felt that most television drama on the Northern Ireland crisis took the view that 'it's a terrible pity what's happening over there and if only the ordinary, decent people on both sides could get together' the problem would be solved. 'Since television drama must by its nature personalise issues,' he continued, 'the standard theme, upon which variations are played, is of personal relationships being ripped apart by the sectarian divide . . .' Reid responded: 'Whatever subject I tackle, I will do so through human beings and through human relationships.' 'In Northern Ireland there is no solution as such,' he continued. 'There is a need for toleration.' Not only must solutions not be offered but also the writer must not take sides for fear of reinforcing prejudices – 'a soapbox is not a very edifying visual image'.

In stark contrast to the 'Billy' plays, BBC Northern Ireland's *Elephant,* broadcast in January 1989, offered a very much bleaker view of the Troubles. The play was based on proposals and ideas put forward by Chris Ryder and Bill Morrison to Alan Clarke to dramatise the relentlessness of killing in Northern Ireland. There was no script at all. Notes given to the production team and actors included:

> The all too familiar pattern of sectarian murders in Northern Ireland is the starting point for this film. Through a series of fictional murders, the film builds an impression of the tragedy each one contains and the terrible regularity of their occurrence here. There will be no attempt to excite or thrill but to genuinely frighten and stir pity – to be truly cathartic . . .

There would be no analysis of why there were twelve steel drawers in cabinets containing files of those who had been killed – the objective was to concentrate on 'the simple cost of the most dehumanising of all acts'. The film was to show just one murder after another. A sergeant at the RUC headquarters at Knock received a props list from the production manager of 'blank firing, fully practical replica weapons as follows':

> 2 x F/P 9mm Browning Pistols
> 2 x F/P Ruger Revolvers (RUC issue type or similar)
> 1 x F/P 'Sawn-Off' Shotgun, DB, 12 Gauge
> 1 x F/P Smith & Wesson 38 Calibre Revolver 4" Barrel
> 1 x F/P Smith & Wesson 38 Calibre Revolver 2" snub nose Barrel

Locations included the Ormeau Swimming Baths, Malone Avenue, Lagan Valley Regional Park, a workshop, a toilet, Sicily Park, a café, Sans Souci

Park, a football pitch, a warehouse yard, a petrol station, the BBC car park, and Dunluce Avenue. Letters had to be sent out, beginning 'Dear Resident' and continuing: 'Please do not be alarmed by what may sound like intermittent gunfire – it's simply a tightly controlled special effects section of the filming . . .'

The provisional title *Victims* was dropped in favour of *Elephant* a reference to the Ulster epigram that you can no more ignore the Troubles than you can ignore an elephant in your living room. This, to Clarke, was the truth, in contrast to the observation he often heard that you can live in Belfast and hardly notice the violence. The viewer saw a man walking down a street, up stairs and down the corridors of the swimming baths to a cubicle where a cleaner was mopping the floor. He reached into his pocket and shot the cleaner dead. Blood marked the bath into which the mop fell. This was not the beginning of a story but the first of a series of killings through the forty-minute film. Only four sentences were spoken in the entire play: when someone was asked two questions and gave replies before being shot. There was no indication who was shooting whom, what sides the killers and victims were on, or what their religious affiliations were.

After transmission, the BBC received an unprecedented number of critical and outraged calls for a programme of this type. It was clear that the drama was too demanding, too avant-garde, for a majority of the viewing public at the time. A minority, however, were deeply impressed and in retrospect *Elephant* was perhaps the most innovative and most powerful television play ever made by the BBC in Northern Ireland. Danny Boyle later was to win greater fame as a director of films including *Shallow Grave*, *Trainspotting* and *The Beach*. Mark Lawson, in his thoughtful review for the *Independent*, observed:

> Elephant (BBC 2), directed by Alan Clarke, was shot in Belfast, as indeed was every one of the cast, repeatedly, wordlessly, dullingly on a loop of cruelty . . . the complete business of the 40 minute play was – and if you did not see it, you will not believe it – people being shot. There were no characters, no plot. It was like a greatest hits for assassins, a hole of the season for terrorists. It was what you might call a silent tragedy . . . if you took his picture literally, you would have to believe that Belfast is like Chicago in Capone's day but the round-dance of death was making the point that the Troubles do not become unremarkable. They are an elephant in your parlour.
>
> There was something elephantine about the way this fact was established. It is, after all, quite a thin point to make. If writers and directors have any business in this jungle at all, it is in telling you how the elephant got there and how it might be removed.
>
> Some tiny political mind somewhere will doubtless be complaining that the play was excessively violent but the argument against killing on television is that it glamorises and sanitises the act and this Clarke precisely did not do. You were shown in elaborate and emetic detail the consequences of one human firing a bullet into another. It might have told you nothing, but in its bleak conception and professional execution

– you rarely heard a word for sound but the recordist Peter Lindsay has provided a track of frightening silence randomly shattered – *Elephant* was hard to forget.

If one person can claim responsibility for the region's phenomenal success in drama in the final decades of the twentieth century it is Robert Cooper. He began as a radio drama producer in the 1970s and soon displayed a flair for finding and nurturing writing talent. He firmly believed that quality of writing was what mattered most, and that radio and television drama could be adapted from short stories, novels and stage plays, as well as from scripts written specifically for broadcast. For example, he persuaded William Trevor to adapt his short story *Beyond the Pale* for radio drama and years later turned it into a television play using exactly the same cast – his first television production.

The creation of the 'internal market', by which regions bid for commissions rather than depend on annual subventions, at first caused consternation in Belfast. 'Northern Ireland will never make a television drama again' was a phrase heard more than once in the corridors of Broadcasting House. Cooper was adamant that this would not happen – the region already had shown its particular expertise in this field. He focused on what the Controllers were asking for: increasingly this was for serials rather than single dramas. An early successful commission – the first with a budget over one million pounds – was *Murder in Eden,* the first serial produced for BBC ONE by the region. This black comedy was a memorable production, with Tony Doyle in the lead and Tina

Prunella Scales, Robert Lang and Ronald Hines in *Beyond The Pale* by William Trevor and directed by Diarmuid Lawrence.

BBC NI

Kelleher in her first television role. Cooper enjoyed the wholehearted backing of his superiors – 'You represent Northern Ireland in drama,' Robin Walsh told him, and Pat Loughery, both as Head of Programmes and as Controller, was particularly assiduous in fostering the making of television drama by the region for network.

From the 1980s onwards, independent companies, apart from producing the occasional thriller located in Northern Ireland, tended to shy away from producing single plays because of the high costs involved. In 1983 the BBC calculated that a play cost around £170,000 an hour to produce and that, while drama accounted for only 6 per cent of output, it absorbed 24 per cent of the annual budget. The golden age of the single play was passing and giving way to the television film. The BBC none the less adhered to its position as a public broadcaster and felt a responsibility to nurture new talent in this area. The challenge for the Northern Ireland Region was to persuade the decision-makers in London to make drama about Northern Ireland for national audiences, when other network companies were cautious about alienating 'mainland' audiences weary of a constant stream of reports of explosions, murders and political initiatives running into the sand. The only way for the region to win drama contracts was to prove that its production and technical teams could find writers of high calibre and create plays of the quality expected in the best-known broadcasting organisation in the world. This became a priority for James Hawthorne when he became Controller in 1978, though he acknowledged that Cecil Taylor, Head of Programmes, 'did the leg work'.

Sophie Ward in
Events of Drimaghleen (1991)

BBC NI

The fact that Northern Ireland, the smallest 'national' region, has been able to gain such a large share of drama production demonstrates a recognition of accumulated expertise and flair. The most ambitious drama project before *Ballykissangel* was Graham Reid's series of six one-hour plays – *McCabe's Wall, Out of Tune, Going Home, Attachments, Invitation to a Party*, and *The Military Wing* – collectively entitled *Ties of Blood*, broadcast in November and December 1985. There were many successful adaptations, including: *Shadows on Our Skins* (1980) and *How Many Miles to Babylon?* (1982) by Jennifer Johnston, adapted by Derek Mahon; *Guests of the Nation* (1983) by Frank O'Connor, adapted by Maurice Leitch; *Aunt Suzanne* (1984) by Michael McLaverty, adapted by Stewart Love; and *Murder in Eden* (1991) by Shane Connaughton, adapted from *Bogmail* by Patrick McGinley. William Trevor adapted some of his stories for the small screen including *One of Ourselves, August Saturday* and *Events at Drimaghleen*. Anne Devlin won the 1985 Samuel Beckett Award for best first play for television for *A Woman Calling* (1984) and went on to write more plays, including *The Long March* (1984), *Naming the Names* (1987) and *The Venus De Milo Instead* (1987).

The 1980s had witnessed a severe reduction in staff across the regions. One consequence was that many who had learned their trade in the BBC set themselves up as independents and other media and film companies emerged to seek commissions from the corporation. Pearse Moore, from Raw Nerve Productions at the Nerve Centre in Derry, produced *Dance Lexie Dance*, one of a series of short films funded by a consortium made up of BBC Northern Ireland, the Northern Ireland Film Council, the British Film Institute and the National Lottery Fund administered by the Arts Council of Northern Ireland.

Shot on location in and around Derry, it is the story of how one man's lonely life is transformed by the simple wisdom of a child. Lexie (B.J. Hogg) and his ten-year-old daughter Laura (Kimberley McConkey) live in an isolated corner of the shoreline of Lough Foyle. Father and daughter have little communication because he works all night at the power station. Then, out of the blue, Laura confesses her dream of becoming a Riverdancer. Lexie seizes this opportunity, and despite his clumsy efforts, he helps her to learn Irish dancing and brings her to the feis. Through the simple fun they have, Lexie learns to laugh again. Directed by Tim Loane and sensitively scripted by Dave Duggan, the film was screened on BBC ONE in December 1996 and was subsequently given an Oscar nomination.

Apart from adaptations, most of the new work continued to feature the Troubles but merely as a backdrop. Martin McLoone, in *Broadcasting in a Divided Community*, subjected television drama about Northern Ireland to a searching and perspicacious analysis. He concluded that the better-received and better-written dramas largely echoed 'O'Casey's humanist anguish about the absurdity of the violence', where concern is generally with the characters rather than with the conflict, which intrudes. In short, he wished that more writers would 'get closer to those (often unpleasant) political realities which lie at the heart of the Northern Ireland problem', and he continued:

> The best drama, to my mind, is that which has come closest to probing, not the tragic circumstances for the 'Romeos and Juliets' of the world, but rather why the Capulets and Montagues are 'at variance' in the first place.

Elizabeth Bourgine in *Love Lies Bleeding* (1993), a powerful drama set in Belfast, which explored differences within the Republican movement and the early days of the current peace process.

BBC NI

Love Lies Bleeding, a 1993 screenplay written by Ronan Bennett, produced by Robert Cooper and directed by Michael Winterbottom, was well received – a response that seemed to indicate that audiences were becoming more used to violent dramas about the Troubles. There were anxieties that the play would be perceived as being much too sympathetic to the IRA, but these were unfounded, mainly because the last scene is of a bloody massacre of hardliners by those in search of a peace process. Primarily a thriller, though unlike Yorkshire Television's *Harry's Game* (1982) and others of the genre, *Love Lies Bleeding* did make some attempt at political exploration. Many aspiring playwrights sought to write about Northern Ireland in a dark way, which was not the kind of drama that had most appeal for British audiences. Cooper recognised that some very fine writing talent was to be found south of the border and increasingly the region set its drama productions in the Irish Republic. *Runway One* was a four-part espionage serial inspired by Irangate, set in Shannon airport, and written by Barry Devlin, the former bass player in the popular group Horslips.

The region secured over thirty hours of television drama commissions for BBC ONE and BBC TWO in 1994–5, a 230 per cent increase on the previous year. Six productions, costing ten million pounds in total, were made in 1994. In getting the green light to make popular drama series, Northern Ireland was clearly beginning to succeed in a highly competitive field. The first was *The Hanging Gale,* a four-million-pound, four-part costume drama which marked the 150th anniversary of the Irish Famine. The series captured audiences of up to ten million and its success did much to help Robert Cooper and his team win the contract to make *Ballykissangel.*

Bus companies in Dublin used to run tours for visitors to 'The Meeting of the Waters' and 'The Vale of Avoca and Glendalough': now the vehicles lined up in Nassau Street, destined for the same County Wicklow beauty spots, simply display 'Ballykissangel' in large letters on their front windows. Around fifteen million viewers watched each episode. Newspapers began to devote as much space to the characters and the actors as they did to those in *EastEnders* and *Coronation Street.* The real life romance between Dervla Kirwan, who played bar owner Assumpta Fitzgerald, and Stephen Tompkinson, the English priest, was followed with intense interest. Millions wept at the death of Assumpta in Father Clifford's arms. The sudden death in January 2000 of Tony Doyle was a hammer blow: he played Quigley, a likable rogue with an eye always on the main chance. The scriptwriter, Kieran Prendiville (author of *Vicious Circle* and *Roughnecks*), had Tony Doyle first in mind as the character around whom his story line was created. Dervla Kirwin and Stephen Tompkinson moved on but other talented actors were recruited, including Lorcan Cranitch and Victoria Smurfit, and a sixth series was being filmed in the spring of 2000. The cast very quickly felt themselves becoming a family unit on location every spring in Avoca – in spite of the arrival of new characters – and this seemed to come over to the viewers. By February 2000 the series had been sold to seventeen countries and was being reported as the most popular programme in Philadelphia and Chicago.

The BBC Northern Ireland Drama Department steadily became more prolific as the millennium drew to a close. By the summer of 1999 it had collected twenty-eight major awards from over fifty international festivals since 1990 and had over forty series, serials, films and single dramas in development.

Kimberley McConkey as the ten-year-old Laura in *Dance Lexie Dance*, a low budget film made by Raw Nerve Productions and screened on BBC ONE in December 1996. The simple story of how Laura transforms the lonely life of her father, B.J. Hogg, by taking up Irish dancing is deftly told and with great charm. *Dance Lexie Dance* was shortlisted for an Oscar.

BBC NI

The Englishman's Wife with Adrian Dunbar and Imelda Staunton (1989).

BBC NI

Stephen Tompkinson and Dervla Kirwan from *Ballykissangel*.

BBC NI

Henri, starring the young Kara Bowman, won three international awards in 1994–5. Graham Reid remained a stalwart supplier of scripts, which included *The Precious Blood* – which portrayed the consequences of the Troubles for two Belfast families – in 1996, and *Six into Twenty-six*, in 1997. Other critically acclaimed productions included: the Sunday evening period drama serial, *Falling for a Dancer*, starring Elisabeth Dermot Walsh and Liam Cunningham, which won a Golden Gate Award at San Francisco in 1999; *Vicious Circle*, in which Ken Stott gave a powerful performance as The General, the most notorious gangster in Dublin's history; *A Rap at the Door*, a courageous drama about 'the disappeared' (Troubles victims whose bodies have never been found) by Pearse Elliott; *Ambassador*, a series in which Pauline Collins played the British ambassador in Dublin; and *A Man of No Importance*, starring Albert Finney as the Dublin bus conductor who wanted to be Oscar Wilde, with Tara Fitzgerald as co-star. Tony Doyle's last great role – which won him an award at the 39th Monte Carlo Film Festival – was as the domineering, pious and disappointed father in *Amongst Women,* adapted from John McGahern's novel. Set in Roscommon in the 1950s, *Amongst Women* was one of the most accomplished productions of the drama department and was one of several in which RTÉ was a partner, albeit a junior one.

The 1994 ceasefires, the growth of the Celtic Tiger, the peace process and – despite the horror of the 1998 Omagh bomb and the unrest surrounding contentious parades – the reduction in violence, led to some fresh thinking on how Northern Ireland and its discontents should be portrayed in television drama. The Belfast novelist Robert McLiam Wilson considered the question in a challenging article in the *Observer* on 12 September 1999:

The Northern Ireland story has committed the cardinal sin of going on too long . . . The ceasefires, the various accords and agreements have failed to form a last chapter. In narrative terms, this is bad news. It's a dreadful pity. For a surprisingly long time, the story was a good one. It was like an all-white title fight on the edge of Europe. The atrocities seemed more shocking, the bad guys were badder, the blood redder. After the first fifteen years, however, it became monotonous. The phrase 'more violence in Belfast today' became as startling and resonant as '*Titanic* still sunk' . . .

All our dramas seem to feature an ex-IRA man with a troubled conscience trying to build some kind of future for himself . . . as representations of the Northern Ireland experience, however, these dramas are disgraceful failures. We have many more window-cleaners here than we

The cast of *Ballykissangel*, the BBC ONE drama on Sunday nights made by BBC Northern Ireland. In the centre is the late Tony Doyle and on the right the late Birdy Sweeney.
BBC NI

Falling for a Dancer, starring Elisabeth Dermot Walsh, Colin Farrell and Liam Cunningham, won the Mini-Series Television Film Festival Golden Gate Award at the 1999 San Francisco International Film Festival.

BBC NI

Tony Doyle playing the irascible and disillusioned former IRA volunteer and farmer, Moran, and his patient and caring second wife, Ger Ryan, in the 1998 dramatisation for network of John McGahern's powerful novel, *Amongst Women*, set in the Irish Midlands in the 1950s.

BBC NI

have IRA men, but you are unlikely to see any films about former window-cleaners with consciences. There are honourable exceptions, of course. Alan Clarke's *Elephant* was an extraordinary piece of drama by any standards. Stewart Parker (*Ruby in the Traffic, Iris in the Rain*) was a distinguished screenwriter and dramatist, and Graham Reid has often produced good work.

He singled out dramas that make the Northern Irish 'cringe with dismay', in which the 'actors are often English, the exteriors are often filmed in Leeds and Manchester'.

Wilson's own remarkable novel *Eureka Street,* described by Simon Hoggart as 'funny, savage, brutal, satirical, ironic and exciting by turns', was adapted into a four-part series by Donna Franceschild in 1999. This drama certainly looked at Belfast and its discontents with an entirely different eye. The two main characters were the antiheroes Chuckie (played by Mark Benton), an overweight Protestant who dreams of wealth and beautiful women and who realises on his thirtieth birthday that he has achieved nothing, and the handsome Jake (played by Vincent Regan), who as a member of a 'debt counselling' team repossesses furniture and washing machines in north Belfast with fiercely loyalist colleagues and keeps the fact that he is a Catholic quiet. Chuckie gets rich by selling non-existent sex aids for £9.99 each and then sends back cheques marked 'Giant Dildo Refund' knowing that few will be cashed. He goes on to get a large sum from the 'Ulster Development Board' to set up a chain of ecumenical cafés in Paris selling potato lasagne and succeeds in bedding the gorgeous American, Max (played by Elisabeth Röhm). A hilarious highlight was a republican poetry reading, during which verses entitled 'From a Sniper to a British Soldier about to Die' is read in Irish; the drunken Jake breaks up the reading and is rescued with difficulty. Here he meets a middle-class and sanctimonious IRA apologist, Aoirghe – 'that's not a name, it's a cough,' Jake remarks – and embarks on a relationship with her. Aoirghe, brilliantly played by Dervla Kirwan, portrayed a woman very different from Assumpta in *Ballykissangel*. Other memorable roles in *Eureka Street* were those played by Des McAleer, the repo man who dreams of a neutron bomb which will only eliminate Catholics, and Chuckie's mother, played by playwright/actor Marie Jones, who has a passionate scene in a bubble bath with her neighbour, played by former *Casualty* star Sorcha Cusack.

Of course *Eureka Street* strained credulity but it was innovative, fast-moving, tightly scripted and alternatively intensely comic and poignant. Liam Fay of the *Sunday Times* found that the production 'swaggers with brazen disdain for all the cosy conventions of the most disreputable of television genres, the hand-wringing Troubles opera'. The serial certainly showed Belfast as a lively city where people wanted, as elsewhere, to get by, to have fun and make love and it gave full dramatic expression to Wilson's view that we are responsible for our actions and that they are not forced on us by history. Not all viewers liked what they saw but it is worth observing that *Eureka Street*, for all its strong language, sex scenes and gritty realism, did not produce a tidal wave of outraged protest which might have been expected two decades earlier. The BBC Northern Ireland Drama Department undoubtedly had played its part in celebrating difference in the region and in dissolving much of its parochialism.

Eureka Street, a drama written by Robert McLiam Wilson and filmed in Belfast which starred Mark Benton as Chuckie.

BBC NI

6

MUSIC
AND THE ARTS

I N 1924 ARTHUR BURROWS, the BBC's Director of Programmes, sent the following instructions to the staff of 2BE:

> Experience shows that different localities have different musical interests. We have no data to work upon in the case of Belfast, but we imagine that a fairly light type of programme will be welcome. Your task, therefore, will be to provide a light type of entertainment, without departing from a high moral tone and good musical standard.

Godfrey Brown, the first recruit and the only person appointed with local knowledge, busied himself putting together the BBC Wireless Orchestra and in assembling singers. Director and conductor of the Belfast Philharmonic Society orchestra and choir, he was well placed to recruit players and other musical performers. He had little enough time to prepare a schedule, particularly as the main burden of providing 2BE's output would fall on his shoulders.

On the opening evening of the Belfast station in September 1924 the very first music played was the national anthem. Almost immediately afterwards the only people who could hear what was being played were the musicians themselves. Included in the evening's programme was Elgar's *Pomp and Circumstance*, Moore's 'Oft in the Stilly Night', and 'The Good Men of Eirinn' by Hughes. The *Evening Telegraph* in Dublin was full of praise:

> There was nothing at which even the highest brows could scoff. The performance of Mr Brown's very capable orchestra did full justice to the items chosen . . . Mr John Seeds, who sang songs by Hugh Wolf, Roger Quilter and others, has a mezzosoprano of fine quality and uses it with perfect judgement. Whatever the future of the Belfast Station may be, its opening experiment proved that listeners-in may confidently expect from its programme music, at least as good, and probably better, than from any of the other stations.

Not everyone shared this view. Brown recalled later:

> I met a friend in Donegall Place and said to him with no little pride in my voice, 'Well, what did you think of our programme last night?' He replied with typical Ulster candour, 'When it was on, it was rotten.' Looking back, I'm now prepared to believe he was not far wrong.

David Curry conducts the BBC Northern Ireland Light Orchestra.

BBC NI

John Vine conducting the Queen's Island Male Voice Choir in the very first 2BE broadcast in 1924.

BBC NI

Tyrone Guthrie, the announcer for the evening, observed in a recording made many years later:

> We had the comforting conviction that nobody much was listening and that it was mostly the cat's whisker department, you know, and that if they did listen they were so amazed and delighted to get anything it didn't much matter what they got so long as it was audible.
>
> Well, we were jolted out of that fairly soon! They wrote us *stinking* postcards to say how terrible we were and how ashamed we ought to be at the rubbish we were putting out. But we didn't pay too much attention.
>
> The great thing was that if you played any classical music, illiterate postcards came to say, 'Why do you play nothing but dirges?' and, if you played popular music, high-class postcards came to say, 'Why must you be so vulgar?'

'I have not yet met the listener who is in the least enthusiastic regarding the orchestral selections,' a letter signed 'Ordinary Listener' commented in the *Belfast News Letter*, and continued:

> They are usually described as 'morbid dope stuff' and 'deadly dreary'. These expressions have come from a score or more of otherwise wireless enthusiasts. In fact 'morbid' has been a byword when we see in the programme the all-too familiar terms andante, allegro, adagio and the 'Third Movement in B Flat', etc. These we might appreciate occasionally if we had not by experience learned to regard them as a symbol of monotony in so far as they appear in the Belfast programmes. Must the local orchestra confine itself to music of this nature as they often do for a whole evening?

Brown and his musicians must have been run ragged in the first few years, because the lines from Britain were so uncertain that most of the musical output had to be produced locally. Even then, when 'simultaneous broadcasts' were being taken from London, there were frequent technical faults which made it necessary for members of the orchestra to be on stand by. In memories jotted down for the twenty-fifth anniversary of the opening of the Belfast station, Brown recalled:

> There was always a good deal of uncertainty, and so it had to be that each member of the Orchestra was provided with a crystal set, and instructed to 'listen in' at 7 p.m. every day, and quite frequently they heard: 'Will the members of the Orchestra please come down to the Broadcasting Station as quickly as possible.'

Often enough the orchestra would be on the air only three-quarters of an hour after such a summons. Brown continued:

> On one occasion the 1st French Horn, not having a night off for some time, took his girl to the Hippodrome. A scene shifter up in the flies was listening to a crystal set, and heard a call for the Orchestra. It was an unusual one at 7 o'clock and asked that the public would assist in finding the Orchestra and so the stage hand informed the stage manager who made the announcement over the footlights. As it happened, the Horn player was one of the first to arrive!

The programme-makers packaged the musical fare as best they could. Early offerings, each lasting two hours, included *A Night of Gladness, A Night of Musical Contrast* and *A Dance Programme for Home Hoppers*. Very little of the musical output was distinctively Irish, let alone, Northern Irish, and established classical music predominated. After listening for several years to the station's music, 'Rathcol', the *Belfast Telegraph*'s music critic, delivered this haughty denunciation of the popularisation of high culture:

> Are we going to go on accepting tamely all that these mighty pundits of superior English stock in the BBC devise for our souls' good? Music is no longer the cherished mistress of the connoisseur. It is now the

handmaid of the million. This is the age of wireless and gramophone Is the world better for it? Is there a real growth of music among the millions?

Such a fetish is this incessancy of music that one of the greatest cares of the BBC wiseheads is to avoid above all things an interval of silence. Music is being degraded by its widespreading. I hear the errand boy whistling a snatch of the Unfinished Symphony and murdering it in the act.

Music for the million is in plainer terms a travesty of music for the half-baked millions who have neither care nor reverence, the millions for whom quality and good taste are naught.

The BBC Wireless Orchestra in Belfast had a permanent membership of thirty – there was no permanent orchestra in Northern Ireland other than this one – but it was frequently augmented. The larger of the two studios in Linenhall Street could contain sixty players but, for example, when Sir Henry Wood came over to conduct the orchestra in the Ulster Hall in November 1928, the number was raised to eighty. The station's most frequent outside broadcasts were of concerts relayed from beyond the stifling atmosphere of the shrouded studio in places such as the Town Hall, Ballymena, and the Guildhall in Londonderry. Brown, who continued to be not only the BBC Director of Music but also conductor of the Belfast Philharmonic Society, organised five of the society's concerts between October 1928 and March 1929. A special symphony concert was given for the Ulster Summer School of Music organised annually by the Ministry of Education in the Great Hall of Queen's University. Broadcasts were arranged with choral societies in Lisburn, Tyrone and Fermanagh. Elgar's *The Kingdom* was performed before a congregation of 1,600 in St Anne's Cathedral on Good Friday, 1930. Amongst the distinguished men invited to conduct the Wireless Orchestra in the studio were: Sir Ivor Atkins of Worcester Cathedral; Sir Hamilton Harty, the illustrious composer who was a native of County Down; and Colonel Fritz Brase, former musical director of the Prussian Guard who had become Director of Music of the Irish Free State Army School of Music. Broadcast choral works included Bizet's *Carmen, A Sea Symphony* by Vaughan Williams, and Offenbach's *Genevieve de Brabant.*

In the autumn of 1930 the BBC made an arrangement with Herbert J. Ireland, the general secretary of the Belfast City YMCA, to pool their resources. A dozen concerts in the YMCA's Wellington Hall followed each Saturday night. The seating capacity was 1,500: reserved seats were 1s. 3d. each and the rest were held down at 6d. each. The concerts were triumphantly successful and on many occasions hundreds were turned away at the door. The series ended on 3 March 1931 when Sir Henry Wood conducted the orchestra before the Duke of Abercorn.

This success encouraged Belfast Corporation to make a similar arrangement – again on Saturday evenings with the same admission charges – for concerts to be broadcast from the Ulster Hall during April, May and June 1931. Wood was back again on 27 June and other guest conductors included the composer and critic, Norman Hay; Captain Brennan, the Belfast city organist; the Newcastle upon Tyne composer, Edgar Bainton; and Colonel Fritz Brase. Free concerts were put on for children in the Ulster Hall in collaboration with the Belfast Education Committee – a total of six thousand were brought to four performances. A rare broadcast of its kind was a concert on 2 April 1931 of selected prizewinners from the feis of St Colmcille in Derry. There was an 'Irish programme' on 8 September 1931, which included W.B. Yeats reading his own poetry and featured Sarah Allgood in *Irish Ballads* with the Wireless Orchestra. In 1932 there were 24 public broadcast concerts, 14 in the Ulster Hall and 10 in the Wellington Hall. The 1933 BBC Year Book declared:

> Sixpence and two and a half hour's entertainment by a symphony orchestra and famous soloists. The two seem, at first, irreconcilable; but co-operation between the BBC in Northern Ireland and a number of public bodies made the relation between them, in 1932, very popular . . . Among these perhaps the most interesting were John Ireland's new Pianoforte Concerto, and 'Morning Heroes', Arthur Bliss's Choral Symphony of War.

Bliss came over to conduct his own work and other conductors that year included Adrian Boult and Sir Henry Wood. In 1933 Elisabeth Schumann was the soprano in a concert of music by Vaughan Williams. The fare, no doubt, was considered overwhelmingly high brow by most listeners but the protests had eased somewhat and, after all, only 3 per cent of the people of Northern Ireland bought licences in 1931, compared with 15 per cent in London, 12 per cent in Berkshire and 15 per cent in Hertfordshire. The microphone was taken to Portrush, County Antrim, during the summer of 1932 to relay dance music and 'concert party' performances.

Technical hitches continued unexpectedly to cut off simultaneous broadcasts from London and members of the Wireless Orchestra were still expected to fill in at short notice. Henry McMullan, then News Editor, remembered:

> The orchestra in the early Thirties on its evening off would always be the evening when the lines went down. We had a system whereby slides were shown in local cinemas saying, 'Members of the Wireless Symphony Orchestra will report to the BBC.'
>
> And everybody got up and came back and started to play. I often wondered whether they played from memory or whether in those days – we didn't have a Music Library in the BBC – they played whatever music was set in front of them.

The orchestra gave free concerts every Wednesday afternoon from the autumn of 1930 onwards in the Belfast Museum and Art Gallery; the seating for four hundred overflowed into the corridors and adjoining rooms. Fitting the allotted programme slot exactly was not easy. McMullan recalled

> one occasion when they were playing in the Long Gallery in the Museum. The microphones were up, of course, and one of them was

fairly near the Conductor, Mr Godfrey Brown; and I suddenly realised they were running about seven minutes out and they were playing the *Blue Danube* waltz and they came to a triumphant conclusion and Godfrey Brown said to them, 'Play it again.' So they did play it twice again: that was broadcasting in those days – it was a lot of fun.

Herbert Thorpe remembered that 'during the giving of a series of concerts broadcast from the Art Gallery of the Museum I was singing in a group of songs at one of them, and at the commencement of the second song my mind went blank and I couldn't remember one word; the accompanist managed to keep on playing during which I walked over and had a look at the copy'.

Much of the BBC's light music came down the cables from London but the Belfast station made its own contribution, *Eight Bells,* an early form of 'navy mixture' in which musical items were linked by patter as if from the quarter-deck of a ship. It was scripted by the Assistant Director, Mungo Dewar, a Scot who probably perpetrated this specially composed song, 'When I Get Back to Tyrone':

> On the side of a hill, where the birds sweetly trill,
> There's a cabin that once was me home.
> And the smell o' the turf, burning bright in the hearth,
> Comes to me far away o'er the foam.
>
> Faith, it's hard to find friendship that wears with the years,
> There's a differ atween then and now.
> We were mates, we were pals, with none o' life's fears
> In Tyrone when I followed the plough.
>
> Sure, how long me oul' heart's been like stone
> But 'twill melt when I get to Tyrone.
> All the folks won't be young, like they were when I wed,
> They'll be older in years with their backs maybe bent.
>
> But we'll dance to Maloney's trombone
> We'll see colleens in Granny's – ochone!
> And we'll sing and we'll shout, till the lamp flutters out,
> On the day I get back to Tyrone.

Dewar's main responsibility was administration and finance and, like other members of staff, a flexible approach was expected. Almost forty years later McMullan remembered that

> it was a fabulous experience. It bore no resemblance to the life as we live it now in the BBC. It was a question of somebody putting his head round the door and saying, 'the Orchestra is on here in two minutes and we can't find Basil or Ray'. And I would hastily don my jacket and rush up to the studio. Literally, people wore dinner jackets in case someone would arrive in the evening wearing a dinner jacket and one would appear rude if one didn't. We all kept dinner jackets. When I say all, there weren't very many of us . . . I was a sort of dog's body. I did

commentaries, did my work for the *Radio Times,* which was what I was really being paid for, announced if there was nobody to announce, occasionally took a small part in plays to make it cheaper if the producer couldn't get within his budget.

Light music was called for in other contexts. *Ulster Weekly*, a magazine programme of news items and features, was introduced with this jingle to a jolly catchy tune:

> Relax now and listen to *Ulster Weekly*!
> *Ulster Weekly*'s on the air!
> With lots of news and views of every topic of the day,
> With a bit of a song, to help you along,
> And chase your cares away.
> We're presenting the listeners' own weekly
> And now we introduce at your call:
> Tommy Thomson, Joseph Keane with his organ
> And compere John Irwin and all.
> We hope you'll all enjoy, every man, girl and boy,
> *Ulster Weekly* while it's on the air!

Light music was an essential ingredient in variety programmes. In 1936 Dudley Hare composed for the *Ballymagraw Gazette* and in the same year there was *Rabscallion,* described as an 'Old-Time Smoking Concert'. Nineteen thirty-six was also the year the powerful transmitter at Blaris turned the BBC in Belfast into a genuinely regional station. The *Belfast Telegraph*'s 'Rathcol' continued to be unconvinced that the service was a boon, however; the disadvantages included:

> The imperfect, uncertain transmission . . . the eternal insistence on music without ceasing, which is breeding a race who hear without listening or else who, listening, have but rarely the power to appreciate. The daily and nightly onslaught of trash. The slow but sure killing of home music-making . . .

Charles Siepmann made his own assessment for internal use:

> MUSIC Here again our Orchestra and our endeavours provide the only prop to the languishing musical culture of Ulster. Our Orchestra gives eight concerts a year which are now reasonably well attended. A second tentative effort to spread interest by a visit to Londonderry proved disappointing. A military band and a brass band supplement our activities and provide useful programme material but there seems little musical consciousness in the province at all and we can only keep our gaze on the future.

On the eve of the war the range of music offered by the region had widened

Richard Hayward was a broadcaster with a remarkably wide range of talents. He acted in the Belfast station's very first plays and wrote and performed vignettes; he was a pioneer in creating realistic sound effects; he was a writer of plays, talks, stories and travel books; and he was a musician and singer, well known for his performance of Irish folk songs.

BBC NI

considerably. The relative merits of classical music and more modern music could be assessed by listeners in *Wanted – A Tune*, with pieces by Schubert and Brahms, and by Gershwin and Berlin, played by the BBC Northern Ireland Orchestra (as the Wireless Orchestra had become) and James Moody's Dance Band. The orchestra offered music by Delibes, Coleridge-Taylor, Glazunov, York Bowen, Walton O'Donnell, and Ravel. Accompanied by Frederick Stone, the Northern Ireland Singers performed extracts from such works as *The Beggar's Opera*, Handel's *Solomon* and Mozart's *Così fan tutte*. *This Symphony Business*, broadcast on Sunday 5 March 1939, was an attempt to explain classical music, with George Nash asking the questions and James Denny providing answers. Gramophone records were played, sometimes as a preview to a forthcoming concert; for example, when Beniamino Gigli sang in the Ulster Hall on Monday 13 March 1939, J.O. Corrin talked about the music on the previous Wednesday. James Moody was the regular supplier of dance music, which he arranged himself for *Accent on Rhythm*. Other light music included *Round the Fire*, a singsong from Lisnabreeny Youth Hostel in Castlereagh, and a singsong at the 'Dug-Out' supper of the Northern Ireland branch of the British Legion. The band of the RUC also performed regularly.

George Marshall was himself an accomplished musician and he naturally took a close interest in the region's musical output which continued to dominate programme schedules. Much of his time was absorbed in an attempt to resolve a dispute with the Bands' Association. Most members of the association belonged to marching bands and, because the region set out assiduously to exclude material which was overtly Orange or Green, much of the usual repertoire was unsuitable for broadcasting. In addition, the quality of playing was often below that demanded by the BBC. Marshall attempted to get round the problem by getting Godfrey Brown to form a station band, made up of the brass section of the BBC Northern Ireland Orchestra and strengthened by musicians drawn from locally based army regiments. He deliberately kept fees offered to the Bands' Association low, and this drew the following comments from a Unionist MP, Sir Wilson Hungerford, in February 1937:

> Unfortunately what we are suffering from in Northern Ireland is that we get on the wireless not what we want to hear but what other people think we should hear. I am at a loss to understand why bands in Northern Ireland have been ignored in this connection . . .
>
> We here in the North of Ireland are unique in the fact that our people, particularly our artisans, are keen musicians, and bands are composed of young men, who, after their day's work in shipyard or factory, spend several nights a week practising music, and who also contribute out of their wages a sum each week to pay for the services of a qualified bandmaster to teach them.
>
> Surely it is not too much to expect some encouragement and support? . . .
>
> Some of our bands are offered engagements, but at what a princely remuneration! Three guineas! And this for a band of 35 players!

Between 1932 and September 1935 bands had been broadcast seventy-three times in programmes generally fifteen minutes long. The association then sent a deputation to Linenhall Street to demand an increase in fees; this was refused and no bands were broadcast for the next eighteen months. There followed a petition to Westminster, protest performances in the Ulster Hall and the Grosvenor Hall ('Come and hear the bands the BBC won't broadcast') and a protracted press correspondence. Finally, Lord Craigavon himself intervened and at a meeting in Stormont with Marshall and the association higher fees were agreed, but Marshall won his point that only prizewinning bands would be invited to broadcast.

The temporary appearance of a broadcasting van in the summer of 1937 provided the opportunity to record music in the home. The first full-length programme made by a mobile recording unit in the region was of a ceilidh in a County Tyrone cottage on 15 October 1937. This indicated a new willingness to 'give expression to Ulster culture'. In 1938 Norman Hay was engaged to co-ordinate 'a group of musicians who were to orchestrate the traditional music of Northern Ireland'. The way in which this was done was not to win favour with traditional musicians but it was to produce a remarkable and popular variety of music which would later win huge audiences for the BBC. The pre-war broadcasts went out in a series called the *Airs of Ulster*.

Brown retired in 1937 and was replaced by Walton ('Bandy') O'Donnell, who had been Director of the BBC's Military Band. The new Director of Music gave strong support to the collection of folk music for orchestration and believed it essential 'that local composers should follow the Northern Ireland folk tune idiom'. Despite his Ulster surname, O'Donnell had no expertise in this area. Henry McMullan, by now Assistant Programme Director, later recalled:

> Bandy came to my office one day and said, 'You know David Curry has got a group and they are playing what he calls Irish dance music and he wants me to audition it and see if it would make a programme.' I frankly didn't know a lot about Irish dance music either. I knew the ceilidh bands because we used ceilidh bands all the time. So I went up and talked to David and his group played a couple of things and when they stopped, he said, 'What do you think?' and I said, 'As far as I am concerned I'd like some of these programmes because they are eminently saleable.' And he said, 'Do you think they are genuine?' and I said, 'I wouldn't like to use the word "genuine". They are a rather sophisticated ceilidh band operation, which I'm quite sure would go down like a bomb in England.' This, of course, was true: it did go down like a bomb on the English and Scottish networks with alacrity and became an absolutely firm ingredient of broadcasting in Northern Ireland.

But was it Irish music? Traditional musicians viewed David Curry's creation, broadcast as *Irish Rhythms,* with disfavour. Yet the orchestration of folk music had been accomplished to universal approval by composers such as Brahms and Kodály – Kodály, indeed, was one of the first to take cumbersome Ediphone equipment into the remote countryside to record traditional Hungarian and gypsy music. Others in Northern Ireland, on the other hand, found the broadcasts too distinctly Irish, as McMullan recalled:

> It came under a good deal of attack in Northern Ireland because, of course, it was suggested it wasn't representative of Northern Ireland. The word 'representative' I came to hate, and various pressures were put on to get this programme stopped because, first it was giving the wrong impression of Northern Ireland and, second, it was a 'foreign' culture.

Regional broadcasting closed down on the outbreak of war. The BBC Northern Ireland Orchestra was disbanded and it looked as if Northern Ireland simply would have a transmitter relaying the Home and Forces Services. In the spring of 1940, however, the BBC in Belfast was back in production, mostly contributing musical and variety programmes to the network. The Ministry of Information, worried about the influence of Nazi propaganda broadcasts, wanted the BBC to reach all of Ireland, as there were so many from Éire serving in the war factories and the forces. The Northern Ireland government was vigilant; Marshall, in turn, was sensitive to the Unionist government's sensitivities. Denis Johnston recorded later:

> I wasn't really in tune, I think, with George Marshall . . . who was really a voice for the Ulster Club, let me put it that way. He was not, I think, interested at all in the South − in fact, the less about it the better. I was very much concerned about the relationship between north and south . . . I actually got a programme called *The Fighting Irish,* advertising the fact that a great many Irish people were doing extremely good work for the Allied forces during the war and it would be a great pity to lose those services, which I think went across very well . . .

Marshall, however, obstructed as much as he could, but artistes, singers, musicians and actors from the South − sometimes brought to Belfast and other times recorded in Dublin − were used for a wide range of programmes, in particular the immensely popular *Irish Half Hour.* The *Irish News* observed:

> The Belfast building is, in fact, erected on a shaky foundation that has produced the cracks in Stormont. When it broadcasts the bright lilting arrangements of Irish dance music by David Curry, or its orchestral arrangements of Irish airs (the two best things it has done), it contradicts itself by drawing on the whole cultural background of Ireland.

Writing in 1944, Deasun O Raghaille, included this assessment of the BBC in Belfast in his booklet *A Listener's Opinion:*

> They introduced new ideas into the broadcasting of ceilidh music. I am not competent to say whether these changes were orthodox from the point of view of Irish music, but from the ordinary listener's point of view they transformed what was becoming the monotonous beat and steady rhythm of Irish dance tunes into lively airs and sparkling melody.
> These Irish tunes as played in Belfast were called 'Irish Rhythms' and

became world famous . . . Why should change in form be deplored? Surely if the music be really alive it must change with the times . . .

Irish Rhythms was, indeed, hugely popular in both the Home and Forces Services. Ursula Eason, who remained in Belfast as acting Programme Director, had her anxieties, nevertheless, and told the Director of Programme Planning in London in 1943 that 'these light music programmes do not reflect the life of the region in the way that we would like to'.

When the war was over there were new opportunities to reflect the life of the region, though not in the way that Ursula Eason had intended. Sam Hanna Bell was more capable and determined than his predecessors at finding people from the Catholic minority who could bring in fresh ideas and new material. It was he who got Broadcasting House to recognise the value of Michael J. Murphy's expertise and to engage Sean O'Boyle, one of the great authorities on Irish folk music. O'Boyle and Peter Kennedy of the English Folksong Society were sent out to make a preliminary survey and then to capture, with the aid of the mobile recording unit, a tradition which in places was teetering on the edge of survival. Over two hundred pieces of traditional music were recorded and most were broadcast in the series *Music on the Hearth* between 1953 and 1956, many of them repeated on the Third Programme. Bell also drew on *Songs of the People,* a series by Sam Henry which appeared regularly in the Coleraine newspaper, the *Northern Constitution.* With Hugh Quinn, the playwright and collector, Bell produced programmes of Belfast street songs in 1952. All of this work created archives of incalculable value to scholars, researchers and programme-makers.

Andrew Stewart gave more encouragement than any of his predecessors to staff making distinctively regional programmes. He also concluded that 'on the

Sean O'Boyle, one of the greatest authorities on Irish traditional music in the twentieth century, was engaged by the BBC at Sam Hanna Bell's request to collect folk music for broadcasting.

BBC NI

artistic side, the kernel of regional activity was an orchestra'. Marshall had been unable to get permission to reconstitute the BBC Northern Ireland Orchestra after the war – concerts could be relayed more cheaply from London. Stewart argued that Ulster had made its own distinctive contribution in Hay's orchestrations and Curry's rhythms, and he added that a 'characteristic of this music is its cheerfulness, unlike the predominant sadness of much of the folk music of the British Isles'. Stewart persuaded the BBC in London that, while Northern Ireland could take serious music from elsewhere, the region could offer light music to the network. Since 1947 the region's musical output had been the responsibility of Edgar ('Billy') Boucher, with the support of the accompanist Havelock Nelson. Musicians, singers, bands and choirs could be engaged, and outside broadcasts could be arranged, but the situation was highly unsatisfactory until Stewart negotiated the formation of the BBC Northern Ireland Light Orchestra. David Curry was conductor for a short while, until Villem Tautsky was engaged and fifteen players were appointed. *Irish Rhythms* continued to be enormously popular and the programme was not only taken by the network but also by several other European stations. *Eight Bells* was revived and there were other lighter offerings, including *Songs from the Shows* and *Stop Dancing*. The players' contracts allowed members of the orchestra to form the core of the Belfast Philharmonic Orchestra, afterwards the City of Belfast Orchestra. *Ulster Bands* relayed Saturday afternoon performances under the pre-war agreement; James Moody continued his programmes of popular music; *Ulster Serenade* provided half-hour programmes of Irish music and song; dances in country halls were relayed in *Country Ceilidhe*; *Come into the Parlour* featured popular Irish tunes and ballads; and *We Make Music* was a compilation of excerpts performed by the Northern Ireland Operatic Society. Havelock Nelson's official title was 'staff accompanist' but he rapidly became a vital force in the musical life of Northern Ireland. Walter Love recalled:

> My mother once told me that she was in the audience in the Guildhall in Newtownards when the BBC was recording a recital for radio. There was a fairly sparse attendance and Havelock instructed the audience to 'clap like hell for the honour of Newtownards'.

Locally produced musical programmes were slow to make a regular appearance

Edgar, or 'Billy', Boucher joined the staff as 'music assistant' in 1947. At first his task was a formidable one as the BBC Northern Ireland Orchestra had been disbanded in 1939. Andrew Stewart, the Controller, realised Boucher's predicament and in December 1948 persuaded the Board of Governors to establish the BBC Northern Ireland Light Orchestra.

BBC NI

on television. The enormous worldwide upsurge in interest in folk music in the 1960s was reflected in the region in television programmes such as *The Folk* and *Patterson People*. Havelock Nelson hosted a mixture of light and more serious music in *The Nelson Touch*. Meanwhile, plans were made to augment the BBC Northern Ireland Light Orchestra, when the governors relented and allowed it to be reformed as the BBC Northern Ireland Orchestra. It took part, for example, in a St Patrick's Day 'spectacular' in 1969 and in television gala concerts. The problem was that there were two symphony orchestras in Belfast and neither was of national standard. The BBC and the Arts Council of Northern Ireland put their heads together and concluded that the obvious answer was to pool resources. An agreement was made to disband the BBC Northern Ireland Orchestra and at the same time to guarantee funding of one million pounds to the new Ulster Orchestra over a ten-year period.

The agreement – between the Ulster Orchestral Society, the BBC, the unions and the Arts Council of Northern Ireland – came into force in January 1981 at a time when Belfast city centre was coming back to life. All but five of the remaining members of the BBC Northern Ireland Orchestra were invited to join the new orchestra which numbered fifty-five players. The orchestra was on hand for the reopening of the refurbished Grand Opera House in Belfast and Friday night concerts in the Ulster Hall attracted capacity audiences. These changes caused much initial angst but the outcome was an orchestra of vastly

Havelock Nelson discussing a score with May Turtle during a rehearsal in 1949.

BBC NI

The City of Belfast Orchestra
rehearsing before a broadcast, with
Maurice Miles conducting.

BBC NI

improved quality, enabling the region to offer concerts to network programmes. In 1996–7 two magnificent concerts to celebrate the opening of the Belfast Waterfront Hall were broadcast on network to an audience of 1.4 million. In the same year the Ulster Orchestra delivered thirty hours to BBC RADIO 3 and twenty hours to BBC RADIO ULSTER. The music department in the BBC, led by the enthusiastic and talented Chief Producer David Byers, unearthed lost, neglected and unpublished works by Charles Villiers Stanford, Cipriani Potter, Arnold Bax and Norman Hay and the Ulster Orchestra's playing of them for BBC RADIO 3 attracted widespread acclaim. The following year a concert for BBC RADIO 2 at Castle Ward in County Down, *Pride of Erin*, featured the soloist Maureen Hegarty and the eighty-four-year-old Larry Adler, who had first been broadcast playing to American troops during the Second World War.

Imaginative attempts were made to win wider audiences for classical music on radio. For example, in *Music Now – The Family Concert* (May 1999, BBC RADIO ULSTER) John Toal introduced popular favourites such as Tubby the Tuba (with Ewan Easton playing the tuba) and a suite from Gershwin's *Porgy and Bess* in a delightfully lively and inclusive manner. *Music Now* was the home for much of BBC RADIO ULSTER's live classical music output and demonstrated the success of the symbiotic relationship between the Ulster Orchestra and the Region. Relays from the Waterfront and Ulster Halls gave the orchestra wide audiences particularly when taken simultaneously by BBC RADIO ULSTER and by Lyric FM. Bill Lloyd wrote, produced and presented a dazzling series of accessible short fillers broadcast during intervals in *Music Now* concerts, *The Musical A–Z*. Lloyd also produced an absorbing series of six programmes for BBC RADIO 4, *The Musical Side of the Family:* in March 1999, for instance, Claire Tomalin explored the remarkable life of her mother, Muriel Herbert, one of the first ever female students of composition at the Royal College of Music, whose music was frequently broadcast in the early days of wireless. In addition he oversaw a *Young Musicians' Showcase* as a curtain-raiser for the BBC network *Young Musicians* final broadcast for the first time from the Waterfront Hall.

The year 1990 saw the introduction of the 'Northern Ireland Curriculum', with its cross-curricular themes of Cultural Heritage and Education for Mutual Understanding, and the founding of the Community Relations Council – both emphasised the importance of understanding and appreciating the variety of cultural traditions of the region. Significantly, James Hawthorne, the first schools producer in Northern Ireland and later Controller, was the first chairman of the Community Relations Council. Pat Loughrey, former schools producer, Head of Programmes and later Northern Ireland Controller, was a founder member of the Cultural Traditions Group in the Community Relations Council. As Controller, Loughrey was acutely aware of the necessity of serving the whole community in Northern Ireland. He set about ensuring that the two main traditions (at the same time recognising that Ulster has a kaleidoscope of traditions) would be properly represented in the schedules. In broad terms, Catholics had acknowledged strengths in poetry, dance, drama, traditional music and aspects of the arts, and Protestants had a reputation for

Julie Felix, the popular ballad singer, visited Belfast in October 1966 to take part in *Swing 'n Folk.*
BBC NI

131

engineering skills, scientific inventiveness, medical expertise, the creation of artefacts and musical flair.

One of the region's most ambitious programmes on music was *River of Sound* in 1995, which traced the development of Irish music from early times and was exceptionally well received. *Sing Carols* at Christmas was another popular television offering. Local popular music fans were turning increasingly to commercial radio stations for their fare but in 1996–7 they were offered a treat in the form of a series of five half-hour television programmes, *Beyond the Line*. As in the Irish Republic, Northern Ireland was beginning to produce groups, such as Ash, Divine Comedy and Watercress, which were attracting attention on both sides of the Atlantic, and Mike Edgar had the opportunity of introducing them in this successful series.

In February 1997 BBC Northern Ireland hosted the Irish Rock and Pop Awards, which featured Radiohead, *Riverdance* star Jean Butler, and U2 drummer Larry Mullan. Mike Edgar and Ulrika Jonsson proved such a success at introducing the stars and groups that they were engaged again for the awards in April 1998. The region was able to host this event, arguably the biggest night in Ireland's musical calendar, because it had the state-of-the-art Blackstaff studios in Belfast's Great Victoria Street. On the night, police were faced with the dual task of shepherding hosts of fans, hoping to catch a glance of famous stars such as Sinéad O'Connor and Ronan Keating, and loyalists protesting against UUP leader David Trimble outside the Unionist Party headquarters nearby in Glengall Street – *Hot Press,* the Irish rock magazine had arranged the show

Michael Baguley who introduces *Come Dancing* surrounded by some of the dancers in the Plaza Ballroom, Belfast.

BBC NI

inadvertently on the same night the Good Friday Agreement was due to be signed. Cries of 'traitor, traitor, traitor' vied with chants of 'we love you Ronan we do, we love you Ronan we do . . .' Accepting U2's award for Best Live Performance, Bono asked: 'What's the difference between Ian Paisley and George Michael?' The answer, he said, was: 'At least George Michael will talk to anyone.' Local musicians who had made international reputations for themselves picked up awards, including Van Morrison, Brian Kennedy, David Holmes, Ash and Shane McGowan. Demand for the exclusive after-show VIP party in the Europa Hotel was so high that over seventy journalists had to be refused admission. In October 1999 BBC Northern Ireland once again produced and screened the *Hot Press* Awards, this time in Dublin. Neil Hannon from Enniskillen was the toast of the night, winning Best Male Singer and Best Irish Songwriter, and his band, Divine Comedy, won the Best Irish Album for *Fin de Siècle*.

Drama, music, talks, poetry readings and short stories have dominated the BBC's output in the arts since 1924. There were radio discussions about music, mostly about concerts due to be broadcast, but it was only after the war that there were programmes about the arts. The most important was *The Arts in Ulster*, a half-hour monthly review, generally broadcast on Sunday evenings between 10.30 and 11.00. In the early 1950s the contributors included David Kennedy talking about literature, James Boyce on drama, Charles Brett on painting and John Cowser on music, with J.J. Campbell as chairman. *Folk Music*

Neil Hannon (left) of *Divine Comedy*, a winner at the Irish Rock and Pop Awards hosted by BBC Northern Ireland in 1998. With him are the presenters Ulrika Jonsson and Mike Edgar.

BBC NI

brought Sean O'Boyle, Jerry Hicks, Sean Dynan, Sam Denton and others into the studio for informal discussions of a kind few listeners had heard before. *Writing in Ulster* brought to the microphone new and established work by Ulster authors and the monthly critical review, *In Ulster Now*, was entirely dedicated to discussion of the arts. In the 1950s the monthly literary programme *Ariel* presented new writing in Northern Ireland. Brief discussions and comment on the arts, particularly after the introduction of regional television, would feature on magazine programmes such as *Studio Eight* and *Scene Around Six* and also on the evening twenty-minute radio programme, *Round up*. Harry Thompson became a popular and sure-footed anchorman in *Look Who's Talking*, an evening television programme looking at the week's scene in Northern Ireland and including features on music, theatre and entertainment. In the 1960s as the radio schedules expanded there were programmes on writers, such as *Robert Lynd* (in which his friends spoke about the life and work of the Presbyterian essayist) and *The Strings are False* on Louis MacNeice in 1966. *Soundings* was a monthly arts review in the late 1960s.

The launch of BBC RADIO ULSTER in 1975 created the airtime for more frequent comment on the arts. In 1977–8, for example, radio output included a fifty-minute weekly review of the arts, a monthly programme on local

The opening concert at the Waterfront Hall in Belfast in 1997 with the Belfast-born internationally renowned flautist, James Galway.

BBC NI

writing and music, and documentaries on subjects ranging from the life of Jonathan Swift to the visit made by Charles Dickens to Belfast. Arts subjects would crop up in Northern Ireland's regular contribution to BBC RADIO 4's *Women's Hour*, such as a discussion with the Belfast-born flautist, James Galway. The showcase programme on television was *Gallery*, produced by Gerry McCrudden, which ranged widely. There were profiles, one of the finest being on the Banbridge-born sculptor, F.E. McWilliam, and on others including the singers Heather Harper and Norma Burrowes; the camera team visited Toronto in 1975 for an international seminar on Irish writers; a retrospective on the acting career of Micheál Mac Liammóir; excerpts from satirical revues; and a review of the *Sense of Ireland* festival in London in 1980.

The poet Paul Muldoon served some years producing some distinguished arts programmes for radio, including the series *Faces of Ireland* in 1976, which assembled actors to read poetry and literary extracts from the earliest times (translated by Kuno Meyer) to the present, on the themes of *Work and Play*, *Love*, *The Irish and Their Creator*, *War and Peace*, *Heroes and Villains*, and *The Irish Abroad*. The presenters were Gerry Downey, Frank D'Arcy, Mary Murphy and Peter Mullan, and scattered throughout the programmes were songs and ballads sung by Risteard Mac Gabhainn, Una O'Somarchan and Paddy O'Carolan, accompanied by James Canning. In *The Great Gazebo*, Muldoon visited the Yeats International Summer School in Sligo; he brought the most distinguished Northern Ireland poets to the microphone; and his *Irish Poetry* series of twelve programmes introduced and explained work stretching over many centuries.

The popular BBC RADIO ULSTER series *Speaking Personally*, in which well-known figures spoke about their lives, was not exclusively about those involved in the arts but amongst those who were heard were the novelist Benedict Kiely, the actor Jack McQuoid, the composer A.J. Potter, and the novelist Jennifer Johnston. Interviewers in this series included Nick Ross, and Frank Delaney, who would later become distinguished in network broadcasting. Gavin Esler and Alf McCreary who became a well-known television news correspondent reporting from across the globe, began his broadcasting career with BBC RADIO ULSTER and amongst those he talked to in the series *Public v. Private* were artists in the public eye, including the sculptor F.E. McWilliam. Judith Elliott produced a wide range of impressive arts programmes, including *Women Writers* in 1984, in which Margaret Walters, Lenny Goodings and Catherine Rose talked generally about the emerging feminist press and Virago and Arlen in particular. Arts discussions became more informal, livelier, more relaxed and no longer strait-jacketed by excessive scripting. The producer who did much to promote this fresher approach was Brian Barfield, especially in his monthly programme, *Studio 3*. Amongst the many absorbing radio arts programmes was *It's Me They Want To See*, written and presented by the actor and writer John Keyes and produced by Ian Kirk-Smith in September 1998: this was a colourful and lively celebration of the great actor–manager Anew McMaster who had trailed his company around the villages and town halls of Ireland for three decades, and it included a raft of distinguished theatrical voices including those of Harold Pinter, Micheál Mac Liammóir, Hilton Edwards and T.P. McKenna.

Tommy Millar was for long the authoritative voice on all music with a touch of tartan, most notably on BBC RADIO ULSTER's Saturday afternoon programme, *Pipes and Drums*.

BBC NI

The cultural life of Northern Ireland had been enriched from the early 1960s by the Queen's University Festival, later the Belfast Festival at Queen's, held each autumn. Excerpts, interviews and critiques were given generous space on radio in *Festival Notebook* before the morning news at 9.00 a.m., in *Morning Extra* and later in *Good Morning Ulster*, and again in the drive-home programme. Arts producers Judith Elliott, Chris Spurr and Stephen Douds saw to it that *Evening Extra Arts Desk* had pace and topicality and the professional and genuinely interested questioning of first Sean McMahon and later of Barry Cowan and Mark Carruthers drew the best out of reviewers and artists. The range of items was wide and included the C.S. Lewis centenary, 1798 bicentenary events, books for children, the William Carleton School, the West

Belfast Festival, the premiere of the film *Divorcing Jack*, Elton John at Stormont and interviews with authors such as Maeve Binchy, Alice Taylor and Bruce Arnold. Sean Rafferty, on weekday mornings in *Rafferty*, featured some of the most entertaining pieces not just on the festival but on the arts in general. Seamus McKee and Michael Barnes gave the Queen's festival full coverage and assessment in the November and December editions of *Arts in Ireland*. The long-running BBC RADIO ULSTER series, *You're Booked*, brought a strong cross-section of writers and critics into the studio to discuss the latest books which, guided by the warm, witty and effective presenter Leon McAuley, resulted in relaxed, friendly and informative conversations. In 1998 McAuley compiled and presented a fascinating series of four programmes on the history of the Irish thriller, *Those Green Remembered Thrills*, the highlight being the Philip Marlowe treatment of the second programme. Contributions to BBC RADIO 4 in the same year included *Reflections*, a series of talks by five Irish writers on the subject of childhood, produced by Judith Elliott. In October 1998, *Mr Joyce's Looking Glass*, a half-hour feature produced by Ian Kirk-Smith, was the opening programme in the BBC RADIO 4 season of James Joyce's *Dubliners* – it received enthusiastic reviews in the London press and extracts were repeated on BBC RADIO 4's *Pick of the Week*. As the peace process got under way and violence eased – in spite of all the excitement surrounding the Good Friday Agreement – *Newsline* on television was able to devote more screen space to arts events, generally introduced by Maggie Taggart. *Gallery* was a regular visitor to the festival, an event which could also feature on network.

Playing Belfast, on BBC ONE in November 1989, had Derek Bailey returning to his native city to produce and direct this programme after many years of making television films about the arts from a London base. Festival events were highlighted against a background of ordinary Belfast people going about their workaday lives in a setting of architecture, Bailey believed, 'more beautiful than rumour has had it'. He linked film sequences with segments from a forty-eight-hour sponsored 'Haydnfest', undertaken by the Ulster Orchestra and Friends of the Ulster Orchestra to raise money for *Children in Need.* The programme included interviews with incoming performers, such as the comedian Jeremy Hardy who commented offstage: 'I'm a bit shell-shocked by the whole thing, really. A lot of people have been trying to convince me it's just like anywhere else, but it isn't!' The Russian concert pianist Nikolai Demidenko observed: 'Belfast is such a special place. I don't like to play in Moscow. I like playing in Leningrad, Siberia and Belfast.' Bailey was concerned to contrast the fear engendered by Northern Ireland's reputation in the outside world, widely regarded as a terrifying place with murder lurking round the corner, and the real-life social vitality noted by surprised visitors. He continued:

> I wanted to use the Festival as a microcosm of the alternative life of Ulster, showing it through the perspective of visiting artists who discover that the Province has a rich cultural vein. Since they come from so many different countries, they present a valuable cross-section of viewpoints.

The sixtieth birthday of the winner of the Nobel Prize for Literature, Seamus Heaney, occasioned two celebratory programmes on 11 April 1999 on BBC TWO Northern Ireland. The first, *Happy Birthday Seamus*, written and presented by the poet, was mercifully free of affectation and pretension; it included extracts from films in the BBC Northern Ireland archive and 'birthday cards' offered by admirers. The second, *Keeping Time – The Poet and the Piper*, was a performance-led film made by Hummingbird Productions featuring the poetry of Heaney and the piping of Liam O'Flynn which celebrated the relationship between the two artists and their respective traditions. One of the most memorable arts programmes in the same year was *The Painted Landscape – T P Flanagan*, a ravishing BBC ONE Northern Ireland broadcast with an arresting impressionistic opening, a compelling commentary by the artist himself and a finely-crafted fading into Flanagan's work from natural images and back out again.

Seamus Heaney in 1972 when he talked about his third book of poems, *Wintering Out*, on *November Review* on BBC RADIO 4.

BBC NI

The Broadcasting Act of 1990 requirement to commission from independent companies at first seemed to present the region with an acute problem, since independents were then almost non-existent in Northern Ireland, but this anxiety proved unfounded as companies emerged. Since that time Brian Waddell Productions has become the largest independent producer in Northern Ireland. The company's credits include three BBC network series of *Gourmet Ireland* with celebrity chefs Paul and Jeanne Rankin and four long running DIY and home improvement series for the BBC. Brian Waddell has also made numerous documentary programmes including *Put to the Test*, a narrative study of the annual Transfer Test examination for 11-year-old children which won the 1998 Royal Television Society Award for best regional documentary. Straight Forward Productions, managed by two former BBC executives Ian Kennedy and John Nicholson, also has an impressive state of productions including three series of *Awash with Colour* for the BBC and *We Shall Overcome*, presented by Nick Ross, which won the best documentary award at the 1999 Celtic Television Festival. Stirling Productions is typical of the growing number of small but successful independent production companies and has made the series *The Pet Set*. Chistera Productions, set up by Moore Sinnerton, a former Head of Schools Broadcasting and acting Head of Programmes, made several arts television documentaries. *A Time to Dance*, screened in 1992, told the extraordinary and moving story of Helen Lewis who, brought up as a Jew in the German-speaking Sudetenland, entered a dance school in Prague only to find the city occupied by the Germans shortly afterwards. Sinnerton made three highly regarded films on Ulster artists in the 1990s: *Gerard Dillon: Painter and Decorator*; *Like a Good Workman* on John Luke; and *Sunshine in a Room*, a film on Tom Carr, screened in 1998 just before he died. The centenary of the birth of C.S. Lewis, the writer and moralist born and brought up in Belfast, was marked by Chistera's *The Man, the Myth and the Wardrobe*.

David Hammond, a former BBC schools producer who founded Flying Fox Films, made television arts programmes for the BBC. His work was always lyrical and includes: *Yellow for the Stars* (1991), in which the painter Neil Shawcross and the children of St Mary's Primary School in Strangford, County Down, paint a mural of their home town (commissioned by Virginia Hardy, Secretary of the BBC in Northern Ireland); *An Ulster Archive* (1992), with archival footage of Tom Carr, Patsy McCooey, Rowel Friers, Joan Trimble and George Watson; and *Something to Write Home About* (1998), in which Seamus Heaney tells the story behind one of his poems.

The regional flagship television programme on the arts was *29 Bedford Street*, named after the office block which served as an overflow for Broadcasting House until accommodation in the Blackstaff building was completed. Hosted by John Kelly it provided in an informal style a lively and varied format in which there were interviews, reviews, music, features and discussions. Amongst those interviewed were Thaddeus O'Sullivan, who directed *December Bride*, the highly praised film of Sam Hanna Bell's novel; the novelist Brian Moore, Seamus Heaney and Kenneth Branagh. Ciaran Carson was interviewed on the publication of his latest poetry collection, *Belfast Confetti*, as well as Conor Carson, the fourteen-year-old Belfast schoolboy who was the youngest ever recipient of the Shell Young Poet of the Year Award. *The Interview* had a simple, unfussy format and the undoubted appeal of the programme was due not only to the prominence of the interviewees – including Seamus Heaney and the stand-up comedian Frank Carson – but to the skill with which the interviewer Roisin McAuley got her subjects to respond.

The most distinctive features of life in Northern Ireland after 1968 were the civil disorder, the political instability and the protracted violence which made the region unique in the latter part of the twentieth century. However, partly as a consequence of major advances in educational provision after the Second World War, Northern Ireland experienced a remarkable cultural flowering which had got under way several years before the onset of the Troubles. During the early stages of the conflict, when concert halls and theatres in city centres either closed or attracted only sparse audiences, the BBC recognised its responsibility as a public service broadcaster and provided citizens with its most significant platform for music and the arts. The return of more peaceful conditions following the paramilitary ceasefires of 1994 coincided with the wholesale refurbishment and reconstruction of town and city centres and the opening of new venues, notably in Belfast, Derry, Armagh and Newtownabbey. By fostering a close relationship with theatres, concert halls, the Grand Opera House, the film and music industries, promoters, artists, writers and actors, the BBC continued to play a pivotal role as a patron of the arts and in stimulating the cultural life of Northern Ireland.

The footballing superstar George Best revealed some honest opinions in an extended conversation with Roisin McAuley in *The Interview* on BBC Northern Ireland in November 1998.
BBC NI

7

RELIGIOUS
BROADCASTS

WHEN 2BE CAME ON THE AIR there had been fewer than two years of peace in Northern Ireland. Between July 1920 and July 1922 the death toll in the six counties was 557 and peace had come to the region only after the adoption of draconian special powers by the new devolved government, the deployment of some fifty thousand full- and part-time police and the outbreak of civil war in the South. One-third of the inhabitants felt no allegiance to the government in Belfast and feared oppression. In the short term the majority, in spite of its triumph, feared the consequences of the Boundary Commission agreed by London in December 1921 and felt embattled and suspicious of Westminster's long-term intentions. The offspring of planters and native Gaelic Irish had blended to a far greater degree than was admitted, but the northern state bore all the scars of bitter divisions going back for centuries. Northern Ireland's problems were uncomfortably parallel to those in the Balkans, where ethnic conflicts erupted alarmingly in the years following the Paris peace treaties. There were fissured communities in western Europe but nowhere was the chasm so deep as in Ulster, where religion was the ethnic divider.

Major Scott and his staff in Linenhall Street were not Ulster men and the Belfast station soon learned it would have to proceed with caution. In any case, head office was acutely aware of its moral responsibilities throughout the United Kingdom and the instructions sent to Belfast applied everywhere. A Religious Advisory Committee was to be appointed forthwith:

> To this committee you should invite the recognised leaders of Roman Catholicism, the Church of England or its equivalent and the United Free Churches. The committee should certainly meet at intervals of about four months, and as often as necessary, and should provide you with a list of folk who can be relied on to give a good address entirely free from dogma . . . Special care should be taken in the examination of the manuscripts of these religious addresses.

Even after-dinner speeches 'by eminent persons at the principal functions in your area' were to be vetted to ensure they would not 'be political in character or highly controversial from a religious point of view'. To a considerable degree these conditions had been imposed by the Post Office, which had given a monopoly of broadcasting to the BBC in 1922 under tight controls which

Opposite:
David Byers of BBC NI conducting the choir during the filming of *Songs of Praise* at the Giant's Causeway.

BBC NI

remained in force until the company became a corporation in 1926.

When the Religious Advisory Committee met for the first time on 3 November 1924, no Catholic representative appeared. Cardinal Michael Logue had refused to attend the official opening of the Northern Ireland parliament in Belfast City Hall by George V in June 1921 and opposition Nationalist MPs were to refuse to take their seats there until 1925. Local councils, such as Londonderry, Newry and Enniskillen, which had declared allegiance to the Irish Free State in 1922, had been put in the hands of commissioners before having their ward boundaries redrawn following the abolition of proportional representation. Catholic teachers had only recently ended their refusal to accept salaries from the new administration. The Catholic Church, finding that the 1923 Education Act denied capital funding to its schools in violation of 1920 legislative guarantees, was in no mood to co-operate with British institutions. Another twenty years were to pass before a Catholic representative agreed to attend the Religious Advisory Committee.

The first meeting of the committee had been convened in some haste because of press criticism and questions in the Northern Ireland House of Commons that the Belfast station had failed to broadcast any religious services. Arrangements were agreed that, in order to give people time to come home from evening church services, programmes should not be broadcast until 8.45 p.m. The religious address was to start at 9 p.m., 'preceded by hymns and followed by programmes, not extending too late into the evening, of sacred and other serious music fitted to the day'. The Catholic Church in Ireland would not provide speakers and so it was decided to take Catholic sermons, talks and services from other stations in the rest of the United Kingdom. Presbyterian addresses from Scotland were to be relayed on occasion for the benefit of the region's largest Protestant denomination.

The Protestant Churches broadly welcomed broadcasting and, according to the *Irish Radio Journal* in 1925, the Church of Ireland Dean of Belfast paid 'an eloquent tribute to the value of wireless in spreading God's message over a troubled world'. The committee might have been expected to have been opposed to other programmes on a Sunday but they approved them 'on the undertaking that the music should be of a high-class nature, and that it be confined to the hours between three o'clock and five'.

Some of the earliest outside broadcasts were of Protestant church services; lines were laid in Belfast to Fisherwick Presbyterian Church and St James's Parish Church, and later to St Anne's Cathedral and Carlisle Memorial Methodist Church. The Church of Ireland cathedrals in Armagh and Derry were linked up, and, finally, the Catholic Church agreed in 1932 to a commemorative service of pontifical High Mass from St Patrick's Cathedral, Armagh. The occasion was the thirty-first International Eucharistic Congress held in Ireland to commemorate the 1,500th anniversary of the beginning of Saint Patrick's mission in Ireland. It was the biggest religious celebration yet seen in Ireland: a million people heard the Archbishop of Baltimore celebrate High Mass and receive the papal blessing from Cardinal Lorenzo Lauri in

Phoenix Park, Dublin. Gerald Beadle went to Armagh to finalise arrangements and broached the question of religious addresses:

> 'I wish you would yourself appear before the microphone,' I said. [The Archbishop] replied, 'You wouldn't let me, you'd censor me.' 'We would not but we would have to restrain you from being rude about Protestants.' He said, 'What do you think I'm here for? What do think I'm employed for?'

In 1936 Charles Siepmann summarised the situation:

> RELIGION Northern Ireland is the only region in which religious services are broadcast during church hours with the express approval of the Advisory Committee. This is rather remarkable. The only difficulty is that the Roman Catholics will not come into line and despite repeated efforts it has not yet proved possible to secure a Roman Catholic member for the Religious Advisory Committee. This, of course, is simply a reflection of the political situation. The relations of the Northern Ireland regional staff with the Roman Catholic Church being entirely cordial.

The Catholic Church finally agreed to send Monsignor A.H. Ryan as its representative to the Committee in 1944. In Britain all Catholic religious addresses were censored by a nominee of the Archbishop of Westminster and it was only when this condition was set aside that the Catholic Church in Ireland agreed to co-operate with the BBC. The Very Reverend Cahal Daly, then Professor of Scholastic Philosophy at Queen's University and later Cardinal and Archbishop of Armagh, joined the committee as a second representative in 1947.

Much attention was paid to the contents of sermons and religious talks and on how they should be scrutinised and passed for approval. Ursula Eason, who was in charge of religious programmes amongst her many other duties, was just as concerned about quality of delivery. In an interview with Rex Cathcart in 1983 she recalled:

> Far too many clergy who came in before the War were only concerned with what they had to say and never for a moment realised that the pulpit is different from the microphone but we rather brutally after the war shook them out of that. We started auditions of people who would probably give a good broadcast so as to let them find out what they sounded like in front of the microphone. We would collect four or five of them together and they would each bring a short sermon written for broadcasting. Then we would record them and all sit round and criticise each of them on play back. They were very co-operative and began to realise that broadcasting is not just the message – five minutes to say what you have got to say about the whole Christian doctrine, which is what many tried to do – but that manner and style of presentation were most important. They were brought to realise that it was utterly unlike what they normally did in church. There were disasters. People who seemed to be good simply could not project themselves over the

Thomas H. Holden at the keyboard of the famous carillon of St Patrick's Catholic Cathedral in Armagh. He made the first of many broadcasts on the bells on St Patrick's Day 1926, though the Church did not permit the relay of any of its services until 1932.

BBC NI

microphone, even though they might have more significant things to say than those who could. That's the danger and it's up to the broadcasters to do something about it.

For two decades after the Second World War religious broadcasts continued to be almost exclusively liturgical and devotional. For most of that time this was true of all the regions and of religious programmes on the BBC Home and Light Services. The energies of the Reverend Moore Wasson, Head of Religious Broadcasting, and his staff were often directed towards organising the region's contributions to network religious services and programmes such as *Lift Up Your Hearts* and *Lighten Our Darkness*. In February 1959 Mrs Mitchell gave a talk *I believe – so I worship* on *Lift Up Your Hearts* to mark the Women's World Day of Prayer, with its theme 'Lord, I believe'. *Thy Word Abideth* was, in effect, a fifteen-minute religious service with devotional music provided by church choirs or the Ulster Singers. Services could be themed: *Towards the Christian State*, for example, was a series of morning services for Lent in 1959 on the duties and opportunities of the Christian state. One of the sermons was given by the Very Reverend J. Ernest Davey, principal of the Presbyterian College in Belfast, with the title 'The State and Toleration' – this was a general talk on the treatment of minorities across the world and not a critical examination of the situation in Northern Ireland.

The first religious television broadcasts were from the studio, such as *It Began to Dawn,* a programme for Easter Day presented by the Reverend Jack Withers. The extension to St Anne's Cathedral – a building which, the *Radio Times* pointed out, 'in the opinion of John Betjeman is one of the most majestic church buildings of the time' – was marked by the televising of the Consecration Service on 17 April 1959. This was not a live broadcast: film of the event had to be taken to London for processing and returned for transmission with overlaid sound and commentary on 19 April. The first live church service contributed to network came from St James's Parish Church in Belfast. The ordination of sixteen priests of the Society of African Missions, Dromantine College, Newry, on 10 December 1961, was also a genuine television outside broadcast. The ceremony in St Patrick's church in Lurgan, County Armagh, conducted by the Most Reverend Dr Eugene O'Doherty, with Father Gerard McGahan giving the running commentary, was the first ordination to have been televised anywhere in Europe. Both the Church of Ireland and the Catholic Church celebrated the fifteenth centenary of Saint

Televising *Morning Service* in the Church of Ireland Parish Church of St James in Belfast. The preacher is Canon Graham Craig.
BBC NI

145

The replica of St Colmcille's currach ready for launching in Lough Foyle in 1963.

Patrick's death in 1961 and, two years later, the fourteenth centenary of Saint Colmcille's missionary journey from Derry to Iona, even though historians did not share their certainty about the accuracy of the dates. The ceremonies included: Pontifical High Mass, attended by three cardinals, in St Patrick's Cathedral in Armagh; a Service of Thanksgiving 'for the life and witness of St Columba' in the Church of Ireland Cathedral Church of St Columb in Derry; a talk, *Sailing to Iona,* by the Most Reverend William Philbin, Catholic Bishop of Down and Connor; and a television presentation by Moore Wasson of the Archbishop of Canterbury, the Most Reverend Arthur Michael Ramsay, preaching at the St Patrick's Day Pilgrimage Service in Downpatrick Cathedral.

Controversy was studiously avoided. *Meeting Point* was launched as a discussion programme on television in the early 1960s but the producers were careful in their choice of topics. The discussion on 25 November 1962 was entitled *Christianity without Religion,* on the idea that acceptance of the Christian faith leads one beyond religion, with Canon Anthony Hanson, Alan Milne and Reverend T.C. Patterson. *Gospel without Myth,* the *Meeting Point* subject for August 1963, was discussed between Monsignor Ryan, Reverend Dr Ernest

Best and Reverend John Young, and chaired by Dr Jim Kincaid, principal of Dungannon Royal School and a future National Governor in Northern Ireland. In February 1963 Sir Tyrone Guthrie talked about religion, drama and life with Reverend Donald Cairns, himself the presenter of a request programme, *Hymns of Praise,* on Tuesday evenings. A programme on Sunday 4 May 1964 took 'a hard look at Sunday schools today' with Harry Thompson, 'a parent and primary teacher' (soon to become a full-time broadcaster), and John Malone, a former Sunday-school supervisor and the inspirational principal of Orangefield Boys Secondary School.

By 1966 *Meeting Point* had become much more courageous. The topic for Sunday 3 April was *History and Division: A Consideration of Historical Factors Making for Separation in Ireland,* with Professor Theo Moody, David Kennedy, Reverend Michael Dewar and Reverend John Young, with Charles Brett as chairman, also screened on BBC ONE. The subject for discussion may have been brave but the choice of panel ensured that no hardline views would be expressed and that there would be a complete absence of acrimony. *De Ecclesia,* 'a consideration of the Constitution of the Church decreed by the Second Vatican Council', on the BBC Northern Ireland Home Service on Sunday 11 December 1966, brought together Reverend Eric Gallagher, Reverend Professor J.L. Haire DD, Father Desmond Wilson and Fergus O'Duffy.

Relations between the main Christian Churches had warmed very considerably since the recriminations of earlier decades and this was reflected in the meetings of the BBC Northern Ireland Religious Advisory Committee. Harmony was increased by the appointment of Father Agnellus Andrew as Roman Catholic Assistant to Head of Religious Broadcasting. Much attention was given to lobbying by smaller Protestant denominations to be given a 'fair share' of religious broadcasts in the region. In 1962 a deputation approached the BBC and Henry McMullan brought the matter to the committee on 26 October. The minutes record:

> This deputation had contended that taken as a whole, they represented a sizeable minority. Since then they had formed themselves into a committee, and forwarded a petition signed by some seven thousand people.
>
> The Committee discussed difficulties which could arise in dealing with such a group of 'Mission Hall' sects. The BBC, of course, could not prevent such a committee being formed, but it was understood that it was in form only a working party.
>
> After a very full discussion, the Committee agreed that whilst approving the principle of minority broadcasts, the matter of dealing with broadcasts from these extreme minority groups be left to the discretion of the BBC.

The ball was then batted on from Ormeau Avenue to the BBC Central Religious Advisory Body. The London committee gave a clear thumbs down to the lobbyists:

> In order to claim the opportunity to share in religious broadcasting the

minority religious group must be *both* sufficiently close theologically to churches in the main stream, *and* sufficiently significant socially or historically . . .

So far as the facts appear at present, the only reason given for these religious groups in Belfast wishing to unite in fellowship is in order to make a claim to a broadcast. It seems doubtful if the BBC could accept such a fellowship as a religious minority within the terms of the main stream policy . . .

What and Why was launched in 1962 in Magee College, Derry, as discussions between students and well-known Protestant clergy and scholars. Church services, devotions and religious talks dominated output and, particularly when programmes were networked, there was close collaboration with the BBC music department. For example, *Songs of Praise* from Balmoral on 13 November 1966 featured Irene Sandford as soloist, the BBC Northern Ireland Orchestra led by David Adams and conducted by Havelock Nelson, and with Edgar Boucher introducing the hymns. A *Meeting Point* programme on 4 June 1967, also networked, was hardly likely to remind British viewers that Northern Ireland had its own special problems of bitter religious division. Entitled *Collared*, Reverend Billy Magee reflected twenty years on what it meant to wear a clerical collar. He said: 'The average church congregation – and even the outsider – wants a tame man on a lead. I must fight like the devil to be free of this kind of bondage. It sets me apart in a way I ought never to consent to. It forces me to live at arm's length from reality.'

Viewpoint, screened on 25 January 1967 and introduced by Harry Thompson, did tackle the question of sectarianism. Called *A Kindling Flame*, it accepted that Catholics and Protestants have 'lived in relative isolation from each other while geographically close' and that in 'such a situation lack of information, misconception, and prejudice breed a quite unnatural fear at the possibility of closer encounter'. The programme regarded apprehension of ecumenism as a major cause of distrust. The title arose from the belief that while 'the flame of religious bitterness has sometimes flared' there is another flame, the kindling of 'mutual acceptance and respect on the part of communities and communions formerly estranged'. In his *Radio Times* preview, the producer Moore Wasson explained further:

> The movement of history has forced a change, and of course the Bible and Christian belief relate the working of the spirit of God very closely to the movement of history. The changing economic situation has brought large numbers of new citizens to the province who are unacquainted with old divisions. Employers increasingly take no account of religious differences. New political attitudes are being born. Christian scholars in all traditions are looking back to the beginnings of the first century and to Christian origins.

The assumption that social, technological and economic advance and improved relations between the main Churches would inexorably lead to greater harmony was not confined to Broadcasting House. It was a view very widely held by liberal members of Northern Ireland's middle classes. Less than two years after this programme, they learned how horribly wrong they had been.

During the first few years of the Troubles the Religious Advisory Committee was at a loss to know how best to respond to the violence. Committee members discussed a programme which looked at the causes of religious hatred, *Who is My Neighbour?*, and clearly could not agree beyond the view that 'there may be a place for more informative types of programmes' and, the minutes of 8 October 1969 continue: 'A suggestion was made that a programme should be mounted showing co-operation between people of different religions, but it was agreed that this could not be contrived by the BBC but must reflect what is already happening.' The committee returned to the question on 17 September 1971 and some members said they would like to see 'the kind of programme that would be built up over a period of months reflecting, say, the life of a smallish town and conveying an idea of all the positive things that were happening – community relations, joint projects and work of churches and social service groups. This would redress the balance in news items that are destructive.' Others were not so sure.

A sea change began with the advent of BBC RADIO ULSTER. By now the view was gaining ground that television was not always the ideal medium for

Children from Lowwood Primary School in Belfast who sang carols in November 1963 on BBC ONE Northern Ireland's *Invitation*.

BBC NI

Songs of Praise from
Bangor Abbey.

religious programmes, apart from *Songs of Praise,* carol services and important ceremonies – too often programmes on religion resulted in visually unstimulating 'talking heads'. Radio was the better vehicle. In fact, the region demonstrated very soon afterwards that meaningful religious programmes could indeed be made for television, which could be both arresting and visually appealing.

Father Jim Skelly joined the staff as Religious Broadcasting Assistant, Northern Ireland and injected a new vigour into religious programmes. *Perspectives* was launched as a new series to tackle controversial topics. Programmes included *Was Jesus God?*; *Passion and Politics,* which discussed symbolism and myths and other issues arising from A.T.Q. Stewart's *The Narrow*

Ground: Aspects of Ulster, 1609–1969; *A Wexford Christmas,* on a group which had revived carols dating from penal times; *The Charismatic Movement*, which also included controversial excerpts from a film on the evangelist Leslie Hale; and *Talbot's Box*, with excerpts from the Thomas Kilroy play. *Hello Sunshine* replaced *Perspectives* and the series won warm praise from Dr Colin Morris, the Head of Religious Programmes, Television, (later Northern Ireland Controller), who said he was 'envious of the imagination and enthusiasm which went into the programmes'. *Where Genesis Begins*, a film about the poet Patrick Kavanagh and the religious influences on his work, won wide praise and was given a showing on BBC TWO.

Moore Wasson retired in 1979, Jim Skelly became the Head of Religious Programmes, and Reverend Ernest Rea (later Head of Religious Broadcasting in London) and Maggie Stanfield were recruited as producers. The breakthrough in radio programmes was first made with *Broadsheet*, a current affairs religious programme which began briefly with Paul McDowell and then had as its presenter Trevor Williams. This swiftly became *Sunday Sequence* in September 1980, a radio series which would in time secure a faithful audience encompassing a great many listeners who would normally tune to a different station when a religious programme came on the air.

By March 1981 *Sunday Sequence* was rightly being described by Skelly as 'the flagship of the department' and when it was suggested to him that the programme was too controversial and not positive enough in its approach to religious problems and subjects, he responded that 'controversy quickened the flow of information which in its turn eliminated ignorance which was so often the basis of fear'. Instead of becoming tired with the passing of the years, *Sunday Sequence* gained stature. In part this was the influence of a new producer, Terry Sharkie, who had a background in news and current affairs. He gave the programme orientation and thrust, and ensured that questions were searching. Part of the attraction of *Sunday Sequence* was that it was not a programme which took refuge in sound bites: it was never felt necessary to close a discussion down after three or five minutes – participants and interviewees were given a chance to expound their views in full and others could respond in detail without, in the words of producer, Reverend Dr Bert Tosh (who would later become Chief Producer Religion), 'blood all over the floor'. Extreme sensitivity and compassion were essential at terrible moments, particularly the Remembrance Day bomb in Enniskillen in 1987. Malachi O'Doherty moved listeners deeply by the care and empathetic way he interviewed victims of violence. Listening at home one morning Moore Sinnerton recalled that it was the silences which affected him the most. Alison Hilliard, returning from London to present *Sunday Sequence* for a while, said in an interview with Dorothy Gharbaoui:

> *Sunday Sequence* has a unique agenda. We can examine issues in the news from an ethical standpoint. Religion in Northern Ireland touches people more deeply than anything else, and any programme which touches people makes for excellent broadcasting . . .

In Northern Ireland people often hear only what they want to hear, whether in broadcast news or in conversation. In this programme, we have access to people's most innermost beliefs, and we try to make them question their attitudes and perceptions. It's not a safe programme nor one that is aimed only at 'religious' listeners. In this region, political circumstances can force people to work out how to apply faith in a practical way.

A similar freshness was being brought by the Reverend Dr Bert Tosh into *Thought for the Day*, a brief, early morning talk which had largely been inhabited by the middle-aged, the male, the layman sounding like a cleric. The scope was greatly broadened and deeply held Christian beliefs were not always *de rigueur*. The two-and-a-half-minute talks were mostly pre-recorded, but on Mondays and Fridays they were broadcast live, allowing speakers to refer to very current events if appropriate. Father Pat Buckley, for example, spoke affectingly about the recent death of his father, while, on a more banal note, in April 2000 a speaker referred to the difficulty he was having with the new British Telecom telephone numbers. In 1999 listeners were invited to submit their 'Millennium Thoughts': seventy scripts were received and ten were broadcast.

This New Day began in the early 1990s as an early Sunday morning programme not overtly religious, with light music and guests who had been generally involved in humanitarian work. One memorable interview was with Edith Devlin who had written about her upbringing in Dublin as a poor Protestant and in later life attracted such huge audiences to her lectures on literature that Queen's University was forced to make the Whitla Hall available to her. *Sunday with Brian D'Arcy* was an engaging magazine of folk religion, meditation, and readings presented by the Passionist priest. *Rhythm and Soul* gave Steve Stockman, the Presbyterian chaplain at Queen's University, free rein to introduce and play contemporary religious music. *Sounds Sacred*, much appreciated by the elderly in particular, was a request programme for those eager to listen to familiar hymns and tunes. *The Protestant Mind,* a four-part series which also went out on network, won much praise: in it Mary McAleese, a Catholic brought up in Belfast's Ardoyne, subsequently a lecturer in law at Queen's University, a member of the BBC Broadcasting Council, and elected President of the Irish Republic in 1997, gave her assessment of the Protestant majority, both as a neighbour and an outsider.

While radio remained the mainstay of religious broadcasting in the region, some fine occasional television programmes were made, including an award-winning feature on Skellig Michael (a remote pinnacle island off the Kerry coast, where monks built a monastery in early Christian times); a biography of the Belfast-born orientalist and expert on wandering medieval Irish scholars, Helen Waddell; a programme on St Patrick's Purgatory on Lough Derg; and a feature on Trinity College Dublin. An ambitious series for the millennium year, a joint production with RTÉ called *On this Rock,* looked at Christianity in Ireland from the earliest times. It avoided a chronological approach, though the first programme explored (for some to an uncomfortable degree) the connections between Celtic paganism and early Irish Christian practices, some of which – such as visits to holy wells – continue to the present day. The second told about the Protestants; the third, the Catholic story (in particular, the Penal Laws, and the nineteenth century renewal and devotional revolution); the fourth, missionary activity from the 1800s onwards; the fifth, *Sacred Space*, on how faith has been and is expressed in metalwork, on vellum and in stained glass; and the last on the zenith and the decline of organised Churches since the middle of the twentieth century.

Particularly in the final decades of the twentieth century, society in Northern Ireland became less formally religious and more and more people were prepared to express doubts openly. As more listeners and viewers were seeking a meaning to life outside organised religion, the broadcasters had to find ways of reflecting these changes. The challenge has been to keep communication going by remembering that much inherited religious language is steadily losing its familiarity.

8

SPORT AND
OUTSIDE BROADCASTS

UNTIL THE BBC BECAME A CORPORATION, the scope for outside broadcasts was limited because newspaper proprietors, fearful that their industry would be ruined by wireless reports, had persuaded the Post Office to restrict items for broadcast. It was not until 1927 that sporting occasions and public events could be covered. The first broadcasts outside the studio were of concerts, religious services and light entertainment from the stage. Special lines were laid to the Ulster Hall, the Empire Theatre and the Wellington Hall, and, from 1931, to the Hippodrome. The concentration on Belfast occurred for technical reasons and only those with sophisticated valve sets could receive a decent signal much beyond the city limits. The first 2BE outside broadcast, describing the launch of a ship from Queen's Island, was made in 1927 and, according to the BBC Year Book: 'The cracking of timber and the rush of water as the ship took to her natural element were conveyed in a most realistic manner to those who were unable to witness the launch.' The microphone was taken to Stormont on 19 May 1928 for the ceremony of laying the foundation stone of the government buildings and, of course, it returned four years later for the opening of the Northern Ireland parliament by the Prince of Wales.

During the summer of 1927 commentary on the Ulster Grand Prix motorcycle races was relayed for the first time and the microphone would return to this event on many occasions. Here is an early report from a commentator, spoken in perfect Received Pronunciation:

> Yes, here they come, here they come. Archer leading, sorry, Foster leading Wood. Hello! Wood has pulled into the pit here. What's the matter with him? Just seems to be filling up with petrol. He's taken his goggles off, having a look at his machine. Foster has gone on and is taking the lead. Yes, he's obviously run short of fuel, shortly than anticipated and is now pushing his machine and away he goes. You'll probably hear him start . . . [*Loud revving*]

In 1928 there were commentaries on the Ulster Tourist Trophy Motor Car Race on the Ards peninsula (Lord Craigavon's sporting passion) and the BBC had two commentators, one in the grandstand and the other at a selected point on the course.

Opposite:
Gerry Anderson on location for
Anderson on the Road.
BBC NI

Until 1930 the Station Director handled most of the outside broadcasts himself but increasingly he had to hand over to the Chief Engineer because he was often a leading guest at such functions. The microphone travelled further: to the dedication of new cathedral bells in Londonderry in 1929; to join summer dances and concert parties in Portrush; and to relay speeches made at the Irish Society's luncheon in Derry on the occasion of the opening of Craigavon Bridge over the Foyle in 1933. In the same year in Belfast the opening of the Royal Courts of Justice was covered, and a commentary on the departure of the Liverpool boat from Donegall Quay. The microphone, the talks producer John Boyd observed later, 'seemed to have the power of making army generals and field marshals tremble at the knees and become tongue tied'. The golf commentator George Nash remembered being at Royal Portrush:

> I was their secretary and the occasion was the opening of the new Championship course for which the BBC had asked for a short eye-witness account. The broadcast was to be given from a Portrush hotel and there I eventually found myself with four or five well-thumbed pages of manuscript damp with the sweat of anguish.

Nash met George Marshall and Henry McMullan in the lobby and mentioned his nervousness:

> 'Well, it's like this,' said Mr McMullan, 'only last week a comedian came into our studios in Belfast, took one look at the microphone and bolted!'

The Maze racecourse in County Down was a regular venue for outside broadcasts. Here is a sample of an early commentary:

> Here we are at the Maze racecourse, you can probably tell by the sound of the crowds outside. The Maze racecourse is just outside Lisburn and today is being run here the second Ulster Derby. There is a marvellous crowd at this meeting, even more than there was for the Coronation Cup in May, and we are in our usual position just behind the popular stand.
>
> Now, the weather here has clouded over. From about twelve o'clock we had brilliant sunshine here until about a quarter of an hour ago. Now it has clouded over but I don't think that Mr R.C. Lyle, who's with me here in the box, will have great difficulty because the visibility seems to be pretty adequate. All ready, Mr Lyle?
>
> Right-O! First of all I'd better give you the runners and riders and owners and they are as follows: Lord Derby's Lazybones . . .

2BE was able to get running commentaries on rugby matches at Lansdowne Road in Dublin and from the Curragh racecourse, but the Belfast station was unhappy about the quality of the broadcasts. John Sutthery went to Dublin in 1938 and swiftly came to a gentleman's agreement with Radio Éireann's Dr T.J. Kiernan, which allowed BBC equipment, commentators and engineers to operate in Éire with the particular intention of covering major sporting events.

He explained to his superiors in London:

> As you are aware, there are a number of events of first-class importance which take place in Eire each year and which are in most cases broadcast by Radio Eireann . . .
>
> The Cork Grand Prix and the Phoenix Park Grand Prix Motor Races are both of absolutely first-class importance, but are handled by commentators who have been rejected from here as unsuitable . . . the Dublin Horse Show is perhaps the most important event of its kind in the world, but is not very satisfactorily handled . . .

Surprisingly, Marshall supported Sutthery but both were rapped over the knuckles by London and the unsatisfactory situation continued.

Strong protest ensued when the BBC in Belfast decided to include sports results in the Sunday news bulletins. On 28 April 1934 the *Northern Whig* correspondent recommended that the presbyteries of Ulster send a resolution 'to those concerned, pointing out the mind of the people of Ulster that this must be discontinued at once'. A contributor to the letters page of the *Belfast News Letter* agreed:

> It has become the custom of the Belfast Station of the BBC to broadcast on Sunday evening, as an item of news, the results of local Gaelic football matches of the day. I am, I think, representative of the majority of the citizens of our loyal province – a respecter of the Sabbath observance as a day of rest. We do not want to hear of exploits in the realms of a sport which holds no interest for most of us – loyal citizens of a mighty empire to whom the Gaelic mind, speech and pastimes mean nothing.

There was such a furore that eventually Lord Craigavon became involved and representations were made to the Director-General. The BBC, in Marshall's words, 'decided to give up broadcasting such results on the grounds that they were hurting the feelings of the large majority of people in Northern Ireland'. Meanwhile, for one-third of the people of Northern Ireland, Gaelic games were the sports of most interest. The GAA did not as yet press hard for running commentaries and, if they had, Marshall would have turned down their request without hesitation.

Because of fears that broadcasts would reduce the number of people paying at the gate to attend matches, Association Football authorities were slow to allow the Belfast station to relay commentaries on their games. As the thirties progressed the scope was widening and, indeed, the official opening of the Lisnagarvey transmitter by the Governor of Northern Ireland in 1936 was a major outside broadcasting event. Raymond Glendinning, a pioneer in getting recordings in the field, on Tuesday 7 March 1939 described the launch of the Royal Mail steamer *Andes* by Lady Craigavon at 11.15 a.m. and provided a commentary on the Darts Final of Down and Antrim League at 9.40 p.m. Two days later Glendenning was taking the microphone 'unobtrusively into the lives of the people of the Glens' in the feature *Dwellers in the Glens*.

From the outset, the Belfast station was anxious to avoid controversy. The Station Director, therefore, ruled firmly that the annual Twelfth procession should not be covered, even though it was one of the largest annual parades in western Europe, much bigger then than now because only a tiny minority could afford overseas holidays. Marshall allowed himself to be courted by Craigavon's government and, after coming to an agreement with the Bands' Association in 1937, it was difficult to resist calls for the parade to be the subject of an outside broadcast. He wrote to the Board of Governors in 1938:

> The next move was a difficult one to counter. It was a request that a running commentary should be broadcast on the procession of Orange Lodges on the Twelfth of July . . . the request for such a broadcast did not come from any insignificant source, but from the County Grand Secretary of the Belfast County Grand Lodge, and was backed up by a Cabinet Minister, the Attorney General and, finally, the Prime Minister himself . . .

Seeking approval from the governors, Marshall wrote again in 1939, reporting that 'a considerable time has to be spent in explaining to Cabinet Ministers and high officials of the Orange Order that such a broadcast would conflict with the BBC's inflexible rule governing such political occasions. This year considerable "copy" was made of the fact that the ceremony of the Pope's coronation was broadcast, and that therefore Ulster's Protestant ceremony should also be included . . .' Marshall warned that the issue would crop up the following year but the outbreak of war postponed the matter.

The German invasion of Poland on 1 September 1939 ended regional broadcasting and it was not until the spring of 1940 that Belfast began to make programmes again as its contribution to the Home and Forces Services. Then, between January 1942 and towards the end of 1943, Northern Ireland was the principal base for United States troops in western Europe. When the first Americans disembarked at Dufferin Quay in Belfast on 26 January 1942, the BBC was there:

> Well, the ship is coming alongside, very much quicker than we expected. Any minute now the gangway will be run up. The troops are lining the decks and they are still looking very serious indeed. They are taking a look and probably wondering who all these people on the quay are. [Cheer] they got a cheer just now from some of the dockers on the quay and they waved back at them. And now the ship is tying up . . . It's so close that the American general on board is shaking hands with some of the officers on shore.
>
> One or two of the men are smiling but most of them look quietly interested. They are pretty stalwart fellows these – they are big tall, big hunky chaps . . . The gangway is being run up and General Chaney,

John Holness, a Harland and Wolff employee, interviewed for a Northern Ireland contribution to the BBC Home Service programme *In Britain Now* in April 1942.

BBC NI

commanding the United States forces in the UK, comes over to meet him. General Harvard who commands this force comes down to meet him. The general who commands this force looks a bit nervous as he comes down to meet all the people here. And now he's on land shaking hands with General Chaney.

Denis Johnston, dressed in uniform as BBC war correspondent, did several outside broadcasts with American soldiers, including GIs who had just sung a rousing tune for him:

> JOHNSTON. Well, that's pretty good boys – is that as good a platoon as you can see?
>
> SOLDIER. The best platoon in the whole battalion!
>
> JOHNSTON. Well, I'm over here: here is a sergeant with an Irish name. How did you get your name?
>
> SERGEANT. Well, that's from my grandparents that came from over here in the northern part of Ireland.
>
> JOHNSTON. You know there's a river here in this part of the world with your name?
>
> SERGEANT. No, I didn't, Sir, until I came over here.
>
> JOHNSTON. Well, what were you in civilian life?
>
> SOLDIERS. I was a bartender by trade in civilian life . . . I was a steeplejack . . . I was a hotel manager – head waiter.
>
> JOHNSTON. Well, what do you think of this country?
>
> SOLDIER. Well, it's a pretty fair country, Sir, but I'd sort of like to be home too. You know how it is. You go from one country to another – you'd always like to be back where you came from.
>
> JOHNSTON. Tell me about the British army coming over.
>
> SOLDIER. We met some of the RAF guys. A pretty swell bunch of fellas. We made some good friends there . . .
>
> JOHNSTON. Did they teach you anything on the way over?
>
> SOLDIER. They taught us a few songs.
>
> JOHNSTON. How about singing one of them?
>
> SOLDIER. How about that one, Johnny – 'The Troopship out of Bombay'?
>
> [*Soldiers sing song in full*]
>
> JOHNSTON. Well, boys, you picked that up pretty quickly. Good luck! Very glad to see you.
>
> SOLDIERS. Very glad to see you too.

Programmes were made with American troops with intriguing titles such as *Ack-Ack*, *Beer-Beer* and *Billy's Welcome Day with the Doughboys*. Finally, when the war was over in Europe on 8 May 1945, the centre of Belfast was filled with huge rejoicing crowds. Henry McMullan was there with the microphone (probably in Anderson and McAuley's department store or the Bank Buildings), struggling at times to make himself heard:

> Belfast is letting itself go, that's plain fact. Whoever first invented the phrase about the reserve of the Ulster Scotch should see the scene

spread out below me here since the Prime Minister's statement. I'm perched up here in a shop window above the great central artery of Belfast. On my right the City Hall, on my left the wide Royal Avenue and stretching away down in front of me the High Street that leads to the docks.

And below me the population of this city – laughing, cheering and dancing – is surging past in great waves of colour and sound in the brilliant sunshine. I, at least, can say it's brilliant sunshine. This is one of those days that is sent for special occasions and Belfast is making the most of it. The colour of the crowd is one of the most exciting things about it . . . The women seem to have brought out every scarlet coat that's ever been imported into this country and pale blue is another that is predominating.

VE Day, 8 May 1945: surrounded by excited crowds close to Belfast City Hall, Harry McMullan interviews RUC Constable Johnson for *Victory Report*.

BBC NI

The whole dingy buildings of the city centre – we make no apologies for their dinginess today, we're proud of it – have broken out into a rash of flags and bunting, elaborate displays of red, white and blue. Plenty of American flags up round us too. America sent her best contingents of troops in the European zone to Belfast – the result: pretty peculiar things happened to the Ulster accent. But Northern Ireland made a lot of new friends, so they are giving a very proud place to the Stars and Stripes . . .

Well, there it is. Tears, cheers, laughter and a feeling that they've worked and suffered and come through with their tails up. That's Belfast today and that's our welcome in Ulster.

The restoration of regional broadcasting in the summer of 1945 did not restore the level of output from the BBC in Northern Ireland to what it had been on the eve of the war. The wavelength had to be shared with the North East of England during the time slots allotted by London, staff had to be recruited, and, though Broadcasting House had been completed in 1941, the building was little more than a shell. However, the mobile recording unit, used extensively by Denis Johnston during the war until he was posted to southern Europe, was still available. When in 1948 the newly appointed Regional Director, Andrew Stewart, discovered that the Plowden Committee's restrictions regarding the rationing of equipment did not apply to Northern Ireland, Broadcasting House was properly equipped. It became possible to broadcast even where there was no telephone connection. For example, when a St Patrick's Day service was broadcast from the Memorial Church at Saul, County Down, a small short-wave transmitter in a BBC van relayed the service to a receiving unit attached to the nearest telephone line two miles away and from there to the main transmitters.

A team of sports reporters, then called 'observers', was drawn together for a busy Saturday. At the end of the afternoon they would speed to Broadcasting House and gather in one studio, where, guided by Kenneth Best, the producer, one by one they gave their reports. All reports had to be scripted and rapid composition and writing were essential. In 1949 the principal sports reporters were: Sammy Walker (rugby); Billy Drennan and Jimmy Hughes (soccer); Jack Carroll (hockey); Jack Turner (tennis); Joe Bell (cycling); Andy Smyth (boxing); Bert McKimm (motor racing); and Billy Mackey (athletics). There was more flexibility in this area than most others because, in addition to the scripted reports, there were interviews conducted by Cyril Hume. The announcer was Ronald Rosser, a familiar voice for many years. Earlier in the afternoon there would be a live commentary on what was judged to be the most important match of the day.

The major outside broadcasts listed in the Annual Report for 1952–3 were: April 1952, the meeting of the British Council of Churches in Belfast; May 1952, the presentation of the Freedom of Enniskillen to the Duke of Gloucester, Colonel in Chief of the Royal Inniskilling Fusiliers; August 1952, Grand Prix Motor Cycle Race on the Clady Circuit; September 1952, speeches by Professor D.A. Hill and the Duke of Edinburgh to the British Association in Belfast; and January 1953, the swearing-in ceremony of the new Governor of Northern Ireland, Lord Wakehurst. This list, of course, reflects what Broadcasting House thought were the most appropriate events for outside broadcasts but it also gives an accurate impression of a then peaceful society. The BBC governors and senior management in London could be forgiven for believing that Northern Ireland was a place where nothing very much was going to happen.

Lieutenant Commander Harry McMullan of the BBC – soon after to be appointed Head of Programmes – watching the arrival at the port of Londonderry of eight German U-boats on 14 May 1945. His eye-witness account was broadcast in the 6 o'clock News on the BBC Home Service on Tuesday 15 May.
BBC NI

161

Those who gave live running commentaries on sports events were amongst
the most accomplished broadcasters of the day, and they were not knocked
from their perch by the arrival of television. A mobile outside broadcasting television unit visited Northern Ireland in November 1955 but a permanent live
transmission facility was not installed until 1957. Sport is news and the labori-
ous business of sending film across the Irish Sea to be processed in London and
returned again meant that by the time the film was back in Belfast it was not
news, it was history. The first televised sporting events were shot by news and
current affairs journalists. Cecil Taylor was told he would have to learn to use
the television camera himself. The sports producer Charlie Freer, who hailed
from Achill in County Mayo, had the task of organising sports results and covering major matches. His first love was rugby and he did not appear to give
any thought to radio or television coverage of Gaelic games, apart from giving
results.

The televising of GAA matches was not the outcome of agonising debate
behind the portals of Broadcasting House – it just happened. Cecil Taylor is
proud of the part he played. As a newsman he became aware that on one
weekend in 1961 three major sporting events were about to happen: a rugby
match between Ulster and Lancashire at the Ravenhill ground in Belfast; a soccer match at Windsor Park in Belfast; and the All-Ireland Gaelic football final

between Down and Kerry at Croke Park in Dublin. Taylor went to see his Head of Programmes, Henry McMullan, and proposed that the news department film all three events. 'It all seems like a good idea,' McMullan replied. 'Would you authorise up to £100 facility fee?' Taylor asked, and this was agreed. Once in Dublin the general secretary of the GAA was astonished: 'And you're telling me the BBC in Belfast wants to do this? You're not pulling my leg?' When Taylor assured him that he had the Corporation's authorisation, the GAA man asked, 'Well, how much would you be looking for?' Taylor responded: 'We would be paying you.' And so, in the first contract between BBC Northern Ireland and the GAA the sum of ten pounds changed hands. Since the age of the video recorder was some distance ahead, the game had to be filmed. Film ran out after nine and a half minutes, and to ensure continuous coverage, Taylor had to hire a second camera – a deft hand was required to change from one camera to the other, especially if the game was an exciting one. Around twenty-five calls of appreciation were received in Broadcasting House for what was the first televised coverage anywhere of an All-Ireland GAA final.

In those early days of televised sports, for the programme *Arena,* all the filming was done by the news department. Taylor even took the initiative in tracking down commentators. 'God, I'd love to do that,' Jim McKeever, captain of the Derry GAA team, said to Taylor when asked to provide a running commentary on the first televised Gaelic match in Northern Ireland, which was in Lurgan. Televised reports in Northern Ireland were still brief and it was generally to network that viewers turned for their sport, and as the 1960s progressed, the news journalists had no time to set aside for sporting events.

Soccer star David Healy celebrates a goal for Northern Ireland against Yugoslavia. International soccer is only part of an unrivalled portfolio of sports rights won by BBC Northern Ireland.
PACEMAKER

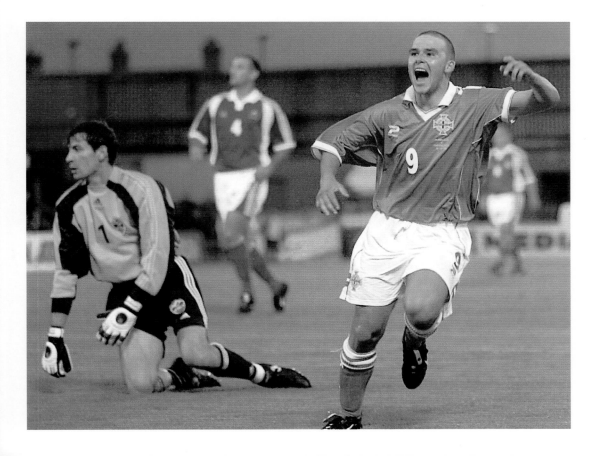

Until the mid-1960s, radio and television outside broadcasts had meant church services, sporting occasions, royal visits, ship launches and the like. Had the Troubles begun a decade earlier, news would have been conveyed overwhelmingly by radio, newspapers and cinema newsreels. From late 1968, outside broadcasts meant covering the Troubles by television camera and radio microphone – until this time 'normal weekly production' in the Belfast studios was a mere thirteen hours of radio and five hours of television. A crash programme of expansion had to be carried out in Broadcasting House, and London authorised a major increase in resources. By 1973 the television studio had high-speed film processing and editing facilities, a mobile vision recording unit and several film units. In addition, the region rented the central Exhibition Hall at Balmoral, used on a 'drive-in' basis by the television outside broadcasts unit, with more than four times the floor space available at Broadcasting House.

Sporting events in Northern Ireland often exposed the divisions in society and tensions arising from the conflict on occasion spilled over onto the terraces. For example, in the weeks following the ending of the IRA ceasefire on 9 February 1996 east Belfast residents blocked the progress of Catholic Cliftonville fans trying to reach Glentoran's Oval ground; Cliftonville

Charles Freer waits with a 'midget recording machine' on the 18th green at Warrenpoint to interview the golfing champion, Harry Bradshaw, in May 1955. Freer was the producer of the BBC Northern Ireland Home Service Saturday night programme, *Ulster Sports Report*.

BBC NI

supporters attempting to get to Shamrock Park in Portadown were set upon, police and civilians were injured and the match was abandoned; Brian Barnes threatened to pull out of the British Veterans Masters Championship at Royal Portrush Golf Club, though he was eventually persuaded to change his mind and won the tournament; and some major events were cancelled, including the Irish Swimming Championships in Belfast. The Sports Council, the Community Relations Council and soccer organisations made a concerted drive to reduce the menace of sectarianism at football grounds and, helped by the renewal of the ceasefire and the peace process, violence on the terraces and in their vicinity was significantly reduced. Disorder was not always intercommunal: the GAA had to grapple with the problem of on-field violence, for example, during the Ulster Hurling Final in 1997 between Dunloy and Lavey when there was a pitch invasion and four players were sent off. Surveys indicated that eight out of ten people believed that sport fostered better community relations. Certainly, there was massive cross-community support for Manchester United, which sustained a flourishing shop in central Belfast, and its manager, Alex Ferguson, found it worthwhile to be a frequent visitor to the region – a phenomenon reflected in a *Home Truths* documentary. Nevertheless, it was clear that during World Cup qualifying matches, Protestants supported the Northern Ireland team and Catholics backed that from the Republic of Ireland.

The BBC was faced with the challenge of reflecting the steady growth of participation in sport and leisure, from 43 per cent to 56 per cent between 1986 and 1996. By 1997, 37 per cent of the population over the age of sixteen were taking part in organised sport, though only 29 per cent of women were participants. In the same year an estimated half a million pounds were being spent per day on sport by the citizens of Northern Ireland; around 8,000 people were in sports-related employment; and £113.8 million of public money were being committed per annum to funding sporting activities. The National Lottery contributed over £6 million in 1997, the main recipients being Gaelic football, soccer and swimming. The most popular pursuits were walking, angling and swimming. Audiences increased, notably in Gaelic games, though attendances at Irish League soccer fixtures declined following the introduction of a two-tier system. The Irish rugby world was rocked by the move to professional status and the introduction of a £30,000 reward for loyalty failed to keep players of international calibre in Northern Ireland. When Ireland played Western Samoa in November 1995 only two members of the team were from Northern Ireland. In an attempt to induce rugby professionals to return the 'loyalty reward' was increased to £50,000 with a free car – this did something to stem the cross-channel flow and in November 1997 six locally-based players were selected for the Irish team which played New Zealand. The triumph of the Ulster team over Colomiers on 31 January 1999 in the European championship final did much to provide rugby in the region with a much-needed fillip. Indeed, interest in specific sports was usually raised to a remarkable degree by the success of local heroes such as athlete Mary Peters (winner of the pentathlon gold medal at the Munich Olympic Games in 1972), footballer George Best, snooker player Dennis Taylor, golfer Darren Clarke, jockey Tony Dobbyn, rugby player Jeremy Davidson and the motorcyclist Joey Dunlop, tragically killed in July 2000.

Once reluctance to cover Gaelic games and sports on Sundays had been steadily dissipated from the 1960s onwards the BBC as a public broadcaster aimed to provide as comprehensive coverage as possible to licence payers interested in spectator sports. Improved technology, camerawork and commentary greatly enhanced the quality of programmes but as the twentieth century was drawing to a close the region, like the network, found itself operating in a fiercely competitive environment. Sports controlling bodies recognised their power to sell rights to the highest bidder, particularly when Sky and other pay-per-view satellite companies were prepared to offer sums greater than those proposed by the BBC and the independent terrestrial companies. The dilemma in Ormeau Avenue was the same as that in London: How much of the licence fee was the BBC justified in setting aside to win sporting contracts?

BBC Northern Ireland was the first organisation to put a Gaelic game on the small screen but in the 1990s there ensued a tug of love between the broadcasters to get rights to cover the games. Until 1998 the broadcaster with no contract or rights could have only news access and that amounted to a total of two reports, each of one minute's duration, within twenty-four hours or during the first available news programme following each match. After that the use of match footage was prohibited. An agreement between the BBC, UTV and the GAA was reached in 1998 to share coverage of the championship. UTV was to present the Sunday programme for the first year and the BBC for the ensuing two years, an agreement which ensured a public service and rapidly-growing audiences. A similar agreement was made between the BBC and UTV to cover

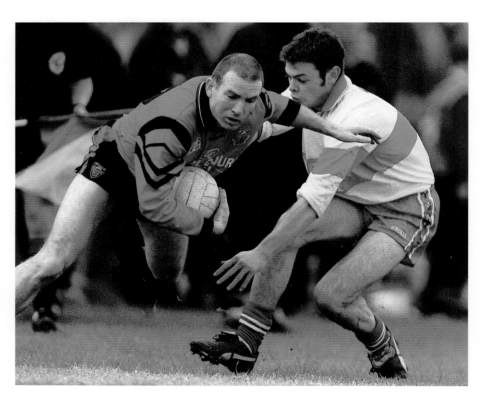

The old and the new of gaelic football – Down veteran Ross Carr, left, in a tussle with Derry's rising star Paul McFlynn.

PACEMAKER

166

Irish League soccer games. BBC Northern Ireland made an agreement with the Irish Rugby Football Union for domestic rugby including international friendlies, interprovincials and All-Ireland League matches. The region signed a four-year contract to televise the Isle of Man TT races, a five-year agreement to cover local road racing at Cookstown, Tandragee, mid-Antrim, Dundrod, Carrowdore and Kirkistown, and it made agreements for the Kerrygold Horse Show in Dublin, the GAA MacRory Cup, Schools Cup Rugby and international cross country events at Stormont. The unrivalled sporting contracts now enjoyed by BBC Northern Ireland owes much to the commitment and hard work of successive Heads of Sport, Joy Williams, Jim Neilly and Terry Smyth.

Contractual difficulties apart, more peaceful conditions allowed for more attention to be paid by broadcasters to sporting events. BBC RADIO ULSTER's flagship programme was *Saturday Sportsound* from 2.30 p.m. to 6 p.m. each week. The early part of the show, which carried live soccer commentary, tended to struggle for audiences in competition with BBC RADIO 5 LIVE but from 4 p.m. onwards more listeners tuned in to hear all of the major local results. *Sunday Sportsound*, from 3 p.m. to 5 p.m. in season, covered Gaelic games with commentators Owen McConnor, Michael Daly, Mattie McGleenan and Brian Canavan. On Fridays RADIO FOYLE had its own *Sportsdesk* with Richie Kelly between 4.30 p.m. and 5 p.m. On BBC Northern Ireland the most important regular coverage was provided by *Northern Ireland Results*, a particularly difficult programme to do because, owing to the vagaries of network's *Grandstand,* presenters Michael McNamee and Denise Watson did not know the duration of the broadcast until they were on air. *Sunday Grandstand from Northern Ireland* gave television coverage of Gaelic games subject to contract arrangements with UTV and the GAA. Special programmes included *King of the Road,* a 1997 documentary featuring Joey Dunlop, and motor bikes were the subject of a feature presented by Alison Comyn, *The Good Bike Guide.*

Significant sporting events could attract particularly large television audiences. Examples include: 89,000 for Northern Ireland versus Ukraine on *Sportsnight Northern Ireland* in 1996; 51,000 for the *Schools Cup Rugby Final,* also in 1996; 104,000 for Ulster versus Stade Français on 9 January 1999; 110,000 for motor bike racing on 11 June 1999; and an astonishing 221,000 for the European Rugby Final between Ulster and Colomiers at Lansdowne Road on 31 January 1999 (around a seventh of the entire population of Northern Ireland). Increasingly, listeners and viewers got sports reports and previews from news and magazine programmes and the faces and voices of such journalists as Jackie Fullerton, Jim Neilly, Adam Coates, Jackie Cummings and Michael McNamee became familiar in most homes through *Newsline, Good Morning Ulster* and *Evening Extra.* Sporting enthusiasts were among the first and most numerous to turn to

Ulster Captain David Humphreys and Mark Blair celebrate victory in the European Rugby Cup Final in Dublin in 1999.
PACEMAKER

BBC CHOICE Northern Ireland, particularly on Mondays, and to local pages of the BBC NEWS ONLINE site and they formed a high proportion of the 35,000 page impressions per week on the BBC Northern Ireland homepage (http://www.bbc.co.uk/ni) being registered by the spring of 2000.

The biggest outside broadcast operation ever undertaken was the Pope's visit to Ireland in 1979. BBC Northern Ireland was the only organisation publicly thanked by RTÉ for the 'help they received from the BBC in the planning and execution of an immensely complicated and successful operation'. On BBC RADIO ULSTER, *Sportswide* was added to the schedule to provide a daily look at sport and leisure across Northern Ireland. News about sport, in addition to detailed reporting of matches and events, was provided with greater frequency as the airtime extended from early morning to midnight. On BBC Northern Ireland, *Today's Sport* was launched in 1984 to precede *Inside Ulster*.

The technology of outside broadcasting was still comparatively unsophisticated in the 1970s. The radio outside broadcast unit was little more than a caravan sporting the BBC logo. Ian Harvey recalled covering the Balmoral Show for *Farm Gate* from the caravan parked beside the Pig Marketing Board stand. Just as the live report began, the heavens opened and Harvey's report was all but drowned by the thunderous drumming of the rain on the metal roof. The following year John Johnston had to broadcast on the show from the same venue. Five minutes before going on air the caravan's pull-out table (held only

Cameraman Peter Jones gets close to the action in a schools cup final at Ravenhill.

BBC NI

Jackie Fullerton interviews
Stephen Ferguson while
cameraman Stephen Clarkson
records the event

BBC NI

by two tiny screws) collapsed under the weight of the heavy equipment on top
of an audio technician's leg, already in plaster. The plaster saved the hapless
technician from further injury, but for the whole of the broadcast Ian Harvey
was under the broken table supporting all the equipment on his shoulder like
Charles Atlas. On another occasion the same duo were in London covering the
Smithfield Show for *Farm Gate* when power was suddenly switched off at the
mains at 6.30 p.m. A generator was started up but it only provided enough
power for broadcasting; the light had gone completely and Harvey could only
read his report throughout by the light of John Johnston's cigarette lighter.

In the 1980s the attention of outside broadcasting was still overwhelmingly
directed towards gathering the sounds and pictures of the Troubles. Events such
as the funeral of Bobby Sands in 1981 and the massive protest against the
Anglo-Irish Agreement in Belfast in November 1985 put the ingenuity of BBC
staff fully to the test.

The 1990s witnessed a rapid improvement in the technology available. In
1994 the region got a new satellite news–gathering vehicle capable of project-
ing pictures back to Broadcasting House and onto screens in less than a second. BBC Northern Ireland's outside broadcasting facility was now capable of
widescreen delivery with enhanced digital effects – one of the first services of
its kind in the United Kingdom. This new equipment was about to be delivered when the PIRA ceasefire was announced, demanding swift coverage of
public reaction. (The next biggest outside broadcasting operation to be
mounted was the visit of President Clinton in November 1995 – at least that
could be planned ahead.) On St Patrick's Day 1994, BBC Northern Ireland's

Religious Unit broadcast its most ambitious edition of *Songs of Praise*, from St Patrick's Cathedral in New York.

Political developments periodically imposed huge demands on outside broadcasts, as the politicians slowly approached the Good Friday accord at Stormont – British and Irish premiers Tony Blair and Bertie Ahern were called in to do what they could to promote agreement and President Clinton arrived at short notice, divulging much of his itinerary to Broadcasting House only the evening before. For years in succession the Orange Order stand-off at Drumcree demanded broadcaster's attention, and the 1998 referendums, election of the Assembly, coverage of Assembly debates and the formation of a new regional executive made for massive calls on the BBC's resources.

The return to near-normal conditions in Northern Ireland encouraged the region to launch *Town Challenge* as an annual ten-week series. Each selected town was asked to provide one team to take part in a treasure trail and a quiz and another to represent it in a physical endurance test. George Jones and Hugo Duncan presented the competition, celebrity guests awarded points to the participants, and the finalists went on to compete for the *Go for It* trophy. In 1997, for example, Stewartstown and Magherafelt competed at the Meadowpark playing fields, and Carrickfergus battled it out with Randalstown at the Carrickfergus marina in a contest which floated fifteen thousand rubber ducks. Having fun and doing silly things were of more importance than winning, and this sort of programme was not to everyone's taste. Liam Fay of the *Sunday Times,* on 4 July 1999, chose *Town Challenge* as a 'specific example of how television can embarrass its viewers':

George Jones gives Hugo Duncan a ride on a lawnmower to emphasise that contestants in BBC Northern Ireland's *Town Challenge* will be given silly things to do.

BBC NI

> The opening show of the current series came from the Crescent in Portaferry and every effort was expended to make the quayside look like a tropical wonderland. The contestants ran about in T-shirts, sandals and shorts. Tweedledum and Tweedledumber impaled their grins on ice-cream cones the size of the Taj Mahal.
>
> The attempt at a sun-licked Caribbean atmosphere would have been almost convincing but for the fat, greasy, Northern Irish rain drops that insolently flopped on to the lens throughout the proceedings.
>
> Occasionally, we caught a glimpse of the cameramen, who were swaddled in hefty anoraks with zipped-up hoods. Now that's comedy.

On the other hand, *Town Challenge* generated a huge amount of local interest and very extensive coverage in the local press, as well as winning a large television audience. 'This is all about town spirit,' Hugo Duncan told the *Ballyclare Gazette* and indeed district councils all over Northern Ireland seized on the enterprise to generate local enthusiasm, often setting aside funds for the teams, providing free buses, and placing advertisements in the press (such as 'LARNE NEEDS YOU! IT'S THE BATTLE OF THE TITANS. LARNE VERSUS ANTRIM . . .'). In a region emerging from three decades of fear an occasional excess of silliness was no bad thing.

Another programme which called for some clowning around was the annual *Children in Need*. This huge fund-raising event consistently generated more interest and provoked more active participation per head of the population in Northern Ireland than in any other BBC region. In 1999, the twentieth year of the appeal was launched a month ahead of the six-and-a-half-hour show by Jackie Fullerton and Shauna Lowry, in company with Pudsey Bear. During the weeks before the live show in the Blackstaff studio, film crews went out to record fund-raising efforts all over Northern Ireland. Examples of how money was generated included: a sponsored leg-waxing session by students of North Down and Ards Institute; a non-uniform day in the Ulster Bank in Main Street, Bangor; children's choirs on Stena Line vessels, which raised some twelve thousand pounds from passengers; a twelve-hour non-stop sponsored fitness session by staff at the Sixmile Leisure Centre in County Antrim; a students' 'Pea Push' in Derry – in which a frozen pea was pushed 200 yards at the North West Institute; and a choice of sponsored kick-a-thon, 'walking the plank', being put in the stocks, or wet sponge throwing at Cascades Leisure Centre in Portadown. On the night itself, 26 November, well over two hundred thousand watched as virtually all the well-known faces and voices of staff in Broadcasting House and Foyle's Northland Road willingly made fools of themselves. Altogether it was a remarkably unifying experience for a people so long rent by division.

Jackie Fullerton and Shauna Lowry, in the company of Pudsey Bear, doing their bit for *Children in Need* in 1999.

BBC NI

9

FARMING
AND GENERAL PROGRAMMES

OR ALL THE INDUSTRIAL AND COMMERCIAL STRENGTH of Belfast and the north-east, agriculture was by far the most important single industry when 2BE began broadcasting. Farming engaged 26 per cent of Northern Ireland's workforce, compared with 6.2 per cent in the United Kingdom as a whole. Since the station's signal – for the great majority of those who could not afford valve sets – only reached a little beyond the periphery of Belfast, programmes for farmers were likely to have a limited take-up. The Ministry of Agriculture, however, was the first government department to realise the potential of broadcasting and seized the opportunity to use the microphone to promote improvement.

Thanks to the Land Purchase Acts, the last of which was promoted at Westminster in 1925, almost all of Northern Ireland's 105,215 holdings were owner-occupied. These family farms, however, were exceptionally small: only 4.4 per cent exceeded one hundred acres, compared with 8.8 per cent in the Irish Free State and 20.9 per cent in England and Wales; and a census of 1937 showed that 37.9 per cent of holdings were below fifteen acres and 82.7 below fifty acres. During the interwar years, times were hard down on the farm in a world of falling prices. The Ministry of Agriculture was as interventionist as it dared under the terms of the 1920 Government of Ireland Act and was determined to do all it could to ensure premium prices for Ulster's produce in the lucrative but open English market.

Civil servants in the Ministry of Agriculture, in effect, wrote the talks for farmers. They won the approval of Charles Siepmann in his report of 1936: 'The talks to farmers are already popular and a genuine public service.' Progress with rural electrification and the more powerful signal from the Lisnagarvey transmitter enabled most farmers to hear the programmes from the autumn of 1936 onwards. The talks were used to inform farmers of marketing legislation to ensure that only clean, graded and fresh eggs were exported, of the compulsory licensing of bulls to eliminate inferior sires under the Livestock Breeding Act, and of legislation designed to raise the quality of exported potatoes. They were told about the latest methods of husbandry and encouraged to change breeds of pigs so that the traditionally fat Ulster ham and bacon could compete with the leaner Danish product. Peter Fitzpatrick established himself as a popular broadcaster to farmers as well as to children. A typical talk he gave

John Johnston (left) and Ian Harvey, presenters of the BBC RADIO ULSTER series *Farm Gate.*

BBC NI

173

was *Farmers' Work and Worry*, on the relatively new art of making silage. Sir Basil Brooke, the Minister of Agriculture in the 1930s, enjoyed coming to the microphone to exhort farmers but the ending of regional broadcasting on the outbreak of war forced him to resort to driving about in a hired tobacco van with a loudspeaker to urge men at numerous markets and fairs to plough up the sward. He also sent a personal letter to every single farmer in Northern Ireland.

Perhaps it was due in part to the effectiveness of BBC talks that Northern Ireland was the only part of the United Kingdom to exceed its quota of ploughed land in 1939–40. Craigavon was allowed to broadcast just before he died, but Ursula Eason's proposals to bring other members of the government to the Home Service microphone were usually turned down. Brooke did, however, get permission to deliver a spirited address entitled *The Plough Versus the Submarine*. When the war was over, the Westminster government had no intention of returning to an open market in farming – the priority was maximum food production and if farmers had to be protected and subsidised then that would have to be done. In short, farmers were prized members of the community and this was to be reflected in broadcasting.

Talks by Fitzpatrick and others, and bulletins on fat stock and other prices, still formed the mainstay of the service to farmers. Professor A.E. Muskett of Queen's University, the expert who came most regularly to the microphone, had a distinctive personal style and became something of an institution. The weekly talks, *For Ulster Farmers*, were arranged under the guidance of the Agricultural Advisory Committee, made up of practical and enthusiastic farmers from all over the province, together with a few scientific research men and some administrators. The committee proposed suitable subjects for broadcasts and reviewed talks already given. A.A. McGuckian, the committee's chairman, explained in 1949 why he thought the talks were so important:

Professor A.E. Muskett of Queen's University, the most regular giver of farming talks in the postwar years. He was long known as a colourful character, well worth stopping for a chat, in the corridors of Broadcasting House.

BBC NI

Farmers are conservative and until quite recently did not take kindly to change or any departure from the settled practice. Now the scientist and engineer have invaded this field of slowly moving thought and probed deeply into the fundamental factors of growth and health in animals and plants.

Attention has been given to the nature and fertility of soils and much work has been put into the study and control of marketing of farm produce. As a consequence of this work a vast new store of knowledge has accumulated, covering every aspect of farm endeavour. The serious problem has been to get this information brought to the notice of farmers in such a manner and just at the right time so that they can and will act upon it and incorporate it in established practice. Few farmers read much agricultural literature and they are suspicious of what professional lecturers have to say.

McGuckian's solution was to bring more farmers to the microphone – 'a splendid medium of disseminating topical and reliable information to the farmers of the province just at the time when it can be of most use to them'. This was hardly a significant change in approach.

The permanent acquisition of a mobile recording unit, followed by the advent of tape recorders, made for more interesting and less stilted programmes. As Robert Coulter, a Scot who became agricultural talks producer in 1953, said to Rex Cathcart in 1974:

> The previous way of preparing a programme had inevitably been in a studio which made two things likely to happen: a) one used experts, speaking with a high degree of knowledge but not necessarily broadcasting in the proper sense, b) one used farmers, practical men from the land, who like others found coming into the studio a terrifying experience and who were inhibited by the whole system. With the coming of the midget tape recorder one could go to their place, to their farm, to their byre, to their pigs, where the broadcaster was the intruder, and they were at home and therefore talked freely and easily, being on their own spot, in their own way of life, their own things around them. The effect of this was quite extraordinary because lots of people who had no interest in brucellosis, coccidiosis or any of the other 'oses' found these men talking in such a vital way from their own direct experience.

Programmes on farming adopted a lively magazine format with five or six items. 'They always said that farmers learned most by looking over the hedge,' Coulter continued, 'and there was something in this recording technique of nonscripted interviews which was a kind of looking over the hedge. So that even in educational terms it brought improvement as well as being friendlier, easier and more relaxing to listen to in the farmhouse and elsewhere.'

John Johnston became the voice and the face of the BBC for Northern Ireland farmers. The flagship radio programme was *Ulster Farm,* a magazine at Friday lunchtime and this was then supplemented by *Farm Gate* every weekday between 6.30 p.m. and 6.45 p.m., later repeated the following morning with an extra market report. *Farm Gate* became so popular that *Ulster Farm* was dropped, particularly as it was in a prime time slot needed for Northern Ireland's increasingly turbulent news and current affairs. *Farm Gate* was broadcast as farmers were coming in for their tea and it concentrated appropriately on farming issues, the state of the market, Department of Agriculture regulations and assistance, meat processing and other aspects of the agriculture business. Nevertheless, the programme began to acquire listeners who were not involved on the land at all. In particular, they appreciated the high quality forecasts, especially if they were interested in gardening. A special bond was established between the forecasters and the agriculture producers, who would keep the weathermen informed on current activities such as ploughing, sowing, hay-making and the like, and on what sort of conditions were likely to spread potato blight or threaten apple blossom in Armagh.

British government policy ensured rapidly growing prosperity for farmers.

The emphasis was on increasing production, on using new and better machinery, on drainage to bring more land into full use, on intensive rearing and on ever more efficient sprays against insect and fungal attack. When the United Kingdom joined the Common Market in 1973 more subsidies became available under the Common Agricultural Policy. The BBC was quick to recognise that the farmers now formed a powerful lobby. *Land 'n Larder*, presented by John Johnston, began as a monthly television programme specifically dedicated to farming and replaced the earlier *Country Window*. It had a magazine format and concentrated on hard farming issues, though it did have lighter items, such as the 'singing farmer' – John Watt from County Antrim, who composed his own country-and-western songs with a local flavour. The only concession to the over-the-shoulder audience was 'Cook with Clare' presented by Clare Connery.

The bonanza brought about by European Community membership looked as if it would go on for ever. Subsidies became available for an extraordinary range of 'improvements', such as the making of concrete roads leading up to rarely used bogland. Ian Harvey, agricultural producer and presenter, remembers this volume of support as 'nonsensical – almost a joke, a sad joke'. Then the bubble burst: taxpayers began to object to the levels of subsidies and the emphasis on higher production at a time when 'food mountains' were becoming enormous. Margaret Thatcher led the charge against the Common Agricultural Policy and major reforms were instituted under the direction of European Commissioner, Ray McSharry. BBC Northern Ireland recognised that it was a public service broadcaster and that it could not in its farming programmes simply be a lobby for the farmers. The complaints of farmers were as loud as before but fewer people with power were listening. Agriculture producers in Broadcasting House now had a difficult task of attempting to ride two horses: they had to reflect the views of farmers and their critics alike, and also the growing concern about the environment, in particular water quality, the removal of hedges and the impact of chemical sprays and leaks from silage pits on wildlife.

The crisis in farming, which became acute in the late 1980s and again in the second half of the 1990s, attracted the attention of the *Spotlight* team. Naturally, the changing times were also reflected in farming programmes, in particular the monthly television series. In the mid-80s *Land 'n Larder* was replaced by *Farm View*, and this subsequently became *Country Times*. *Country Times*, unashamedly, was no longer a series about farming, but was about the countryside, for the benefit of both the urban and rural viewer. It also memorably ventured overseas on two occasions. In a co-production with RTÉ, the programme team made *Growing Freedom*, eight programmes about farming in eastern and central Europe shortly after the dismantling of the Berlin Wall in 1989. The producers and crew soon discovered that the trappings of the police state had not disappeared overnight. Secret police, sporting standard handlebar moustaches, dressed in standard grey suits and wearing standard red ties, kept vigil in the hotel lobby and corridors in Warsaw, took the crew's passports, conspicuously followed them in an orange Lada and imprisoned their chief contact, Elisabeth, overnight. Ian Harvey and Jim Miley were horrified at the problems facing Polish farmers entering a new era. At Schmachtenhagen LPG, a commune in the former East Germany which had become a co-operative, Harvey was determined to film a majestic shot of ten green Deutz combine harvesters sweeping through the vast field of corn, and members of the co-operative were only too happy to comply. A couple of minutes after the huge machines had started to move forward two of them broke down and had to be towed away. For years the co-operative had had no money to buy spare parts and the combine harvesters were breaking up before the television crew's eyes. The programmes also filmed in Hungary, Moldavia and Moscow.

Another *Country Times* production involved an examination of the experiences of some Ulster men who farmed in Africa. The first programme was about Zambia, where President Kaunda invited Alister and Paddy McGuckian of Cloughmills, who had already made a part of the desert grow in Saudi Arabia, to help stimulate the economy. When they got to Zambia, Chieftainess Chiabe of Chiawa pleaded with the McGuckians to help her people along the Zambese River, who were dying of starvation. The programme told the story of how the area was transformed, given an infrastructure and found an export market for resin from pressed marigolds – used in animal feed to take the pale look off egg yokes and chicken skins. Zimbabwe was the location for the second programme, which examined the achievements of Billy Hughes, who had emigrated from County Armagh in the 1940s to become the country's leading tobacco farmer, and Paddy Millar, who also farmed tobacco as well as cattle, was originally from the Cregagh Road in Belfast. Ominously relevant in spring 2000, three years later, the programme gave an early indication of the coming land crisis in Zimbabwe, and the plight of white settlers affected by enforced land confiscation.

Country Times followed a magazine format, combining current affairs with feature material on rural life. A single programme could cover both the implications for agriculture of cross-border institutions and a feature on how a thatcher carries out his work in the 1990s. It set out to be a journalistic programme but audience figures were often disappointing – in part this was due to the difficulty of establishing a loyal band of viewers for a monthly programme and also because for much of the year when *Country Times* was on BBC TWO it was competing against *EastEnders* on BBC ONE. Nevertheless, the programmes contained many high quality items, some of them included in the network series, *Country File*.

Programmes devoted exclusively to farming were confined increasingly to radio. *Farm Gate* continued to give a vital service to farmers and when, for a time, items on farming were incorporated into *Evening Extra*, the protests were so strong that the dedicated farming slot was restored. An additional *Farm Gate* was provided on Saturday mornings in place of *Country Living*. The BBC radio network series on Monday mornings, *Farming Week*, went round the regions and was produced and put out from Belfast once a month. This programme was heard not only all over the United Kingdom but also by the British forces stationed in Germany.

Ian Harvey was drawing the programme towards its close one morning at 6.30 when the studio door burst open and in walked Ruth McCrum, the cleaner. With her duster and Pledge in her hand she asked in a loud voice: 'Are you busy?' Harvey indicated with his eyes that he was. 'Will I come back later?' She then emitted a burst of the unrestrained laughter for which she was famous. Once again alone in the studio, desperately attempting to prevent his voice from collapsing, Harvey closed the programme with these words: 'From all of us here in Belfast, goodbye.' A listener in Germany nearly drove off the autobahn he was laughing so much, and wrote to Harvey to tell him about it. Central control rang down and asked: 'Was that planned? Was it rehearsed?' Steve Wright subsequently recorded Ruth's laugh and used it frequently on his popular network radio programme, *Steve Wright in the Afternoon*.

Cherrie McIlwaine, the presenter of *Gardeners' Corner*, a Saturday morning programme on BBC RADIO ULSTER with a large and loyal audience.

BBC NI

Agriculture programme staff no longer formed an autonomous group, but features and news items on farming were regularly included on *Newsline*, giving the industry a higher viewing audience than it had ever obtained. Gardening, in contrast, retained its dedicated slots on both radio and television – after all, it was reckoned to be the biggest participant leisure activity. Carefully scripted talks gave way to question and answer sessions, gardening tips and visits to gardens in the long-running and immensely popular programme *Ulster Garden*. In the late 1960s Crosbie Cochrane regularly chaired panels including Eric Mayne, Dick Grubb and Norman Martin to answer questions put by members of horticultural societies. In more recent times Libby Hunter and then Cherrie McIlwaine proved to be accomplished and natural presenters of its successor, *Gardeners' Corner*. Listeners found the format of magazine programmes, gardening roadshows round Northern Ireland and summer phone-ins highly effective. Bookings for roadshow events stretch far into the future.

Gardening was an obvious area for co-operation between North and South. The first joint production between BBC Northern Ireland and RTÉ was *Room with a View*. Ian Harvey was about to set off for Dublin to discuss the next series when he turned to his wife Sue and asked: 'What are we going to call it?' 'Greenfingers,' she said without hesitation. *Greenfingers* delighted gardeners all over the island and aficionados came to feel that Gerry Daly, Crosbie Cochrane, John Cushnie and Helen Mark were their personal guides and friends. The series was designed to show the ordinary person how to create a garden and, before serious 'makeover' gardening programmes became the rage, *Greenfingers* used time-lapse filming to demonstrate how a garden could develop from scratch. The series was then commissioned out to Straight Forward

Productions, an independent company set up by Jan Kennedy, a former Head of Programmes, and John Nicholson, a former chief producer of agriculture.

Brian Waddell Productions made *Gourmet Ireland,* presented by Paul and Jeanne Rankin, a network series which was very popular with viewers. The programmes could be said to provide tangible evidence of Belfast's revival because Paul Rankin had returned from Canada with his wife, Jeanne, to open Roscoff, which became one of the city's many fashionable restaurants. Following a second successful series, *The Rankin Challenge* brought a certain professional *savoir-faire* into the viewers' own kitchens, when the well-known chef visited homes around Northern Ireland.

Awash with Colour, by Straight Forward Productions, was made as an afternoon programme for network on BBC TWO but on BBC Northern Ireland viewers could watch it again in the evenings. This was a teach-yourself-painting series, presented by the County Tyrone artist Dermot Cavanagh, in which celebrities, generally television personalities, were invited to learn to paint in attractive locations in Ireland. On 12 March 1999 Shaun Usher of the *Daily Mail* encouraged his readers to watch the programmes:

> I must draw your attention to *Awash With Colour.* This is a VCR alert, because the programme goes out early in the afternoon and many people have no chance to sample it. Simple, fascinating, blessedly free of gimmicks – since it's made in Northern Ireland, where they don't understand that incessant background music and lots of jump-cuts encourage concentration – *Awash With Colour* follows painter Dermot Cavanagh from Dublin to Donegal.

Awash with Colour – this teach-yourself-painting series had a simple, unfussy format and great charm in the absorbing and instructive way the County Tyrone artist, Dermot Cavanagh (left), guided celebrated amateurs like Joanne Salley, a former Miss Northern Ireland, in painting techniques.

BBC NI

Each week he stops somewhere pretty and makes a picture. Er . . . that's it. More than enough, too, for enjoyment and discovery. Peering over Cavanagh's shoulder while the picture grows, one starts looking at objects instead of just seeing them. Director Jane Kelly and producer John Nicholson understand the value of that, letting their pleasantly low-key tutor stand and stare . . .

Here is solace for the spirit and balm for the eyes. Please join the class.

When Charlie Dimmock from BBC's *Ground Force* went to County Fermanagh to learn to paint at Tempo Manor for the autumn 1999 series, the tabloids gave her a great deal of attention. The singer Mary Black was taken to Annagasson in County Louth, Jan Leeming chose Drogheda in the same county, the pop singer Brian Kennedy painted a seascape at Ardara in County Donegal, master chef Lloyd Grossman was brought to Narrow Water Castle at the foot of the Mourne Mountains, and former boxing champion Barry McGuigan took his lesson in his County Monaghan home town of Clones.

Maggie Taggart talks with Zoë Ball, of BBC RADIO 1's *Breakfast Show*, when she was in Northern Ireland for the BBC RADIO 1 Roadshow from Portrush in July 1999.

BBC NI

The natural television presence of the former Olympic gymnast Suzanne Dando had been obvious when she appeared as a co-presenter in the first series of *Awash with Colour*. She presented *The Pet Set* in 1999, made by Sterling Productions for BBC Northern Ireland. The programmes avoided the treacly approach, so alluring to makers of features on pets. The magazine format included 'The Vet Set' and 'The Wild Set' and programmes featured such items as: puffins on Rathlin island; visits to the Belfast and Dublin zoos; the Grove veterinary practice outside Ballymena in County Antrim; celebrities such as Frank Bruno and Bill Oddie talking about their pets; the USPCA dog shelter at Carryduff; and a feature on barn owls with pupils of Altayeskey Primary School near Draperstown in County Londonderry.

One of BBC Northern Ireland's biggest annual undertakings is the screening of *Making a Difference*, an event which aims to pay tribute to unsung local heroes. The process of nomination begins several months beforehand and then culminates in a full evening's entertainment, broadcast the following night. The February 2000 edition was launched on 6 December 1999 in the Europa Hotel by Patrick Kielty, Carol Smillie and Desune Coleman (Lenny in *EastEnders*) to encourage nominations. Prior to the event a number of films were made about some of those nominated. Annabel Croft, the former tennis star, met Sister Eileen Hannon, nominated by past and present pupils of St Catherine's College, Armagh, for her dedicated coaching in tennis for so many years. Coalisland man David Campbell was nominated for setting up the Lifelong Learning Programme in Moneymore, County Derry. Stephen McCoy from Toome, County Antrim, nominated his sister Yvonne because she

had devoted her life to him and helped him to come to terms with the terrible injuries he sustained in the 1989 Kegworth air crash in which forty-seven people died. The final five-hour television extravaganza featured such personalities and groups as: Shauna Lowry, *Casualty*'s singing receptionist Rebecca Wheatley; the new manager of the Northern Ireland football team, Sammy McIlroy; Ulster-born jockey Richard Dunwoody; the Afro-Celts Sound System from London; Tricia Penrose from *Heartbeat*; the girl band Honeyz; and the well-loved Belfast actor, James Ellis. The programme also witnessed well-known personalities, such as Diane Harron, Wendy Austin, Rose Neill and Sean Rafferty, doing things not normally expected of them – for example, Donna Traynor teamed up with actors Joe Savino and Desune Coleman for their own versions of 'Baby it's Cold Outside' and 'Endless Love'. The purpose of all this was summed up by Controller Pat Loughrey: '*Making a Difference* is unashamedly a celebration of all that's good in our community.'

A kaleidoscope of celebrities pack the stage in the Grand Opera House, Belfast, for *Making a Difference* in 1999.

BBC NI

10

BBC RADIO ULSTER
AND BBC RADIO FOYLE

OR THE FIRST FIFTY YEARS of its existence the BBC in Northern Ireland could be described as a part-time station. It made and broadcast its own programmes in time slots assigned to it and relayed network output during the remaining transmitting hours. During the Second World War the small staff in Ormeau Avenue made modest contributions to the Home and Forces Services. Local output was not particularly demanding even by comparison with that in the 1930s. Here is a sample of three successive days of the Northern Ireland Home Service in 1952:

WEDNESDAY 8 OCTOBER

6.15–6.20 Northern Ireland news
10.45–11.00 Joan and Valerie Trimble on the piano

THURSDAY 9 OCTOBER

6.15–6.20 Northern Ireland news
10.00–10.20 Folk Music: discussion with Sean O'Boyle

FRIDAY 10 OCTOBER

6.15–6.20 Northern Ireland news
6.20–6.40 *Sporting Preview*
7.00–7.30 *The Singing Blackbird,* a play by Joseph Tomelty
7.50–8.00 *The Week at Stormont*

When Northern Ireland finally got its own wavelength in 1963 the change was not very great: local output could be given more satisfactory scheduling and London programmes replaced those which had been coming from the North East. The locally produced BBC radio output on Tuesday 12 November 1968, for example, totalled a mere forty-three minutes – and that during a month when Northern Ireland was sliding towards chaos. Pressure to increase the service came not only as a result of violence but also from commercial radio. Downtown Radio was on the air with much longer local programmes than the BBC in Belfast and could often break the news of critically important events sooner than Broadcasting House. A combination of technological progress, a growing demand for consumer choice and mounting discontent with opt-outs led to the decision in 1974 to create BBC RADIO ULSTER. Controller Richard Francis outlined his plans to the advisory committees:

Walter Love has long been one of the most recognised voices in Northern Ireland.

BBC NI

183

There had necessarily to be a short period of preparation, but we took the view that it was in the interests of the community to commence the service as soon as possible. There would be 4/5 hours of programmes per day to begin with, and concentrated increases on weekdays, Monday to Friday. Eventually there would be a seven-day operation. The difference between Radio Ulster and the four networks was that we would have a new campus of our own on which to create programmes not subject to the requirements of network. We would opt-in to other programme services, selecting judiciously from 2, 3 and even 1.

BBC RADIO ULSTER would begin with *Good Morning Ulster* at 6.45 a.m., opt in at 8.00 a.m. for the national news, and then return with *Round-Up Reports* to 9 a.m. There would be bulletins at 10 a.m. and 11.00 a.m. and a band of programmes from midday to 1.00 p.m. and, in stages, output would be stepped up to twenty-one hours a week. Stage two would be a p.m. band and stage three 'a weekend programme build-up'.

Good Morning Ulster quickly established itself as essential listening for news and current affairs, becoming the flagship BBC RADIO ULSTER programme. Early output included *Lunchbox*, a weekly family magazine; *PM Ulster*, a drive-home news, current affairs and listings programme from 5.30 p.m. to 7.00 p.m.; *Eleven Tonight*, mainly concerned with news; and *Up Country*, a weekly magazine from rural Ulster.

Up Country, generally presented by Helen Madden, who won a British Airways award, was a particularly engaging series which put into practice the philosophy and ethos Richard Francis hoped to cultivate in the new service. Amongst the programmes were: *Ballycastle – Ould Lammas Fair*, in which local people recalled their memories of travelling in a jaunting car, while others spoke about horse dealing, being a palmist and selling the traditional home-made candy 'yellow man'; *Herring Fishing*, about the methods and perils of fishing off the County Down coast, and how the herring are smoked; *The Forge, Pettigo*, on making horseshoes in this Fermanagh village on the Donegal border; and *Ulster Fleadh Cheoil*, a visit to the great traditional music festival held that year at Clones in County Monaghan.

By comparison with commercial stations and BBC RADIO 1, BBC radio programmes still had a formality, some would say a stiffness, which suited dedicated BBC RADIO 4 listeners very well but threatened to encourage others to tune in to independent broadcasters. The tyranny of the script still prevailed – Bert Tosh, then minister of a Presbyterian congregation, remembers how stultifying he found this insistence when a service was relayed from his church. There were those who were adamant that, because the BBC was a public service broadcaster, standards had to be maintained. Don Anderson, who had done much to get Downtown Radio off the ground, was brought into the BBC with a particular remit to find suitable programmes to fill the rapidly expanding airtime. To pack the schedules from dawn to dusk with the kind of beautifully crafted and scripted features which had been produced, for example, by Sam Hanna Bell, would have involved crippling expense. In any case, licence

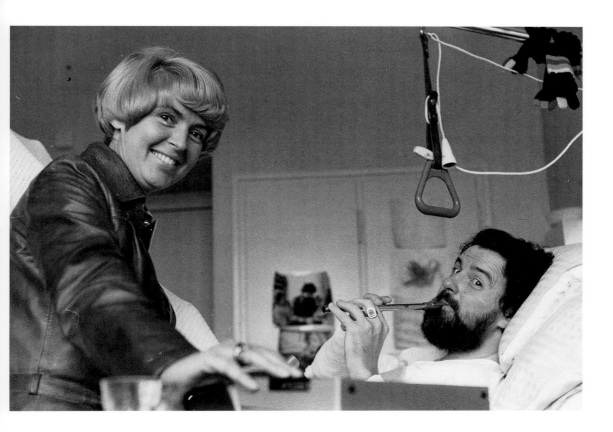

payers wanted variety and light entertainment at a time when hourly bulletins were filled with news of atrocities and tragedies.

Gloria Hunniford, with her relaxed, chatty style, heralded the dawning of a new era. Dan Gilbert joined the BBC in 1956 from newspapers and became Head of Radio Current Affairs thirteen years later. He recalled in 1994 how Gloria Hunniford began her BBC career as a reporter:

> Back in 1969, at the start of the Troubles, we were recruiting new reporters – mostly people with a journalistic background – and found ourselves short of a female voice. It was my wife who suggested we tried a young singer who had just been interviewed about a record she had made. Her name was Gloria Hunniford. Not many people realise she began as a hard news reporter at a time when the news couldn't have been harder.

'You are not coming in to do the knitting and cooking bits,' Gilbert told her. 'You are going to be out there among the bombs, bullets and barricades.' When the expansion of BBC RADIO ULSTER moved on to stage two she was given her own programme, *A Taste of Hunni*, produced by Harry Adair, who was to have a long and distinguished career making radio and television programmes. *A Taste of Hunni* very quickly won the affections of a very large audience. Walter Love remembered:

> Even as recently as 1960, when I was taking part in a record request programme, everything on radio was scripted. It was Gloria, with a

Gloria Hunniford, the presenter of the popular *Taste of Hunni*, with James Galway in Lucerne after his road accident. Here she is recording an interview in hospital for the Northern Ireland edition of *Women's Hour* for BBC RADIO 4. BBC NI

185

magazine chat called *A Taste of Hunni,* who changed all that and at the same time introduced that particular informality between broadcasters and the public which has been such a feature of radio in Northern Ireland ever since.

Such was the success of the programme that Gloria Hunniford became a local celebrity. When she was eventually head-hunted by Ulster Television her departure was a painful experience for Broadcasting House, but the ice had been broken, revered traditions had been shattered and the programme-planners had found the formula to appeal to listeners through the morning and through the afternoon.

Mary Clark assesses quality and value for money in a shoe shop for her BBC RADIO ULSTER programme, *Consumer Desk,* in 1981.

BBC NI

Paul Evans, as Editor General Programmes, played a key role in shaping BBC RADIO ULSTER. He had an unerring sympathy with the audience and carried that with him into television where he was instrumental in developing such notable successes as *Making a Difference* and *Town Challenge.*

By the end of the 1970s the output of BBC RADIO ULSTER had been increased to sixty hours a week. More space could be given to sport, in *Sportsound* and *Sportsweek,* and for those working the land in *Farm Gate* and *Ulster Farm*; and to programmes with special music interests, such as *As I Roved Out,* on Irish folk music, *Star Brass,* on award-winning bands, and *Make Mine Country,* on country-and-western music. Paddy O'Flaherty won an award as the best country-and-western disc jockey of the year. During the 1980s other specialist interests were being catered for, including: *Talk it Through,* a programme aimed at a female audience; *Consumer Desk,* in which Mary Clark investigated and exposed consumer issues and problems; *Belfast Villages,* for those fascinated by local history and traditions; and *Popround* broadcast from youth clubs around Northern Ireland.

Barry Cowan, a heavyweight in any discussion programme, attempted to hold the ring in *Witness Box,* a series in which important issues – including the EEC, the existence of God, abortion, the border, Direct Rule, and capital punishment – were debated by people with opposing views. *Break Out,* begun in September 1989, arrived in the BBC RADIO ULSTER schedules during Northern Ireland Disability Week the previous year – a week sponsored by the BBC, during which fifty features concerned with disability were broadcast. The presenter, Alison Jordan, and the interviewers were all disabled one way or another, and all the items were concerned with aspects of disability, ranging from diabetes arising from alcoholism to what was involved in going fishing as a paraplegic. *Places Apart* brought the microphone all over Northern Ireland to give listeners the feel of a district, to introduce them to people who made a difference there and to explore intriguing aspects of its past. The producer, Louis Edmondson, commented: 'This programme is about places which are on the map but not known because people often drive straight past them.' *Love Forty,* produced by Terry Sharkie and presented by Walter Love on Sunday afternoons, was directed at the elderly. This series set out to be 'life affirming', to show that there is a great deal going for existence in the later years. Love himself said:

> I've been talking to RADIO ULSTER listeners for several decades, so I'm a familiar voice they trust. Radio has that special capacity of talking to people, and gives it special significance for those who may be less mobile and unable to get out and about.

Most of the music played was drawn from the 1940s, the golden age of cinema and radio, and the programme dealt with concerns such as retirement homes, travel abroad and even dating agencies.

BBC RADIO ULSTER increased its output again in 1983, this time to seventy hours a week, by filling the afternoon completely. *Three to Five* was launched on St Patrick's Day, with features from Toronto and New York. As other broadcasters discovered, the afternoon slot from 2.00 p.m. to the news at 5.00 p.m. proved to be a particularly difficult one in which to maintain a steady audience. Paul Clark proved himself to be a sure-footed and trusted presenter of *Three to Five,* as he blended a selection of music with conversations and information about local events, sales of work and fundraising efforts. In 1984 Wendy Austin was given her own twenty-five-minute programme before 9.00 a.m. called *Morning Extra* with producer Rosemary Kelly. Subsequently extended to fifty-five minutes, the programme ranged widely with serious interviews on health issues, local disputes and so on, interspersed between lighter items. 'Wendy Austin's is the caring voice at the BBC in Northern Ireland,' Dorothy Gharbaoui wrote in 1989, '. . . you hear her no-nonsense tones helping the battered edges of society find status, comfort and recognition.' The problem with the scheduling of *Morning Extra* was that many listeners still expected hard news and current affairs at that time of the morning.

Anxiety about income caused the BBC to axe the weekday PM *Ulster* for a time, but it was revived and extended from one hour to one and a half hours. Special interest programmes included *Mainly Money, Mainly Motoring* and *Mainly Micro*, produced and presented by Mike McKimm. By 1985 BBC RADIO ULSTER was broadcasting eighty hours a week but there was some concern that a certain blandness was creeping into mid-morning and mid-afternoon programmes. However, a steady diet of serious programmes could be picked out of the schedules, such as *On Friday it's John Simpson*, and its successor

BBC RADIO ULSTER presenter, Paul Clark, taking advice from Tina Nee and Godwin Avenorgbo.

BBC NI

Behind the Headlines, presented by Brian Garrett, who also featured in *Legal Opinions*.

Talk Back was the brainchild of Martin Dillon, a producer, investigative journalist and writer with a special distaste for blandness. It began as a daily current affairs magazine slot starting after the midday news and running to 1.00 p.m. Dillon was himself the producer, Barry Cowan the anchorman, and David Malone – with a pirate radio background – the researcher. The phone-in type of programme had rapidly gained in popularity, particularly in the commercial sector, but this was a phone-in with a difference: it unabashedly courted controversy on burning issues of the day, light years away in style from the courteous and decorous discussion programmes broadcast two decades earlier. The programme was a runaway success and its eight telephone lines were regularly jammed with 120 calls an hour.

Talk Back was also a magazine programme with interviews – sometimes hard-hitting but never unnecessarily so – which, in themselves, were usually enough to set all eight lines buzzing. Interviews, often preceded by pre-recorded reports, in the early programmes included: Paddy Devlin on the peace line seventeen years on; Chief Superintendent Frank Milner on dog fighting; an

Audio supervisor, Davy Neill, prepares to 'mic' the Prime Minister Tony Blair before an interview on *Newsline*.

BBC NI

Irish neo-Nazi, who blamed the Jews for the Troubles, was responded to by Mervyn Taylor TD; Pascal O'Hare and Kevin Boyle on the Diplock courts; Rachel Tingle and David Norris on whether homosexuality is over-promoted in schools; Nell McCafferty on Yuppies becoming Dinkies; and (on 6 January 1987) Sammy Wilson, Peter Thompson, Brian Feeney and Jim Kirkpatrick on the Belfast City Council's decision not to adjourn for the first time since the 1985 unionist boycott.

The huge popularity of *Talk Back* continued year after year, and it grew still further when David Dunseith became the presenter in 1989. Ten years later, in 1999, the programme's daily listenership was 120,000, almost 39 per cent of Northern Ireland's radio audience. In the week before the Orange march from Drumcree was due to take place in 1997, 21,000 people – that is, approximately one in fifty of the Protestant population – called the *Talk Back* switchboard. In *Northern Protestants: An Unsettled People* Susan McKay describes a conversation she had with Dunseith about the programme. He told her that the programme attracted callers of all persuasions; it had a dedicated following among 'Bible-believing Protestants', who often rang to warn of signs that 'the last days' were coming. A woman faxed him a handwritten letter, asking him if he did not realise that 'all you say and think is recorded in heaven' and

David Dunseith with
Mo Mowlam, the Northern
Ireland Secretary of State in
the *Talk Back* studio.

BBC NI

warning him that he was facing 'a lost eternity'. One caller telephoned to say that she was a middle-class citizen of north Down who had to spend thousands of pounds sending her children to public schools in England because the political situation had not been sorted out. 'I'm fed up with the unarticulated people of Northern Ireland attacking Mo Mowlam,' she said. The programmes had intended, as well as unintended, lighter moments and set pieces written by some of Northern Ireland's finest journalists, such as Eamonn McCann, Fionnuala O Connor and Malachi O'Doherty. It was on *Talk Back* that The Hole in the Wall Gang made its broadcasting début.

BBC RADIO FOYLE was launched in September 1979 as an opt-out service from BBC RADIO ULSTER, beginning with twenty hours a week on VHF 93.1, FM only. The station was on the air in the early mornings, at noon, and in the afternoons, and it was to contribute to the Belfast newsroom and provide weekly programmes for BBC RADIO ULSTER. Ian Kennedy took up the position of Managing Editor almost immediately on his return from Dubai, where he had been helping to set up an English language television station. Kieron Gill was News Editor, Jim Lindsay as reporter and Austin Hunter as sub-editor, with Dick Phillips and Michael O'Donnell as producers. The Controller, James Hawthorne, reported that he believed the team to be 'a strong and enthusiastic one' and 'greatly looking forward to making the BBC's presence felt in the north-west'.

Early indications were that the new service was getting a good audience on both sides of the River Foyle and that the VHF signal was being picked up as far away as Muckamore in County Antrim. Before the year was out, indeed, the Home Office had given approval for a medium wavelength for the station. Londonderry was then one of the most battered and restless parts of Northern Ireland and major population movements during the early part of the Troubles had resulted in the river becoming a religious, as well as a geographical, divide. Even choosing a neutral name for the station was a cause of much anxiety; Lady Faulkner, the National Governor who took a keen personal interest in the new service, believed the title 'Radio Foyle' to be 'inspired'.

Just before Christmas 1979 its premises in the Northern Counties Building were hit by a large car bomb left outside the Post Office in the city centre. Work was unaffected and the station carried out its first outside broadcast at the Guildhall Christmas tree, the programme highlight being a rock climber lowering himself from the highest point of the Guildhall. On 10 January 1980, the Board of Governors in London passed on this minute:

> Mrs Stella Clarke led the Board in congratulating the staff of BBC RADIO FOYLE on their coolness and courage in maintaining an uninterrupted service in spite of a bomb explosion which wrecked their offices on 19th December.

The second explosion, in June 1980, was much more destructive. Valerie Buchanan, then a production assistant, recalled: 'We were warned to leave the building. The next day we had to work in a station with no roof and I joked with one of the contributors to bring a hard hat. He never showed up.' The Controller reported:

> The offices which are housed on the second floor of the Northern Counties Building were extensively damaged. The sheer resilience of the staff ensured that no output was lost despite operating from a studio area which was open to the elements. By 9.30 a.m. on the Monday morning office areas had been prepared for use by the staff. The damage incurred was greater than that experienced from the December bomb and as a result temporary alternative accommodation will be used for the Radio Foyle operation. The general repair work to the Northern Counties Building is estimated to take at least eight months . . .

Temporary premises were made available by Magee College at Rock Road and BBC RADIO ULSTER broadcast editions of *On Friday it's John Simpson* and *Sunday Sequence* from its studios.

BBC RADIO FOYLE celebrated its first birthday on 11 September 1980 – unfortunately a day when Du Pont announced the closure of its Orlon plant with the loss of over four hundred jobs. In a special edition of *What's West*, broadcast also on BBC RADIO ULSTER, the Mayor of Derry and other public figures paid tribute to the work of the station. Preliminary audience research indicated that the 'station has gained and held a considerable audience from both sides of the political and religious divide. Indeed the mid-day record request programme achieves an audience high enough to figure in the audience research figures for the whole of Northern Ireland.'

Not everyone believed BBC RADIO FOYLE was equally appealing to both sides of the divide, however. Articles in the *Derry Journal* and elsewhere reported that the UDA had referred to BBC RADIO FOYLE as 'the sectarian station' and that other loyalists referred to it as the 'Bogside Broadcasting Company', adding that the vast majority of presenters, interviewees and backroom personnel were Catholic. The *Derry Journal* columnist 'Jed' pointed out the error: the managing editor, news editor, current affairs producer, senior reporter, chief engineer, three other engineers and two programme secretaries were not Catholics. It was nevertheless true that BBC RADIO FOYLE was regarded with considerable suspicion for some years hence by Protestants in the area. Meanwhile, Ian Kennedy warned that a new commercial station, Northside Sound, would shortly start broadcasting and appealed for funding to provide weekend programmes. The commercial competitor eventually was Downtown Radio, but just over the border Highland Radio presented stiff competition, particularly for those seeking popular music.

During these years of continuing violence and the H-Block hunger strike the most vital service in BBC RADIO FOYLE was local news, much of which was relayed not only to BBC RADIO ULSTER but also to network. It was also a good forum for local discussion but in terms of quantity the main output was music and light entertainment. A programme which attracted a lot of praise was *The Killing of Lord Leitrim*, a documentary broadcast in 1983 on the notorious murder of a ruthless north Donegal landlord in 1878 by members of the Fenian Brotherhood. By 1984 BBC RADIO FOYLE was producing two hours of programmes per week for BBC RADIO ULSTER, and on an open day that year some seven thousand local people turned up, some going home because the queue was so long. Staff in BBC RADIO FOYLE faced the same sort of risks as others covering the Troubles. One reporter was struck in the face by a rubber bullet fired by the security forces during a republican funeral. The station car was attacked by loyalist demonstrators on one occasion and stolen by republicans on another. The station was once occupied by Sinn Féin councillors, who were protesting against the broadcasting ban in the late 1980s. Paul McFadden recalled: 'I had a row with some of the councillors outside the studio. It was particularly galling because no one was working harder than us at the time to put across the news fairly and include their views.'

The most illustrious BBC RADIO FOYLE broadcaster to emerge was Gerry Anderson, whose mix of chat, music, asides, musings, interviews and competitions won him a devoted audience. His talent and appeal was quickly recognised in Broadcasting House and his morning programme – in the year 2000, 10.30 a.m. to noon – was broadcast both on BBC RADIO FOYLE and BBC RADIO ULSTER. Anderson won fame when he highlighted the controversy surrounding his city's name – should it be Derry, or Londonderry, or both, Derry/Londonderry? His solution – Stroke City – has become his personal catch phrase. (The term is now widely used and has even been heard at formal meetings in the higher ranks of the civil service and the government.) During the week which followed the Omagh tragedy in August 1998 many presenters on BBC RADIO ULSTER and BBC RADIO FOYLE were praised for their programmes which managed to be sensitive and caring, devoid of self-indulgence or sentimentality. Since the bombing occurred within BBC RADIO FOYLE's area, the station, not for the first time, found itself covering a local story which immediately became an international one. As Managing Editor Ana Leddy recalled: 'People really turned to us. Some stumbled blindly into our reception area at the time, not knowing where else to go with their grief.'

In 1999 a telephone call from a listener whose son had been beaten up in the city centre sparked a week of coverage on the station. It won widespread acclaim for bringing members of the public and city officials together in the hope of developing a strategy for tackling the growing problem of unprovoked attacks in the city. BBC RADIO FOYLE also provided outside broadcasts for the local hospital's fortieth anniversary celebration, the local psychiatric unit open day, the Cancer Research *Relay for Life* event, and produced a special cross-community carol service in Omagh for transmission on Christmas Eve.

In the late 1990s BBC RADIO FOYLE had much good news to report and the almost complete return of peace presented the station with a challenge. The newsroom producer Eimear O'Callaghan and presenter Paul McFadden agreed: 'We were being used to bombs going off and people being attacked. Now we must be more proactive and imaginative in what we do.' The station carried a great deal of live music, especially during the Easter music festival. Frank Galligan was not only a well-known musician but also presented a daily music, arts and entertainment programme from 9.00 a.m. to 10.30 a.m. Hugo Duncan, a seasoned musician, had his own country-and-western programme on both BBC RADIO FOYLE and BBC RADIO ULSTER. In *Saturday Club*, Eamon Friel provided an eclectic mix of music – in his own words 'from the Beatles to Bing and Abba to Altan'. *Sean Coyle*, every weekday from 1.30 p.m. to 3.00 p.m. and popular with listeners, was a mix of music, requests and dedications. Mary Harte and Mark Patterson proved themselves accomplished broadcasters on a range of local, national and international issues of interest to Derry and its hinterland. Paul McFadden's *The Morning Programme* was nominated for a Sony Breakfast News and Talks Award. At the height of the 1999 Drumcree standoff – on the day the Prime Minister was due to address the House of Commons on the previous week's Stormont talks – Tony Blair agreed to do a live interview on the programme. 'Imaginative use of local politicians in these discussions revealed a side to our elected representatives rarely glimpsed by listeners,' said Ana Leddy, then Managing Editor, in an interview with *Ariel* in April 2000.

A major programme of refurbishment, costing over three hundred thousand pounds was approved in 1997, to include a new radio car, replacement of both main studio sound desks and the introduction of the latest digital storage and editing system. This enabled BBC RADIO FOYLE to provide an hour-long news and current affairs programme each day and to broadcast a full, nine-hour daily schedule. In the spring of 2000 BBC RADIO FOYLE, nominated for the second year running, won the accolade prized by broadcasters, the Sony Station of the Year Award.

BBC RADIO FOYLE staff in 1999.
From left: Colm Arbuckle, Frank
Galligan, Eimear O'Callaghan, Paul
McFadden and Ana Leddy,
Managing Editor.

BBC NI

Twenty years after it was launched BBC RADIO ULSTER had become the most listened to single radio station in Northern Ireland – one in three of the population was tuning in to its programmes – and over the previous five years it had won five Sony awards for Sport, Specialist Speech, Specialist Music, Comedy, Local Radio Personality and Current Affairs. By the mid-1990s it was broadcasting from early morning to midnight, providing a distinctive local voice, together with local bulletins on the hour and regular traffic, travel and weather reports, providing, in effect, the most comprehensive information service in the region. *Good Morning Ulster*, extended by thirty minutes, attracted the highest listening audience in Northern Ireland. *Your Place and Mine* encouraged real input by the community by linking up local studios in Newry, Armagh, Enniskillen, Omagh, Ballymena and Coleraine. The emphasis was on light items such as conversations with, or about, talking parrots, world whistling champions, totem pole designers, female undertakers, clan gatherings, remote-control church organs, new arts centres, a mobile solar washeteria, and an interview with Jackson Blakely from Moira, County Down, winner of the UK Articulated Lorry Driver of the Year Award.

John Bennett on weekdays between 9.00 a.m. and 10.30 a.m. built up a loyal following with his music-based programme, which included celebrity interviews, occasional live music and phone-in story-telling and competitions with titles such as 'Duncher Dip'. The local studios were also extensively used to involve the widest cross section of the public in an unpredictable mix in the joint BBC RADIO ULSTER / BBC RADIO FOYLE programme *Frankly Anne-Marie*. *On Your Behalf*, presented by Linda McAuley, was launched in 1995 to provide sound consumer advice. *Breast Cancer Awareness Week*, a bi-media initiative which provided vital health information, won a Sony Gold Award in 1998; local charities reported that as a result of the programmes an increased number of women came forward for screening and advice. Other special interest programmes were launched, such as *Exam Slam*, a support service for GCSE and A level students approaching the examinations season; *Computers Don't Bite*, which set out to explain the apparently inexplicable; *Men's Health Awareness Week*; and *Personal Finance Week*. A five-part series of *The Other Foot* had Frank Galligan and James McClelland travelling the length and breadth of Ireland looking at current attitudes to the peace process.

BBC RADIO ULSTER attempted to cater for all musical tastes in programmes, which included: *Friel's Fancy*; Walter Love's *Jazz Club*; John Bennett's *Sunday Club*; Tony McAuley's *Country Roots*; Frank Galligan's *New Country*; *John Anderson*, with the band leader's unusual blend of classical, rock, pop, choral and swing music; John Toal's *Music Now*; *Mary Johnston*; *Country Afternoon with Hugo Duncan* ('the wee man from Strabane'), and *Pipes and Drums* – 'music with a touch of tartan' – presented by Tommy Millar. Impossible to categorise was *Just Jones*, an extraordinary mélange which filled what many broadcasters regard as the 'graveyard slot' of the late weekday afternoon. George Jones's

John Bennett with the popular group, the Corrs, in 1999. Bennett's blend of interviews, telephone chats, story-telling, music, and 'Duncher Dip' along with other competitions has a large and loyal audience on weekday mornings.

BBC NI

Stephen Coyle, a Strabane boy who was seriously injured in the Omagh bombing, was airlifted to a Belfast hospital by the RAF. Later, during the filming of the documentary *Omagh: The Legacy*, Stephen was able to enjoy a more relaxed helicopter flight.

BBC NI

zany, fast talking patter, almost insufferable good cheer, listings, together with phone pranks and the mysterious, down-to-earth voice of 'Sadie', won an unusual mixed audience of schoolchildren, women working at home, men on building sites and even the elderly.

The departure of Sean Rafferty to BBC RADIO 3 weakened the more serious element of morning broadcasting after 9.00 a.m. and he had been an accomplished presenter of *Evening Extra*, a newspaper of the airwaves launched in the autumn of 1996. Rafferty – who won the Best Regional Broadcaster of the Year Sony Silver Award in 1996 – was replaced by Mark Carruthers who rapidly ensconced himself in the programme and in the affections of listeners. Just as *Newsline* brought in specialists on business, the arts, the money markets, social problems and sport to expose them to a general viewing public, so *Evening Extra* adopted a similar and pacy format.

Towards the end of the millennium BBC RADIO ULSTER had become the United Kingdom's most successful regional radio service. In 1996–7 eight out of Northern Ireland's top ten radio programmes were from the station, with seven being speech based. Listeners turned to BBC RADIO ULSTER, in addition to BBC RADIO FOYLE, in the aftermath of the Omagh bomb in August 1998. The Annual Report observed:

> Programmes throughout the schedule responded to the needs of listeners, playing specially requested music, opening phone lines and allowing people to pour out their sorrow and their sympathy. Presenters sometimes struggled to keep their composure as the tide of grief flooded over them. Listening figures were the highest ever recorded and one

The *Good Morning Ulster* team from left: Conor Bradford, Seamus McKee and Wendy Austin.

BBC NI

community psychiatrist told us we had provided a mass counselling service for the entire province. In recognition of this BBC RADIO ULSTER won a Gold Sony Award for its response to the tragedy.

Omagh was the worst single tragedy of the Troubles, yet it occurred when the main paramilitary groups had agreed that the war was over. Much thought and discussion was devoted to considering how the victims should best be remembered. The government appointed Sir Kenneth Bloomfield, who was also BBC Northern Ireland National Convenor at the time, to hear and receive evidence from the survivors and their families and to make recommendations. The problem that physical memorials could themselves be divisive and targets for attack was cause for concern. It was BBC RADIO ULSTER that provided the most appropriate memorial in *Legacy*, very brief oral memoirs of loss and pain every weekday morning just before the nine o'clock news. In the words of Pat Loughrey:

For many of us in Northern Ireland, the reverberations of the past persist. Grim events forgotten by many are alive every day in the minds of others. Thus, *Legacy* was born, a unique segment on BBC RADIO ULSTER that has made its mark far beyond these shores. It is a vivid, poignant oral history of what the Troubles have meant – and continue to mean – to so many.

Few had done more to persuade political representatives with diametrically opposed aspirations to sit down and talk to each other than former US Senator, George Mitchell. Here he is (left) being interviewed by Barry Cowan for *Seven Days*.

BBC NI

11

CHILDREN'S, SCHOOLS
AND
IRISH LANGUAGE PROGRAMMES

ATTEMPTS TO GET SCHOOLS BROADCASTING established in Northern Ireland before the Second World War were a complete failure. One reason was that the Education Advisory Committee, which first met in November 1924, was composed largely of head teachers of prestigious grammar schools who were not convinced that the wireless set had any right to be in a classroom. An exception was Major Rupert Stanley, director of the Belfast Education Committee of Belfast Corporation, an Englishman and an expert in wireless telegraphy and telephony; his enthusiasm for the radio in education, however, does not seem to have been shared. The committee preferred to advise on improving talks early in the evening and invited one of their fellow members, Professor R.M. Henry of Queen's University, to speak on classical civilisation.

Few of the elevated members of the Education Advisory Committee seem to have bothered to listen to programmes for schools when they were broadcast by network. There were no rank-and-file secondary teachers and not a single primary teacher on the committee – had they been invited to join, they probably would have been refused permission to attend by their principals. When Gerald Beadle became Station Director in 1926 he succeeded in galvanising the committee to arrange a demonstration of schools broadcasting in the Ulster Minor Hall on 14 December. The Minister of Education, Lord Charlement, was not exactly helpful in his speech to the meeting. Wireless had done 'an enormous amount of good to heighten the cultural standards of the community' but could the schools meet the expense involved? As reported in the Advisory Committee minutes, he continued:

> £50 is needed for a set and most regional committees would prefer to spend this amount on improving sanitary arrangements or accommodation . . . When all is said and done, wireless could never be more than a supplementary aid in schools, and could not attempt to replace the teacher. Children must be coaxed to and led in the direction of knowledge, and a teacher would teach more in an hour's personal teaching than could be done on wireless in the course of a year.

No Northern Ireland school appears to have responded to requests from producers for reactions to education programmes. However, there were good

Opposite: David Hammond on location with school children. in the 1960s. An accomplished interpreter of traditional ballads, Belfast street songs and songs from the flax mills, he was for long a schools producer who brought Seamus Heaney and other rising artists and writers to the microphone and to the screen for the first time.

BBC NI

reasons for not listening: early demonstrations of wireless in the classroom for teachers had been ruined by a succession of technical hitches, and reception from the Daventry transmitter was often too weak in any case. The committee continued to oppose the making of schools programmes in Linenhall Street and yet, as George Marshall reported to the Board of Governors in 1939, topics of local interest were what teachers seemed to want:

> Northern Ireland, being a self-contained unit with a two-thirds Protestant and loyalist majority, has always been more concerned with questions of politics and religion than anything else, as well as a strong predilection for everything pertaining to the six counties of which Northern Ireland is composed. Those, therefore, connected with education in the Province have always retorted to the Corporation's suggestions about the use of wireless in schools that Ulster topics should be provided for the scholars, and that until this is done, little or no progress will be made.

Fewer than one hundred Northern Ireland schools were taking network education programmes on the eve of the Second World War. Some of those which did found the programmes not to their liking, and Laurence Lynch, a Catholic science teacher, wrote an article to the *Irish News* after attending a demonstration and conference organised by the Regional Director:

> Looking at the programmes listed for the coming year, I read that the talks to children will include one on 'The Succession of Life on Earth', another on 'Evidences of Evolution', again another on 'Causes of Evolution' and still another on 'The Ancestors of Man' . . . it is obvious that the BBC has departed very far from the ABC in its apparent desire for good. In doing so it is making it impossible for all teachers to welcome its efforts to help in the work of education, and depriving particular schools of services to which they have a right.

Some of the liveliest and most imaginative programmes to issue from the studios of Linenhall Street were for children. *Children's Corner*, soon after renamed *Children's Hour*, was a forty-five-minute teatime programme begun in 1924, and was an instant success. A charitable organisation run by the programme, the Radio League, had over three thousand children as members in the Belfast area and so many letters poured in that a short programme was launched before each broadcast to be given over to readings from them. Evva Kerr, a music teacher, was the first producer and organiser and she impressed the inspector sent over from head office in 1926, who reported: 'She reads well and sings pleasantly. They take little or nothing from London for the *Children's Hour*. What I heard was distinctly good.' *Children's Hour* mission was to entertain: those invited to take part sang songs, told stories, read poems and played musical instruments and were referred to as 'aunts' and 'uncles'. Richard Hayward – actor, playwright and travel-writer – sang Irish folksongs. However, when Beadle became Station Director he put a stop to chatter between the participants (later this would be considered essential), insisted on stories of higher literary merit, increased the number of talks, introduced competitions and abolished the labels of 'aunts' and 'uncles'.

Evva Kerr moved to Scotland and in 1932 Ursula Eason was appointed to run *Children's Hour*. Fifty years later, in a conversation with Rex Cathcart, she recalled:

> It never occurred to me that I might not be welcome, provided I could do the job. I did get a number of letters criticising the fact that I was English and my accent, saying they couldn't understand me and why didn't I speak plain English. But what I felt was very wrong was that I should pretend and try to put on a local accent. I would use local words, like 'throughother' and 'scunner'. I was aware that quite a lot of the stuff we were doing was quite outside the local audience and that we must draw material from the province but it was quite hard to find writers . . . I was very keen to do a lot of folklore programmes, traditional stories and the great sagas. I remember doing a three-part drama on Cuchulainn. I would have liked to have done more. Of course, what we didn't do in *Children's Hour* were stories about the present day in Ulster. That was to come after the war.

Cicely Matthews, presenter and organiser of *Children's Hour*. Over the years hundreds of young people were invited by her to appear before the microphone in the hugely popular feature, 'I Want to be an Actor'.

BBC NI

Practically every word in every programme broadcast by the BBC in Belfast was scripted. Ursula Eason remembered that 'the script to me was a lifeline' because she was initially so nervous but, she added, 'what a lot of poor broadcasting, actual performances, as a result'. As acting Programme Director during the war, she got the opportunity from the spring of 1940 to make half-hour contributions from Belfast for the Home Service's *Children's Hour*.

Walter Love made his début as a broadcaster at the age of eleven in 1946. Then a pupil of North Road (now Strandtown) Primary School, he was often confined to bed by asthma and sought company in the wireless. For him the highlight of the week was *Children's Hour*. '*Children's Hour* fired the imagination of countless thousands and here in Northern Ireland we were fortunate that this important aspect of broadcasting was in the caring hands of a wonderful lady.' Like so many others, the young Walter wanted to enter the competition 'I want to be an actor' and he wrote to Cicely Matthews and was thrilled to be called in to Broadcasting House:

> I had always imagined Cicely Matthews as being very tall with dark hair. She was, in fact, small and dumpy but that didn't matter. Cicely had a great facility for making her young charges relaxed. Perhaps too much so at times. In one live studio Christmas party the youngest son of the Head of Programmes was one of the guests. All the children came up to Cicely at the microphone, where she asked them in turn what they wanted for Christmas. 'What do you want Kinley?' asked Cicely. 'I want

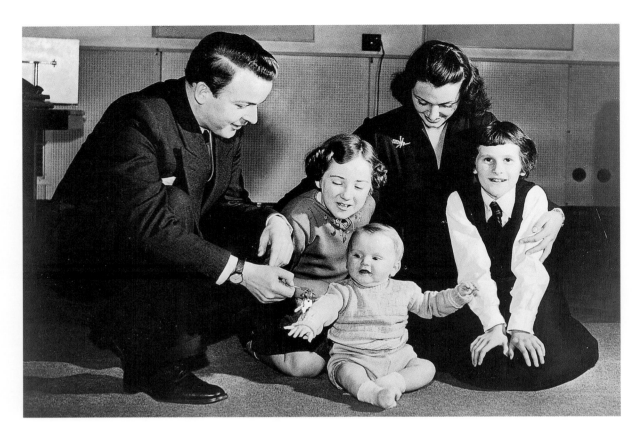

The Button Brown family, from left: Button (Patricia Stronach), Mrs Brown (Eithne Black), Hetty (June Rogers), Mr Brown (Maurice O'Callaghan) and in the foreground Binkie (one-year-old Kevin McCrudden who is now a floor manager with BBC Northern Ireland).

BBC NI

to go to the lavatory' was the unexpected reply.

Cicely Matthews, a talented actress married to Graeme Roberts who not only wrote plays but had acted in 2BE productions back in 1924, spoke later about the origins of 'I want to be an actor':

> There had been so little before and the first request week I only got seven cards and the only Northern Ireland item they wanted was George Beggs singing. So I thought, 'I'll change all that' and I developed a lot of programmes that children took part in themselves. I suppose the most popular was 'I want to be an actor'.
>
> 'I want to be an actor' ran for 255 plays and 1,350 children took part. Altogether, it meant the children felt they had something that was specially prepared with them in view.

Children's Hour had an enormously popular serial about a farm, *The Button Brown Family,* read by Peter Fitzpatrick and written by the engineer John D. Stewart, the first foray into broadcasting by this versatile scriptwriter and playwright. Eddie McIlwaine, the *Belfast Telegraph* feature writer, recalled in 1994 how he was always waiting in anticipation for the rattling of Mr Brown's bucket which signalled the start of the next episode.

At its first meeting in 1947 the Regional Advisory Council expressed concern that the take-up of schools broadcasts was so poor in Northern Ireland. Strictly speaking, educational broadcasting was solely the responsibility of the Schools Broadcasting Council which had three representatives from Northern

Ireland. Stephen Murphy, the Education Officer for the North West England region was asked to include Northern Ireland in his area of responsibility. Murphy went to Belfast and found that the most determined opponents of the BBC in Northern Ireland producing its own schools broadcasts were the local Schools Broadcasting Council representatives, in particular the Belfast Education Committee director, Stuart Hawnt. The Northern Ireland Ministry of Education inspector wrote to Murphy in 1951 and agreed that 'every recognised school should be provided with a radio installation', but, the letter continued:

James Boyce, one of the BBC's best-known broadcasters in Northern Ireland.

BBC NI

> There is room for doubts on three points:
>
> (1) I am not sure that the proper function of school broadcasts is clearly understood, save by an enlightened few.
> (2) I have no evidence that the rank and file inspectors, particularly the older hands, have much knowledge of school broadcasts . . .
> (3) . . . while the Ministry approves of broadcasts, it is not quite so happy about ancillary activities . . .

Two years later the three Northern Ireland representatives wrote a paper insisting that there was no reason to have special programmes for Northern Ireland or a regional school broadcasting council. In 1956, Leslie Davidson, the new Education Officer, wrote in despair: 'Williams (Senior Chief Inspector) objects to the idea of a Northern Ireland council because the Ministry does not want any educational body in Northern Ireland under its control.' Unaware of these objections, the Education Advisory Council pressed for programmes with Ulster content and Davidson made notes of a meeting in November 1956:

> Problems of 'Northern Ireland accent' in production. Genuine Ulster voices were not essential . . . It was better to under-emphasise the Northern Ireland brogue than to over-emphasise it. What should be avoided was the professional actor's 'Dublin brogue' . . .

Davidson worked hard to promote schools broadcasts and when the number of registered schools reached four hundred the three Northern Ireland representatives had to drop their resistance. A Northern Ireland programme committee was formed and James Hawthorne, a mathematics teacher, was appointed the first producer.

From the outset Hawthorne and the committee took the view that there was little point in replicating material that could be produced just as easily by network. The need for programmes on local topics, long expressed by teachers and utterly ignored by their three representatives who never consulted them, would be met. The first series, *Today and Yesterday in Northern Ireland*, was designed for pupils aged between ten and thirteen. An article in the 1961 spring issue of the *Northern Teacher* outlined the forthcoming series:

James Hawthorne, the first producer of BBC Northern Ireland's schools department, set up in 1960. Hawthorne later set up the television service in Hong Kong and returned as Controller of BBC Northern Ireland in 1978.

BBC NI

The aim of the series is to widen the children's interest and to increase their knowledge and experience of the province and its affairs . . .

While each programme will be self-contained, nevertheless it is hoped to indicate in some of them the connections which Northern Ireland has with the United Kingdom, with the Commonwealth and with the rest of the world. The nature of the programmes is such that they may well provide teachers and children with inspiration for further exploration of topics and ideas . . . What a pity that less than fifty per cent of schools in the North are equipped to make use of this opportunity.

The first weekly schools broadcast was made on Wednesday 26 April 1961 at 1.40 p.m. The first programme was on the Giant's Causeway, its geological and legendary origins; and subsequent topics included the first inhabitants of Ulster, fruit growing in County Armagh, and forestry in the Sperrin Mountains. Only 284 schools registered with the BBC but the audience was clearly impressive – no fewer than 10,000 pupils' pamphlets, published to accompany the programmes, were sold for the first series. Essentially the programmes were about local aspects of geography, history and literature. In the 1962 spring series *More About Transport* looked at the Dublin–Belfast train, the Enterprise, containers and trailers, arriving by sea, and arriving by air, and included in *Buying and Selling* were programmes entitled *The Cattle Dealer*, *Our Coal Supplies*, *Marketing Eggs*, *Potatoes*, *Belfast and the Tea Planter* and *The Shopkeeper*. The 1962 autumn series was divided into four sections: *The Landscape of Ulster*, *Early Settlements*, *People in Industry* and *The Stories of William Carleton*. Leslie Davidson was impressed, reporting that the series was 'kindling children's imagination and deepening their experience'. He listened to *The Textile Worker* with a class in County Armagh and found that after the programme 'the children were freely communicative about their own family history, as with the little girl who knew all about the "half timers" because her "Daddy's grandmother had been one"', and he continued:

> One class asked to be shown through the mills at Tanderagee and another school wrote that the programme 'brought home the current situation in our village, its apparent poverty, the decline of the linen industry, its imminent liquidation and the exodus of the workers since the mills closed down two years ago'.

A programme on the Belfast Ropeworks produced a similar response.

At a time when talks producer John Boyd was still having to deploy all his diplomatic powers to get permission to record writers from the Irish Republic and to broadcast talks on Ulster's social and economic history by leading academics, the decision was made to launch a secondary school series entitled *Two Centuries of Irish History*. Hawthorne did not flinch at tackling controversial and divisive issues from the past such as the 1798 rebellion, the Union, Catholic emancipation, the Home Rule Bills, and Ulster on the brink of civil war in 1912–14. However, this was the O'Neill era, a time of growing optimism and greater openness and the ground-breaking series was universally praised and had an extraordinary impact. A book on the series with the same title was a runaway bestseller.

Encouraged by this success, the BBC agreed to approve an expansion of the schools department: David Hammond specialised in literature, Douglas Carson in history and Tony McAuley in geography, and Eric Twaddell was appointed education officer to maintain liaison with the schools and London and to act as secretary to the advisory committee. *Modern Irish History: People and Events* was a series concerned with the period from 1588 to the present day and it set out to encourage an interest in the past by a vivid recreation of events and the people, famous or obscure, who helped to shape them. Long before the present emphasis on evidence-based learning, these programmes were dramatised documentaries, using newspaper reports, speeches, diaries, trial transcripts, secret service papers, emigrants' letters and other contemporary records. *Irish Geography*, also for secondary schools, had titles which included *Sealink*, *In the Forest*, *Home Produce*, *Tory Island*, *Water: Conservation and Supply*, and *The Port of Belfast*. *Explorations* introduced secondary pupils to the poems, short stories, plays and novels of Irish writers, such as Sean O'Casey, Edna O'Brien, Louis MacNeice and Brian Friel. Produced by David Hammond, the first series of *Explorations* was both written and presented by Seamus Heaney, the future

winner of the Nobel Prize for Literature.

The staff of the schools department immediately identified with Sam Hanna Bell and John Boyd, for they were setting out to provide for young people the same opportunity to understand and appreciate the culture, traditions and landscape of Ulster and of its past. They looked to these two men as mentors and inherited their dedication and sympathy with their subjects. The schools programmes were made with the same painstaking attention to sound effects, atmospheric music and scripting as had been previously given to *It's a Brave Step* and *Fairy Faith*. The producers were assiduous in seeking out new writing talent and were the first to employ Heaney to write scripts and to bring the poet to the microphone. Rosemary Sutcliffe, one of the finest children's authors of the day, in 1973–4 wrote sensitive and dramatic documentaries and plays on stories drawn from Irish heroic tales and episodes in early Irish history such as *Deirdre and the Sons of Usnach*, *Midir and Etain*, *The Escape of Red Hugh*, and *The Flight of the Earls*.

Ulster in Focus became BBC Northern Ireland's flagship primary television series and it covered a wide range of historical, geographical and literary topics. *Dusty Bluebells*, a programme on the lore of street songs produced by David Hammond, was acclaimed by teachers and pupils alike. An even greater success was *Green Peas and Barley-O*, directed by Bill Miskelly, made for children between the ages of seven and nine. Filmed and dramatised in part at the Ulster Folk Museum, it told the story of a fictional character, Jimmy Gillespie, set, in the first programme, in 1917. Over four programmes, Jimmy was portrayed at home, at school, at the hiring fair, and on the farm. *Green Peas and Barley-O* was packaged as one programme for an evening showing, with the title, *Pot Hooks not Spiders* – the instruction given by the teacher in a handwriting class. *Ulster in Focus*, originally for ten- to thirteen-year-olds and changed for the upper end of the primary school only, remained popular and was being taken by 65 per cent of schools in 1988.

The lists of writers, actors and broadcasters used by the schools department reads like a who's who of the arts and entertainment world. Liam Neeson, later to win fame in *Schindler's List* and in other Hollywood roles, was first brought to the microphone by Douglas Carson in *Robert Emmet*. Neeson made his television début in a programme for nine- to eleven-year-olds, *Railways* – he acted all the parts as a ticket collector, signalman, driver, engineer and passenger guard. Ian McIlhenny and Denys Hawthorne took part in many programmes. Veteran actors, including J.G. Devlin, Margaret D'Arcy, Harold Goldblatt, and Michael Duffy, made regular appearances. The roll call of scriptwriters included Seamus Heaney, James Simmons, Derek Mahon, Rosemary Sutcliffe, Sam Hanna Bell, Michael Longley, Medbh McGuckian and Paul Muldoon. The cream of the region's broadcasters were delighted to be actors and presenters, including Charles Witherspoon, Walter Love, Larry McCoubrey, Helen Madden, Sam Hanna Bell, Michael Baguley, Barry Cowan, Seamus McKee and Donna Traynor.

Much of the drive behind the development of educational broadcaasting in the late eighties and early nineties came from Pat Loughrey, a former teacher who joined the department in 1984 as a producer of programmes on Irish history. He produced radio documentary series on Ulster settlements in Canada, the United States and Australia, and in 1987 was responsible for the highly acclaimed BBC RADIO ULSTER series *The People of Ireland*. He edited the subsequent book of the same name. In 1988 he was appointed Head of Educational Broadcasting and in 1991 he became Head of Programmes, responsible for all of the local output, news and current affairs and general programmes on radio and television, and later Controller, BBC Northern Ireland before moving to London in 2000.

Sea changes began to transform the education system with the phased introduction of the Northern Ireland Curriculum in the 1990s and from then on schools began to demand programmes directly related to curriculum and its various key stages. *See Here!* was aimed at pupils about to become school

Charles Witherspoon, the well-known radio actor, and author of several successful *Children's Hour* serials and of many feature programmes.

BBC NI

leavers and covered topics which could be broadly categorised as social and life
skills. This series was also taken by further education colleges, youth clubs, vol-
untary groups and Youth Training schemes. Imaginatively dramatised as vox
pop television, *See Here!* dealt with such issues as personal relations, early preg-
nancy, honesty, and drugs – programmes of a kind which fall flat on their faces
if not produced with flair. The twelfth programme confronted sectarianism: the
character, who could not be identified as a Catholic or a Protestant, moved
from petty paramilitary crime to killing for the cause. Paul Brady's 'The Island',
used as the theme music throughout, most effectively intensified the impact.

One Potato, Two Potato, described as 'educational fun for younger listeners',
was a radio series for children aged between five and seven; the programmes
became one of the longest-running and most successful schools series. Libby
Smyth and Michael McDowell so obviously struck a chord with listeners that
they have presented the programmes throughout. This miscellany series aimed
to create an awareness of living in Northern Ireland and it successfully tackled
issues of heritage and identity. In 1988 Eric Twaddell reported that approximately six hundred schools used the series but the figure did not reflect the
full extent of uptake: around three classes per school listened each week, 'i.e.
listening audience each week could be 3 x 600 x 30 pupils per class = 54,000
listeners!'

The most popular secondary radio series in 1988 was *Labhair Leat* – by that time Irish language broadcasting had matured. In 1936 the Ulster branch of the Gaelic League asked the BBC to transmit programmes in Irish, particularly lessons in the language. Marshall delivered an outright refusal:

> After careful consideration we decided we could not undertake to do so. The number of Gaelic speakers in Northern Ireland is negligible and, as far as schools are concerned, the proportion of those where the Irish language is taught is quite small and is practically confined to secondary schools . . .

The Regional Director was even more definite during the war when the Dominions Office had the temerity to suggest the introduction of 'a Gaelic period into the programmes broadcast from the Belfast Station, ostensibly for the Gaelic speaking people in Northern Ireland . . .' Marshall responded:

> I do not quite understand what the Dominions Office mean by the introduction of a Gaelic period into the programmes . . . you might point out that there are no Gaelic speakers in Northern Ireland, by which I assume is meant Erse or Irish . . .

After the return to regional broadcasting, songs sung in Irish, for the most part collected by Sean O'Boyle, were heard more frequently but Irish language broadcasting in Northern Ireland did not begin until 1981.

Under the auspices of the then Controller, James, Hawthorne, the groundwork was done by Eric Twaddell, who at London's behest brought back to Broadcasting House mounting evidence of an unmet demand – Twaddell recalls that it was he, an Ulster Protestant with no knowledge of Irish, who compiled the detailed report which made further resistance impossible. Paul Muldoon, the poet and arts producer, seemed to be the only person with sufficient Irish to launch a series and he engaged Gerry Stockman of Queen's University to present a fifteen-minute programme once a week. Kieran Hegarty was appointed in 1983 as the region's first dedicated Irish language producer. (Stockman had to be brought in for part of the interview to vet the quality of Hegarty's Irish.) By degrees this output was increased to between four and a half and five hours a week by the beginning of the new century. In the 1991 census returns some 143,000 indicated some knowledge of Irish though, no doubt, many of those could be categorised as aspirational. The real test would be audience figures.

Labhair Leat, the longest-running Irish language school series, was directed at secondary schools to GCSE level. To this was added *'A' Level Irish,* dealing mainly with literature and writers, and Primary Irish. *Béal Beo* was a ten-part learning series for adults which gained impressive audiences. Irish language

Deirbhile Ní Churraigín, presenter of *Now You're Talking,* a 30-part Irish language series for adults on BBC Northern Ireland.

BBC NI

education moved to television with *Now You're Talking*, thirty twenty-five-minute programmes which won audiences of between 50,000 and 70,000 – far beyond what was expected. The inspiration came from a successful series in Wales with the same title. Scotland's parallel series was entitled *Speaking Our Language*, clearly inappropriate for Northern Ireland and especially in Broadcasting House where the unanimous view prevailed that any hint of politicisation of the language had to be avoided. Impressive support materials accompanied all of these programmes.

The Irish language unit bought in sixty-five of the hugely popular children's programmes, *Tellytubbies*, to be made into an Irish version. After the first showings it was clear the gamble had paid off: viewing figures reached fifty thousand. The first Irish language documentary, *Dá mBíodh Ruball ar an Éan* (If the Bird had a Tail), on the life of novelist Seosamh Mac Grianna of Donegal, was shown in 1991. Others which followed included: *Gaeil Bhéal Feirste* (Irish in Belfast) 1992; *An Ciúin Mac Ádaimh* (The Quiet MacAdam) 1993, on a noted Presbyterian linguist of the nineteenth century; *An Droichead* (The Bridge) 1993, on the Foyle hospice; *File an Pobail* (Poet of the People) 1994, on the acclaimed Donegal poet from Gortahork, Cathal Ó Searcaigh; and *Súil Aniar* (Eye from the West) 1997, a look at the Telifís na Gaeilge station (now TG4) after its first year on the air.

Eric the Viking, a BBC Northern Ireland Education Department production for the series *Ulster in Focus* in 1994.

BBC NI

All television programmes in Irish had English subtitles from the outset. Amongst other television programmes were: *Sneachta Dearg* (Red Snow), a magazine series covering a range of material from political issues to arts, music and comedy; a twenty-six-part short animation series; *An tÁiléar Draíochta* (The Magic Attic), an education series for six- to eight-year-olds in both English and Irish; and five-minute animation programmes on Cuchulainn, also in both English and Irish. In common with other departments of the BBC, commissions were put out to independent producers. For example, Westway Film Productions is making *Dolmen*, six dramatised stories located around a Neolithic portal tomb at six different periods of Irish history.

Eirinn is Alba, Scots Gaelic meaning 'Ireland and Scotland', was a major joint production between BBC Northern Ireland, BBC Scotland and RTÉ, first broadcast in February 2000. This series of six forty-minute television programmes examined the historical relationship of Ireland and Scotland, and included issues such as religion, migration, emigration, the arts, and relationships with England. The thread of identity is one that runs through all the programmes.

The heart of the Irish language output was the daily radio programme, *Blas* ('taste' or 'accent'), Monday to Thursday, and on Friday *Karen na hAoine* ('Karen [Ní Gallachoir] on Friday') – magazine programmes on topical items, events, listings, cooking, music and concerts. On Saturday Brian Mullen presented a wide-ranging mix of popular music from across the globe, jazz, blues and rock in *Caschlár* ('Spin programme') and on Sundays Colm Mac Aindreasa wrapped up the week with a selection of traditional Irish, Scots and Breton music in *An Dlaoi Mhullaigh* ('The Ridge Sheaf') – the last wad of straw on the roof which binds all the rest of the thatch together. BBC Northern Ireland is now responding to the increased debate within the community on language and cultural identity, and producers are regularly in contact with representatives of the Irish Language, Ulster Scots and Cantonese communities to develop new programmes

At the same time that listening figures were rising for Irish language education programmes on radio, they were falling for other programmes. Young people turned to the radio for popular music and chat but became ever more resistant to 'serious' radio programmes. By 1988 the secondary English series *Explorations II* was being taken by 15 per cent of schools, *Early and Medieval History* by 10 per cent; and the response to a new series, *Contemporary Irish History*, was exceedingly poor. Radio schools broadcasts for secondary schools were phased out but primary series, still with large audiences, were retained. *Hurley Burley* was brought in for pre-school children and *Radio 321* as a mathematics series for seven- to eight-year-olds.

For pupils at secondary level television had to be the principal medium, the two regular series being *Study Ireland* and *Poetry*. The most recent series of *Poetry* included criticism of the work of Ciaran Carson, Elaine Gaston, Michael Longley, Seamus Heaney, Eilish Martin, Medbh McGuckian, Paul Muldoon and Cathal Ó Searcaigh. The most significant series of the decade was *A State Apart*, powerful and moving programmes, written and presented by Jim Dougal, on the history of Northern Ireland from the late 1960s to the Good Friday Agreement of 1998. Two new primary television series were *I Do This* – home, work and play for seven- to eight-year-olds – and *Primary Focus Geography*, with programmes on traffic surveys, quarries in County Antrim, environmental threats to Strangford Lough, and Du Pont synthetic fibres. *I Do This* set out to give pupils opportunities to learn about some of the jobs that people do and some of the goods and services that people need: on a trip out from the planet Golivia, Screen and AN-10-Eye crash-land somewhere in Northern Ireland and, while they wait for their spaceship to be repaired by the AA (Astral Automatic), they explore and hear people talking about their work.

From the beginning, the education unit made programmes for network and it was one of these, *United*, that won the region its first BAFTA award, for the Best Schools Drama in 1999. Produced by Michael McGowan, it told the story of how, in a small rural Ulster town, the main character decides to form a Manchester United supporters' club and the complications which arise from attracting an unexpected range of applicants, from born-again Christians to extreme republicans.

From the outset in 1961 all education and learning programmes were accompanied by support materials. It is difficult to imagine, nearly forty years on, how pamphlets for *Today and Yesterday in Northern Ireland* and other early series filled such an enormous void. There were no textbooks worthy of the name on Ulster history, geography or literature. Patrick Carty's *Classbook of Irish History*, used widely in the Irish Republic, was crude propaganda outlining seven hundred years of the glorious struggle against alien oppressors. Hugh Shearman's works, sometimes brought into the classroom, were passionate defences of the unionist position. The BBC's pamphlets – 8d. each at first – were designed, illustrated and printed to a standard previously unknown in the Northern Ireland classroom. At last material on local landscapes, events and people was being made available and for many years the BBC was virtually the sole provider. By the time the quality of pamphlets began to fall, the educational publishing industry was surging forward, North and South.

In the 1990s the region began to produce support materials in new ways. The tapes for *Now You're Talking* were an essential accompaniment for those intent on using the series to learn Irish. The most ambitious project was the making of the interactive multimedia CD-ROM, *A State Apart*, in 1999. Based on material collected for the series, it used personal testimonies, video footage, photographs, newspapers, election results and maps to allow the user to become immersed in the history of the Troubles over thirty years. Co-funded by the Community Relations Council using monies allocated by the European Union's Peace and Reconciliation Fund, this multimedia package history could be viewed and witnessed from the perspective of both individual citizens and key politicians who had helped to shape events. The package also allows schools with Internet access to visit the website associated with the CD-ROM. From the site, pupils can access updates and links to other sites which deal with Northern Ireland's history and politics. In short, this flexible package offered a new, stimulating and challenging approach to teachers of history, placing emphasis on sources of evidence and personal perspective. Increasingly, the support provided for education broadcasts is being supplied by BBC ONLINE – 'hard copy' will disappear and the principal channel of support will be http://www.bbc.co.uk/northern ireland/education.

Schools broadcasting in the region began when Lord Brookeborough was still Prime Minister and got under way while Captain Terence O'Neill and the BBC, with a shared philosophy, were attempting to extend the middle ground. Assumptions that ancient wounds had healed, though scar tissue would remain, and that Northern Ireland's society was moving towards integration, were shattered in 1968–9. For the next quarter of a century and more the schools department was broadcasting to young people being raised in a society convulsed by violence, hatred and recrimination. Many children were not only caught in the conflict but also drawn into it to become activists in the front line. Northern Ireland's divisions were reflected in, and to some extent perpetuated by, the education system. In the 1990s the most far-reaching fair employment legislation in the western world integrated all but the smallest workplaces but it was not – and almost certainly could not – be applied to the schools. In this world of euphemisms, such as 'controlled' and 'maintained', children were kept apart by both the eleven plus qualifying examination and by religious affiliation. In spite of a vigorous integrated education movement, over 95 per cent of children were being educated separately at the start of the new millennium. The remarkable achievement of the BBC in this fissured field was that in schools broadcasting it established itself as a neutral third party. The BBC made available scarce resources in areas where – partly because of the uneconomic size of the market – the publishing industry rarely ventured. Schools broadcasts, and the accompanying pamphlets, teachers' notes and other support materials, made it possible for teachers to bring topics into the class-room they had been previously too frightened to attempt, either from lack of confidence or for fear of being branded by their pupils as traitors. In this way the BBC makes a significant, though unquantifiable, contribution to the process of healing in a bitterly divided society.

12

THE
DIGITAL AGE DAWNS

T HE DIGITAL AGE IN BROADCASTING began in Northern Ireland in September 1998 with little publicity and its arrival was virtually unnoticed during a time of exciting and hectic political change. BBC CHOICE Northern Ireland was in the van of this technological revolution; a brand new channel with a fresh approach, it set out to enhance and enlarge the current analogue output, while at the same time retaining the ethos of BBC Northern Ireland.

BBC CHOICE network transmits through the day until 10.00 p.m. from Monday to Friday and then, for the next two hours on average each night, the output of BBC CHOICE Northern Ireland is entirely regional. There are extended news and sports bulletins and *11th Hour*, presented by Ralph McClean, has established itself as a vibrant magazine with particular appeal to the young and young at heart. BBC CHOICE Northern Ireland not only delivers news, features, in-depth coverage of local issues, sport and live music performance but also draws on the BBC's immense library of old film and other archive material, such as the 'and finally' lighter items from *Scene Around Six*. For many viewers the main attraction is the opportunity to see repeat items and programmes.

The potential audience created by the digital revolution is awesome. This fact is particularly appreciated by those born and brought up in Northern Ireland but who are now living elsewhere, because BBC CHOICE Northern Ireland can be received anywhere in the United Kingdom. BBC ONLINE has an even bigger potential audience and can be accessed anywhere in the world where there is a connection to the Internet. The core of the online service is news which has developed rapidly and very successfully and now is updated almost continuously. Other non-news sites have been created with their own dedicated teams. The *Across the Line* site provides news and gossip on the rock and pop scene across Ireland and includes MP3, that is, the facility to download and listen to unsigned local bands, singers and groups, giving them an unrivalled opportunity to seek recognition and hoped-for contracts. A particularly large and popular site is Sport which has been receiving an impressive number of hits. Others include: the *Ballykissangel* site, which includes a mock-up local newspaper detailing the characters and goings-on in this fictional village; the *On Your Behalf* site, for those concerned with consumer issues; *Angie's Gallery*, for weather information; and the *John Bennett* site, which not only

Opposite:
Christine Bleakley, who was the first presenter on BBC CHOICE Northern Ireland, in September 1998.

BBC NI

contains audio clips of recent interviews with celebrity guests but also enables those overseas to send in requests and display electronic greeting cards for friends and family at home. Education is one of the largest sites and makes a great deal of support material for schools broadcasts available online and, in addition, has an expanding interactive element. Interactivity is a particularly important part of the *Talk Back* site, which has its own producer, and allows listeners via the web to vote on certain issues and to make a significant contribution to this immensely popular community debate programme. *Hearts and Minds* is available on video on the web and is of special value to those abroad who want to keep abreast of current affairs and opinion in Northern Ireland.

The advent of BBC CHOICE Northern Ireland and BBC ONLINE Northern Ireland was a significant step forward in extending consumer choice in the region. As late as thirty years after 2BE began transmitting its first weak signal the BBC Northern Ireland Region patently was failing to serve the whole of the community. The 1960s witnessed notable attempts to abandon the earlier timidity and to cultivate a culture of openness, but during the seismic inter-communal upheavals from 1968 onwards it was apparent that much more remained to be done. Sir Kenneth Bloomfield memorably observed that the BBC should be a window through which we can look at the rest of the world, and it at us, and a mirror in which we can view ourselves. During the violent 1970s and 1980s the rest of the world often looked through the media window at Northern Ireland and much of the energy of reporters, producers, presenters, camera staff and sound recordists in Broadcasting House was directed at enabling outsiders to attempt to understand the Northern Ireland imbroglio.

At the same time the people of Northern Ireland were looking into the mirror and many, from both sides of the divide, raged at the reflection. Throughout the thirty years of the Troubles the BBC had worked hard to fulfill its responsibility to all sections of the community. During the 1970s – at a time of terrible violence in Northern Ireland – the Controller Dick Francis and News Editor Robin Walsh set the high journalistic standards that were needed to report the Troubles with objectivity, impartiality and fairness. Robin Walsh ensured that editorial values were maintained, first in his role as the guardian of journalism across the Nations and Regions of the BBC and then during his time as Controller, BBC Northern Ireland.

Pat Loughrey built on this solid foundation with his drive and clear-sighted determination. In particular his passion for inclusiveness ensured that viewers and listeners could enjoy a wide range of programmes across all the genres within a schedule designed to provide for the needs of all the communities. Pat encouraged the development of television drama, making BBC Northern Ireland one of the standard-bearers for quality film-making within the Corporation. In 2000 he became the Director of Nations and Regions in the BBC, responsible for all output in Scotland, Wales, Northern Ireland and English Regions. His successor, Anna Carragher, who had returned to her native Belfast from London as Head of Programmes in 1995, on her appointment as Controller in August 2000 took over management of an annual budget of £60 million. She also had overall responsibility for over 300 staff (rising to more than 600 with the re-integration of BBC Resources), almost 600 hours of local BBC television output, more than 8,000 hours of radio from BBC RADIO ULSTER and BBC RADIO FOYLE, a growing slate of network programming and rapidly expanding online services with well over one million page impressions every month. The professionalism of the schedule planners, programme-makers and staff, and their determination that the organisation must serve all in the community, ensured that by the beginning of the new millennium the BBC in Northern Ireland had come close to Bloomfield's ideal and was truly a public service broadcaster.

SELECT BIBLIOGRAPHY

BBC, *Extending Choice: The BBC's Role in the New Broadcasting Age* (London, 1992)

—— Year Book (issued annually from 1928)

BBC NORTHERN IRELAND, *Review of Operations* (Belfast, 1991)

—— *BBC Northern Ireland: Annual Review*

BOYD, JOHN, *The Middle of My Journey* (Belfast, 1990)

BRIGGS, ASA, *The Golden Age of Wireless* (London, 1965)

BUTLER, DAVID, *The Trouble with Reporting Northern Ireland* (Belfast, 1949)

CATHCART, REX *The Most Contrary Region: The BBC in Northern Ireland 1924–1984* (Belfast, 1984)

FRANCIS, RICHARD, 'Broadcasting to a Community in Conflict – the Experience of Northern Ireland,' lecture to the Royal Institute of International Affairs, Chatham House, London (22 February, 1977)

THE HOLE IN THE WALL GANG, *Give My Head Peace* (Belfast, 1999)

KYLE, KEITH, 'Ulster and the BBC,' in Karl Miller (ed.), *A Listener Anthology: August 1967–June 1970* (London, 1970)

LOUGHRIN, GRÁINNE and MARIAN MCCAVANA, *The Radio Catalogue* (Belfast, 1993)

MCINTOSH, GILLIAN, *The Force of Culture: Unionist Identities in Twentieth-Century Ireland* (Cork, 1999)

MCLOONE, MARTIN (ed.), *Broadcasting in a Divided Community: Seventy Years of the BBC in Northern Ireland* (Belfast, 1996)

MCMAHON, SEAN, *Sam Hanna Bell: A Biography* (Belfast, 1999)

1924–1949 Silver Jubilee: The BBC in Northern Ireland (Belfast, 1949)

O'DOCHERTY, MALACHI, 'The Cold Eye,' in Maurna Crozier and Richard Froggatt (eds), *Cultural Diversity in Contemporary Europe* (Belfast, 1998)

INDEX

All page numbers in italics refer to illustrations.